STUDIES IN THE HISTORY
OF CHRISTIAN MISSIONS

R. E. Frykenberg
Brian Stanley
General Editors

STUDIES IN THE HISTORY OF CHRISTIAN MISSIONS

Alvyn Austin
China's Millions: The China Inland Mission and Late Qing Society, 1832-1905

Chad M. Bauman
Christian Identity and Dalit Religion in Hindu India, 1868-1947

Michael Bergunder
The South Indian Pentecostal Movement in the Twentieth Century

Judith M. Brown and Robert Eric Frykenberg, *Editors*
Christians, Cultural Interactions, and India's Religious Traditions

John B. Carman and Chilkuri Vasantha Rao
Christians in South Indian Villages, 1959-2009: Decline and Revival in Telangana

Robert Eric Frykenberg
*Christians and Missionaries in India:
Cross-Cultural Communication Since 1500*

Susan Billington Harper
*In the Shadow of the Mahatma: Bishop V. S. Azariah
and the Travails of Christianity in British India*

D. Dennis Hudson
Protestant Origins in India: Tamil Evangelical Christians, 1706-1835

Patrick Harries and David Maxwell, *Editors*
The Spiritual in the Secular: Missionaries and Knowledge about Africa

Ogbu U. Kalu, *Editor,* and Alaine M. Low, *Associate Editor*
*Interpreting Contemporary Christianity:
Global Processes and Local Identities*

Donald M. Lewis, *Editor*
*Christianity Reborn: The Global Expansion of Evangelicalism
in the Twentieth Century*

Jessie G. Lutz
Opening China: Karl F. A. Gützlaff and Sino-Western Relations, 1827-1852

Stephen S. Maughan
Mighty England Do Good: Culture, Faith, Empire, and World in the Foreign Missions of the Church of England, 1850-1915

Jon Miller
Missionary Zeal and Institutional Control: Organizational Contradictions in the Basel Mission on the Gold Coast, 1828-1917

Andrew Porter, Editor
The Imperial Horizons of British Protestant Missions, 1880-1914

Dana L. Robert, Editor
Converting Colonialism: Visions and Realities in Mission History, 1709-1914

Wilbert R. Shenk, Editor
North American Foreign Missions, 1810-1914: Theology, Theory, and Policy

Brian Stanley
The World Missionary Conference: Edinburgh 1910

Brian Stanley, Editor
Christian Missions and the Enlightenment

Brian Stanley, Editor
Missions, Nationalism, and the End of Empire

John Stuart
British Missionaries and the End of Empire: East, Central, and Southern Africa, 1939-64

T. Jack Thompson
Light on Darkness? Missionary Photography of Africa in the Nineteenth and Early Twentieth Centuries

Kevin Ward and Brian Stanley, Editors
The Church Mission Society and World Christianity, 1799-1999

Timothy Yates
The Conversion of the Māori: Years of Religious and Social Change, 1814-1842

Richard Fox Young, Editor
India and the Indianness of Christianity: Essays on Understanding—Historical, Theological, and Bibliographical—in Honor of Robert Eric Frykenberg

Christians in South Indian Villages, 1959-2009

Decline and Revival in Telangana

John B. Carman & Chilkuri Vasantha Rao

WILLIAM B. EERDMANS PUBLISHING COMPANY
GRAND RAPIDS, MICHIGAN / CAMBRIDGE, U.K.

© 2014 John B. Carman and Chilkuri Vasantha Rao
All rights reserved

Published 2014 by
Wm. B. Eerdmans Publishing Co.
2140 Oak Industrial Drive N.E., Grand Rapids, Michigan 49505 /
P.O. Box 163, Cambridge CB3 9PU U.K.

Library of Congress Cataloging-in-Publication Data

Carman, John B.
Christians in South Indian villages, 1959-2009: decline and revival in Telangana /
John B. Carman & Chilkuri Vasantha Rao.
pages   cm. — (Studies in the History of Christian Missions)
Includes bibliographical references and index.
ISBN 978-0-8028-7163-3 (pbk.: paper)
1. Christians — India — Telangana — History — 20th century. 2. Christians —
India — Telangana — History — 21st century. 3. Telangana (India) — Church history —
20th century. 4. Telangana (India) — Church history — 21st century.
I. Vasantha Rao, Chilkuri.   II. Title.

DS432.C55C37   2014
275.4'84 — dc23

2014020234

www.eerdmans.com

Contents

	PREFACE	xi
1.	**Studying and Restudying Village Christians**	1
	Review of the 1959 Study	1
	Returning to Achampet in 2008	3
	Principal Discoveries	6
	Issues Important in the Original Study and Issues Important Today	8
	Explaining the Order of Chapters in This Study	9
2.	**A Brief History of Developments in Telangana**	14
	Telangana: A Region in North-Central Deccan	14
	Hyderabad and Telangana before 1948	15
	Indian Independence and the End of Hyderabad State	17
	Village Social Structure and the Position of Dalits	18
	Changes in Society during the Past Fifty Years	22
	Political Systems in Andhra Pradesh	23
	New Urban Connections of Village Christians	26
	Participation of Some Village Christians in Politics	28
3.	**Christianity in India and Telangana**	31
	Thomas Christians and Roman Catholic Missions	31
	Earliest Protestants and Dalit "Mass Movements"	34

CONTENTS

	Yerragantla Periah: Pioneer Dalit Christian Leader	37
	British Methodists in Hyderabad State	38
	C. W. Posnett and the Medak Cathedral	41
	Medak Diocese in the Church of South India	44
	Dalit Theology and Its Development	45
	Spreading Pentecostal and Other Independent Churches	48
4.	**The Village Religion Surrounding Christians**	51
	Village Hindu Cultural Environment	51
	Christians' Participation in Hindu Rituals Fifty Years Ago	52
	Lifecycle Rituals	54
	Burial Practices Observed by Many Christians	56
	Remembering Departed Elders	59
	Christians Celebrate a Hindu Calendar Festival *(Dasara)*	60
	Amulets and Black Spots	61
	Christians Possessed by Village Goddesses	62
	Black Magic (Witchcraft) and Counter-Magic	63
	Bhakti in Village Religion	68
5.	**The Older Congregations in the Jangarai Section**	72
	Comparing the Situation in 1959 with More Recent Developments	72
	Sustaining the Old Pattern in the Two Large Congregations	76
	Worship and Preaching	80
	Disintegration of Congregations without a Resident Pastor	85
	Intermarriage and Its Consequences	86
	Addressing Problems in Pastoral Care	88
	Ambajipet: Lay Leadership in a Diminished Congregation	92
	Conclusion	97
6.	**The Independent Churches**	99
	Twenty-Five New Churches in Twenty-Five Years	99
	Anticipation of Current Trends: Sadhu Joseph's Healing Ministry	101
	Ministry of Some Independent Pastors	104
	Five Women in an Independent Church	109

Contents

	Worship in an Independent Style	113
	Preaching of Independent Pastors	116
	Tharamma of Medak: The Healed Victim Who Became a Healer	119
	Conclusion	123
7.	**New CSI Congregations of Different Kinds**	125
	One Small Multi-Caste Congregation at the Pastorate Headquarters	125
	Beginnings of Mrs. Deevenamma's Lay Ministry	127
	Six Christian Families in the Gypsy Settlement	129
	Mrs. Deevenamma's Healing Ministry and the Horeb Prayer Church	131
	Merging Traditions in Worship and Pastoral Care	136
	Conclusion	137
8.	**Christian Adaptations of Hindu Practices**	139
	Dual Adjustments in Becoming Christians	139
	Adaptations Noted in 1959	140
	Christians and the *Jathara* Festival	142
	Adapting Traditional Forms of Music and Drama	145
	Other Current Adaptations	148
	Christian and Hindu Involvement in Adaptation	151
9.	**Distinctive Beliefs of CSI Christians**	154
	Understanding the Christian Message in One's Own Language	154
	Beliefs Reported in the 1959 Study	155
	Giving Christian Meanings to Hindu Terms	159
	Prominent Beliefs Expressed in Recent Interviews	161
	Conclusion	168
10.	**Healing and Conversion**	171
	Multiple Meanings of "Conversion"	171
	Previous Conversions in the Jangarai Section	173
	Recent Conversions after Healing	174
	From Group Conversions to Individual Decisions	176

CONTENTS

Hindu Efforts to "Reconvert" Christians — 178
Greater Hindu Tolerance of a Christian Minority — 180
The Legacy of Yohan — 184
Conversion as a Call to Ministry — 186
Conclusion — 188

11. Challenges Facing the CSI Congregations — 189
Introduction — 189
How Christians Relate to Their Religious Environment — 189
Baptism and Church Membership — 193
Prospects for the Recovery of CSI Village Congregations — 196

12. Challenges Facing a Divided Church — 200
How Christians Are Counted — 200
Strengths of Multi-Caste Congregations — 203
Dalit Theology and Village Churches — 206
Prospects for Village Christians in Telangana — 208

APPENDIX — 214
Sermons Preached in CSI Congregations — 214
Sermons Preached in Independent Churches — 217
Sermon Preached in the CSI Church in Chinna Shankarampet — 223

GLOSSARY — 226

BIBLIOGRAPHY — 235

INDEX — 240

Preface

This project began as a restudy of the Church of South India (CSI) congregations described in *Village Christians and Hindu Culture*. By the end of that 1959 study, their future seemed uncertain. Would they grow because of many new dramatic conversions, or would they slowly dissolve into the larger Hindu society around them? There was, of course, a third possibility, that they would continue more or less unchanged: each Christian congregation living as a small community in the Dalit hamlet at the edge of a larger village, and also living on a religious "edge," on a boundary where the Christians continued to participate both in Christian worship and in Hindu rituals.

As co-author of *Village Christians,* John Carman twice urged Christian scholars in India to undertake a restudy of the same congregations in order to answer these questions. Finally, in 2008, the opportunity arose for him to undertake such a follow-up, working with Chilkuri Vasantha Rao, professor in the Department of Biblical Studies of the Andhra Christian Theological College (ACTC) in Hyderabad. From May through December 2008, he conducted the initial fieldwork in the Wadiaram pastorate of the CSI Medak Diocese. He was aided by eight students from the diocese, then enrolled at ACTC, who spent most of May visiting villages in the western part of the pastorate where there are or were in the past CSI congregations. Each student was assigned two villages, sometimes gathering information about each Christian family, sometimes talking with elderly members of a congregation no longer functioning, and sometimes interviewing the pastor of an independent church in that village. During the following months, while classes were in session, they met with Vasantha Rao to report on their findings. One of them, Erolla Prabhakar, was able to return to the Wadiaram pastorate several times during the year for additional research. Two years later, in May 2010, the eight students returned to the same villages to seek answers to questions specific to each congregation.

Vasantha Rao spent from May to December in 2008 visiting the same villages and some others, as well as translating and writing up reports conveying the information that he and the students had gathered, which he sent to Carman in numerous email files. In January 2009 Vasantha Rao came to the United States to begin a one-semester appointment as a senior research fellow at Harvard Divinity School's Center for the Study of World Religions. He and Carman shared the results of both the old and the new studies in a course entitled "Christian-Hindu Interaction in Some South Indian Villages." By the end of the semester, the outline of a book was emerging, an outline that has grown and changed during the past five years.

Vasantha Rao returned to full-time teaching at ACTC in June 2009. A year later, he began a four-year term as principal. Since returning to India, he has supervised some additional research by the eight student assistants and translated reports and interviews from Telugu into English. Carman utilized all this material in drafting the chapters of this book. During the past five years, three trips to Hyderabad enabled Carman not only to visit some of the congregations that were being studied, but also to discuss various aspects of the study with Vasantha Rao and the students.

Both Vasantha Rao and Carman, more than a generation apart, spent their early childhoods in Telangana, the part of Andhra Pradesh that was formerly in Hyderabad State. At the time, Carman's father was in charge of the Baptist mission hospital in Hanamakonda, ninety miles northeast of Hyderabad. After fifteen years in the United States and Holland, Carman returned to India for six years as an American Baptist missionary, the first four years affiliated with the Christian Institute for the Study of Religion and Society in Bangalore. From 1963 until his retirement in 2000, he was professor of comparative religion at Harvard Divinity School and for sixteen years was director of the Center for the Study of World Religions. His primary research has been on the South Indian Vaishnava tradition of Ramanuja, which he later compared with conceptions of God in other theistic religions.[1]

Vasantha Rao grew up in Hyderabad City and became a presbyter in the Medak Diocese, where he has had pastoral experience in villages like those described in this study. Chapter 8 in this book, on Christian adaptations of Hindu rituals, draws on his 1988 B.D. honors thesis, later revised and published

---

1. *The Theology of Ramanuja: An Essay in Interreligious Understanding* (1974); with Vasudha Narayanan, *The Tamil Veda: Pillan's Interpretation of the Tiruvaymoli* (1989); *Majesty and Meekness: A Comparative Study of Contrast and Harmony in the Concept of God* (1994).

Preface

as *Jathara: A Festival of Christian Witness*. The thesis itself was partly inspired by the chapter in *Village Christians* on "The Meeting of the Gospel with the Village Mind." The thesis involved observing both the Hindu "Pilgrimage of the Seven Streams" and the Christian festival that adapted some of the rituals in that Hindu pilgrimage. Participants in both pilgrimages were interviewed. Similar Christian pilgrimages are now taking place, often annually, in many pastorates in the Medak Diocese. Vasantha Rao's later graduate studies were in the field of Old Testament/Hebrew Bible, culminating in a Th.D. from the University of Hamburg.[2]

While the current study is intended to serve as a scholarly sequel to *Village Christians*, most readers of this book will not be acquainted with the earlier study. For that reason, this book includes summaries of a number of topics discussed in *Village Christians* that are critical to understanding the present situation and some of the changes that have taken place. The earlier study began with ten months of research by P. Y. Luke and his wife, Devapala. Many of the conclusions reflect their considered judgment as church leaders with much experience in village congregations. In this second study, shorter periods for research benefited greatly from the assistance of eight theological students familiar with the region, who have been enthusiastic about their opportunity to participate and eager to use what they have learned in their own ministry. For reasons to be explained later, church records, which were so detailed fifty years ago, are no longer kept. Vasantha Rao and the eight students have gathered a large number of stories about individuals and families. The longest ones (which had to be abbreviated) concerned two healers and a former magician. As far as possible, despite translating and editing, attempts have been made to let individual Christian voices be heard. Such research does not enable a demonstration that these voices are representative, though we believe that many of them are.

The new development that has greatly altered the Christian presence in this region is the establishment and growth of many independent churches, which are not part of the Church of South India. Instead of conducting all research within the familiar confines of the Medak Diocese, it has been necessary to expand the study to include some information about a few of the independent churches, relying on the generous cooperation of several independent pastors.

A larger and more balanced picture of the Medak Diocese would need to include more information about the urban churches, with a detailed description of at least one congregation in the twin cities of Secunderabad and Hyderabad. Villages are now more closely connected with the growing metropolis than they

2. *Ecological and Theological Aspects of Some Animal Laws in the Pentateuch* (2005).

were fifty years ago, and the pastoral care of the CSI village congregations is largely supported by the city churches. Regrettably, it was not possible to enlarge this study to provide a more comprehensive picture, which would make much clearer the differences between rural and urban Christians in economic status and education, as well as what they share in both belief and practice. We suspect that the growth of independent churches is taking place in the cities at least as rapidly as in the villages. There are many important questions that require another study to answer. It must be left for others to determine whether such new investigation and reflection can and should be undertaken.

The earlier study was one of fifteen studies conducted in different countries and in churches with different circumstances.[3] This study differs from *Village Christians* in several respects. It is not a church-sponsored project and does not make recommendations for changing the functioning of either the Church of South India or the independent churches. Both authors are ordained Christian ministers as well as professors, but do not have the continuing pastoral responsibilities that the Rev. P. Y. Luke had fifty years ago. They do have a strong interest in the vitality of Christian churches, and try to convey what they have learned about the aspirations of the Christians with whom they have become acquainted. They have tried to identify those issues that are important for the congregations studied, both now and in the future. They think that it is worthwhile for educated Christians in India to have a fuller understanding of rural churches and for those elsewhere to include these congregations in their overall picture of World Christianity.

We close this Preface by expressing our appreciation to all those who have made this project possible and have assisted us in various ways. We begin with the eight students at the Andhra Christian Theological College in Hyderabad. As noted above, in May 2008 they were ministerial candidates in the Church of South India, Medak Diocese. During this vacation month such students are normally assigned to assist a presbyter in some village congregation. These students, however, were assigned to villages in the Wadiaram pastorate in order to help in our research. In May 2010 they returned to those villages to obtain additional information that would answer remaining questions. Without the help of our student researchers we would have much less to report, and without their enthusiasm it would have been more difficult to present a balanced picture, especially regarding the bleaker side of our findings. All eight of our assistants have now finished their theological course and in May 2014

---

3. The project was first entitled *Studies in the Life and Growth of the Younger Churches*, but after 1960 it was renamed *Churches in the Missionary Situation — Studies in Growth and Response*. See Mackie, ed., *Can Churches Be Compared?* 16.

Preface

were ordained as Presbyters in the Church of South India. We list them here, along with their ministerial assignments in the Medak Diocese in 2013-14.

Rev. Erolla Prabhakar, Komalancha village, Banswada Pastorate
Rev. Mulki Ravi Kumar, Bachepally village, Pitlam Pastorate
Rev. Aasadi R. Solomon Raj, Dharmaram village, Nadipally Pastorate
Rev. Mekala Prasad, Duddagonda village, Gorrekal Pastorate
Rev. Kamalapati Ravikumar, Gangaram village, Sadashipet Pastorate
Rev. Kalikonda Suresh, Bebipet village, Chittapur Pastorate
Rev. Pothraj Jeevankumar, Kistapur village, Jannaram Pastorate
Rev. Methari Steven Kumar, Kallada Pastorate

Our entire project would not have been possible without the unwavering support of the Most Rev. Dr. B. P. Sugandhar, who was the Bishop in Medak and also the Moderator of the Church of South India when we began our study in 2008. He appreciated the value of a restudy of the same congregations fifty years later. With the concurrence of the Ministerial Board and the Executive Committee of the Diocese, he authorized the student assignments in 2008; he strongly supported the study leave for Vasantha Rao in 2008-9. We must also thank Bishop Sugandhar's successor, the Rt. Rev. Tallari Kanakaprasad, Bishop in Medak when we concluded our study in 2011. He responded positively to our request that the eight students be reassigned to the same villages in May 2010. We also thank the Rt. Rev. Dr. P. Surya Prakash, Bishop in Karimnagar, for his encouragement and help, especially with the arrangements for Vasantha Rao's year of leave from his teaching responsibilities at ACTC. We are grateful to the ACTC Board of Governors for sanctioning that leave.

During the first year of our study (2008-9), the ministerial staff of the Wadiaram Pastorate helped to introduce us and our assistants to the CSI congregations in the Pastorate, especially those in what had been in 1959 the Jangarai Section. The Rev. Sarangula Devavaram, then the Presbyter-in-charge, was our genial host. The Rev. Kota John Wesley, then Presbyter in Toopran, and the Rev. Deenadayal, then Presbyter in Chinna Shivnur, also accompanied Vasantha Rao and some of our students in various visits. The Rev. Nambala Prasanna Kumar was then the Deacon at the new church in Chinna Shankaampet, which is important in our study. The Rev. Nithin Kumar was at that time a ministerial candidate assigned for a year to the large congregation in Banda Posanipalli; he also made regular visits to other congregations that we were studying. After graduation and ordination as a Deacon, he was assigned to another congregation in this same Pastorate.

There are many whose names and stories appear in this book to whom we are grateful. Here we mention those who also helped us with our research.

Mrs. Tharamma, the school teacher who became a healer and established the independent church in Medak, gave us a detailed account of her own healing and its consequences. Mrs. Raduva Deevenamma Mithra, who spent many of her post-retirement years visiting villages in the Wadiaram pastorate and established the church in Chinna Shankarampet, not only related her own life story but also directed us to many of the new Christians for whose healing she had prayed. Her friend, Miss Dr. Mahima Paranjyothi, helped many in some of these villages with her homeopathic medical practice and also accompanied Mrs. Deevenamma in many of her evangelistic tours. She helped us to become acquainted with the small congregation in Ambajipet of which she was a mainstay.

We gratefully remember the late Pastor Burgupalli Sanjeev Kumar (called Pastor Sanjeevi), who founded and led the independent church called the "King's Prayer House," affiliated with the International Outreach Church. This church is located in the market town of Chegunta, less than a mile from the Wadiaram pastorate headquarters. He introduced us to other independent pastors, with whom the CSI clergy had little or no contact. Just a few weeks before he succumbed to illness in May 2011, he arranged for interviews with five women in his church. He also related how he founded the church.

Finally, on the Indian side of this project, we want to recognize Vasantha Rao's own family: his wife, Kantha Evangeline; their son, Samuel Stanley Jones; and their daughter, Parimala. They not only gave general encouragement, but also made specific contributions: Kantha's interviews of women in Wadiaram, Sam's work in organizing the files, and Parimala's role in accompanying her mother and in recording the conversations were a remarkable help.

On the American side of the project, Professor Donald Swearer, then Director of the Center for the Study of World Religions at Harvard Divinity School, encouraged our application for the funds that enabled this project. Dean William Graham and the divinity faculty welcomed us and made possible the joint course in which we shared our preliminary findings. At a later stage Robert Eric Frykenberg and Paul Wiebe, both of whom have written much of great relevance to this study, read and commented insightfully on two previous drafts. Carman's daughter Alice Iyer and son Peter gave a close reading to and many helpful comments on the earlier drafts; his daughter Tineke Vandegrift added her thoughtful encouragement. In addition to reading through many drafts, his wife Ann has given much secretarial assistance and continual encouragement in what has become a six-year project.

To all who have encouraged and helped us, we express our continuing thanks.

JOHN B. CARMAN
CHILKURI VASANTHA RAO

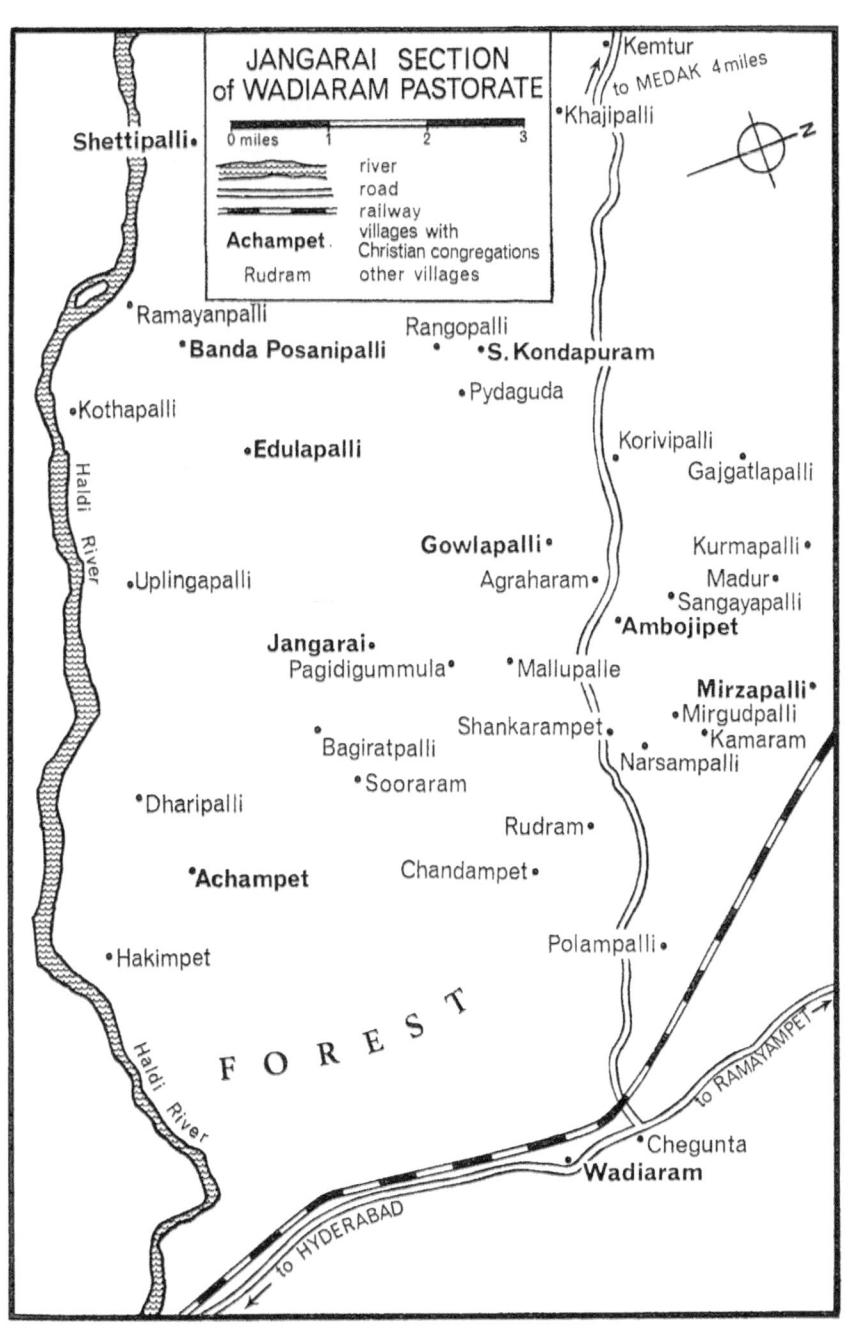

Villages in the Jangarai Section in 1959. (Spelling of names has sometimes changed.)

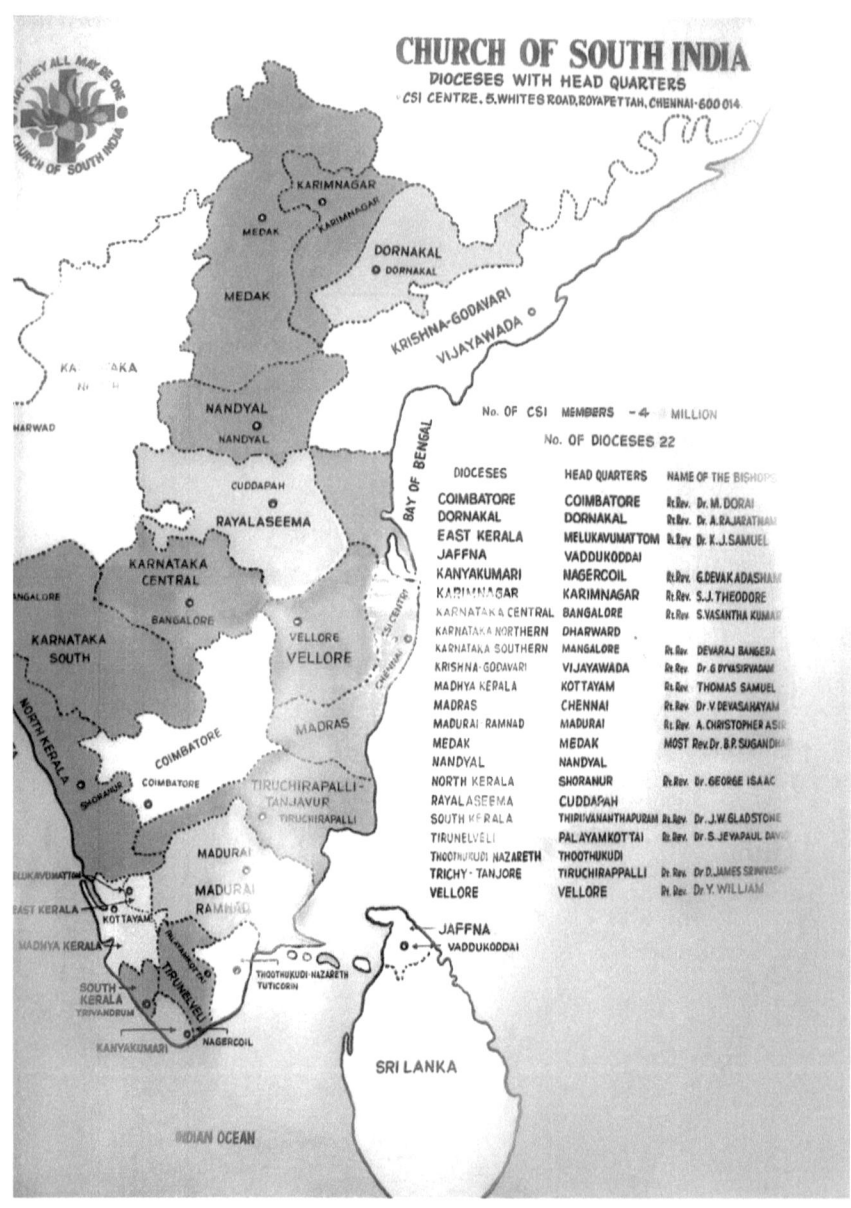

Dioceses in the Church of South India, circa 2005.

Mrs. Deevenamma with Lambada Christians outside the Medak Cathedral, where they were baptized and which they visit four times a year.

The Church of South India Cathedral in Medak, the center of the Medak Diocese and now also a tourist attraction.

Mrs. Deevenamma leading a group of Christians returning to Chinna Shankarampet, after attending a service in the Medak Cathedral.

The Horeb Prayer Church in Chinna Shankarampet.

Old-style worship hall on the veranda of the parsonage, in Bandaposanipally, the oldest congregation in Wadiaram pastorate, founded in 1914.

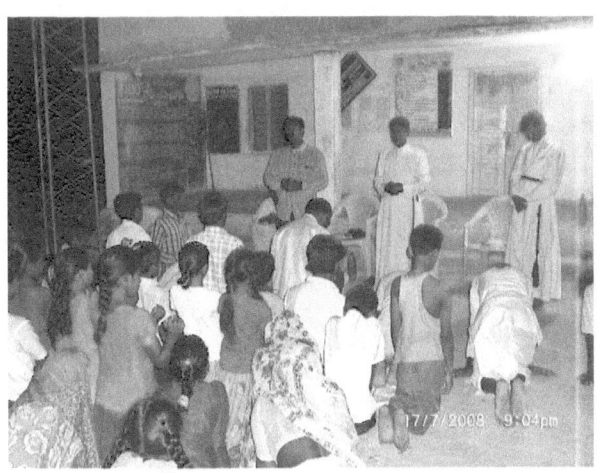

Worship in a courtyard in Edulapally,
where there is a long-neglected congregation.

Ruins of the old church-parsonage in Jangarai.

The new church building under construction in Jangarai; Chilkuri Vasantha Rao and his family are standing in front with some members of the congregation.

A woman in a pink sari behind
a lighted cross in Tonigandla village,
in the neighboring Ramayampet pastorate.

Two women praying with arms raised in Jangarai.
This festival service took place in the community hall.

The new church building in Ambajipet, some funds for which were given by a Presbyterian church in Busan, South Korea.

Pilgrims around the hilltop cross during the pilgrimage festival (Jathara) at Luxittipet.

CHAPTER 1

Studying and Restudying Village Christians

Review of the 1959 Study

This book began as a return to the churches that were the subject of a study more than fifty years ago. They are village Christian congregations in the Wadiaram pastorate, which belongs to the Medak Diocese of the Church of South India (CSI), a diocese containing churches in and around the city of Hyderabad and stretching northward for more than one hundred miles. The original study, made in 1959 by the Rev. P. Y. Luke, a presbyter in the Medak Diocese, and his wife, Devapala, resulted in the publication of *Village Christians and Hindu Culture* (1968).[1]

This was one of several studies (fifteen were eventually published) commissioned by the International Missionary Council, which became part of the World Council of Churches. Supervision of the studies in South India was assigned to the newly founded Christian Institute for the Study of Religion and Society in Bangalore. Its director, Dr. Paul Devanandan, gave John Carman, then a research fellow of the Institute, the task of working with Mr. Luke on this study and writing up the results.

The Institute was concerned about the isolation of urban Christians in India. In cities such as Bangalore and Hyderabad, the friendships and social contacts of educated Christians were largely with other Christians: Christian families arranged for their children to marry other Christians. Some church leaders bemoaned the isolation of Christians from the rest of Indian society. The Institute sought to encourage Christians to learn more about their Hindu neighbors and to work with them in various projects to improve and reform Indian society.

---

1. Luke and Carman, *Village Christians.*

The situation in the village congregations that Luke and his wife studied could hardly have been more different from that of urban Christians. More than half the Christians had married non-Christians, and most Christians had a pattern of life that was both Christian and Hindu. Here is how it was summarized in *Village Christians:*

> At the pastorate headquarters in Wadiaram is a little shrine of the local goddess, Mankali; it stands inside the compound behind the church hall. At this shrine the villagers offer sacrifices to the goddess on a few special occasions, and they call the entire church compound the "Mankali Compound." This churchyard with two names is symbolic of the spiritual condition of village Christians in the pastorate; both Christian and traditional beliefs and practices exist side by side.
>
> Most Christians have a Hindu or Muslim name as well as a Christian name. Some tie a cross round their necks, and on the same thread put a Hindu charm or talisman. Once when the author (P.Y.L.) was invited into a home to pray with a woman in acute pain, he found the sacred ashes of Kamudu (kept from the bonfire at Holi) smeared over her body in order to ward off the evil spirits. Christians give thank-offerings to Christ, and also pay considerable sums to the wandering religious mendicants of their own caste. They meet regularly to worship Christ, but also on occasion sacrifice a chicken to Poshamma, the goddess of smallpox. They respect their presbyter and sometimes bring him through the village to the evangelist's house in great procession, yet they consult a Brahmin about auspicious days and hours and ask him to draw up horoscopes for various purposes. They keep a picture of Jesus Christ on the wall of their house, but in a niche in the same wall they have a little image of their household goddess, Balamma or Ellamma. They want the blessings of "Lord Jesus" without incurring the displeasure of any of the village goddesses. Each year many of them celebrate twelve or thirteen Hindu festivals and one Muslim festival (Muharram) as well as the two Christian festivals of Christmas and Easter. In Kondapuram, the washerman who came back from Sadhu Joseph's healing services and started attending Christian worship said that he could not possibly be baptized because of the religious duties he had to perform for the whole village. To this an elder of the congregation replied, "It does not matter. You can do both. We are doing both and yet we are Christians. We carry out our traditional duties at the village sacrifices, except that we do not eat the meat offered to idols."[2]

---

2. Luke and Carman, *Village Christians*, 165.

Studying and Restudying Village Christians

This earlier study was received with much consternation and some skepticism by Mr. Luke's colleagues in the diocese. It was embarrassing that the Lukes' findings differed so sharply from the enthusiastic reports of progress that had been sent to Methodist churches in Great Britain that were supporting the work of the diocese. The embarrassment may have been greater because the situation so resembled that of which Protestants in India had often accused Roman Catholics: a mixture of Christian and Hindu customs and a compromise of Christian principles.

This was not the only striking discovery that the Lukes made, however. From the perspective of Christians in the big cities, the level of village Christian belief and practice was minimal, and in recent years there had been very little Christian preaching to Hindus. Yet in several villages there were some Hindus attending Christian worship, and a few of them were seeking baptism. Some of these people had attended the healing services of a lay Christian, Sadhu Joseph, who said that Jesus had prevented him from committing suicide and had healed him of leprosy. A few Hindus had had their own encounter with Jesus in a dream, who restored them to health. While the earliest members of these congregations had all come from one or both of the two Dalit castes,[3] Malas and Madigas, some of the new converts came from so-called higher castes that had previously shown no interest in becoming Christians.

The directive for the World Council studies asked the investigators to look for "signs of life and growth" in the churches studied: these were expected to be found in "the Church's encounter with its environment." The 1959 study therefore looked for such signs, seeking for them in responses both to the village Hindu society and to the specific Christian inheritance of church members. These might "be indicated by points of tension and costly personal decision, but also be present in those less conscious" attitudes that help to mold their lives.[4]

Returning to Achampet in 2008

This present study had already begun when investigators came more than six miles in an auto-rickshaw over a dirt road prior to arriving at the Dalit section of the village of Achampet. The congregation there was one of those where Mr. and Mrs. Luke had lived for three weeks during their study of the Jangarai section of the Wadiaram pastorate, forty-nine years before. At the

---

3. Officially "Scheduled Castes," formerly called "outcastes" or "untouchables." See also note 8.
4. Luke and Carman, *Village Christians*, xiv.

time, this congregation, while not the largest in the section, seemed to have gone the furthest in developing a distinctive Christian style of life appropriate to its village setting.

Near the village, people on the road signaled for the auto-rickshaw to stop. Garlanded in traditional style, the authors rode the last two hundred yards very slowly. This procession was accompanied by the drums that members of this Dalit caste (the Madigas) had for centuries been obligated to beat on all local ceremonial occasions, including sacrifices to the village goddesses, funeral processions, and weddings within their own Madiga community. The warmth of the welcome and the enthusiasm of the drummers were no less than a half century before.

Turning a corner, however, it was clear that something important had changed. Instead of the old parsonage, whose veranda served as a worship hall, there were now two sheds housing cattle and a third shed storing wood. No "evangelist" (lay pastor and teacher) had been stationed in this congregation for the past thirty years, and it had been three years since the presbyter in charge of the pastorate had paid a visit. Without regular repair, the walls of the parsonage-church had crumbled, after which the land had been occupied by three families of the village's other Dalit caste, the Malas, none of whom had become Christians. These families claimed that they had originally given the land on which the parsonage had stood. Since the land was no longer being used to provide a home for an evangelist and his family, they were simply reclaiming it. They took the stones from the parsonage and its well for their own houses, filled the well with debris, and up to that time had successfully thwarted all the Christians' attempts to reconstruct their church building.

The congregation's sense of its identity, however, had not disappeared. In part this was because its membership had included all within the Madiga caste community. Many of them gathered for a worship service led by the CSI pastors who were with us. This visit was not the first since our 2008 study began. One of our student assistants had already learned a good deal about this nonfunctioning congregation. Unlike many CSI congregations nearby, it had maintained a church roll with information about each family. That inquiry quickly made clear that there had been another major change, for the Madiga families were no longer the only Christians in Achampet.

About twenty years ago, two men from Achampet (one from the potter caste) had made the trip every Sunday to attend worship at a Pentecostal church in the market town of Chegunta.[5] They had appealed to the pastor for someone to be sent to Achampet to start an independent church. Pastor Devadass, formerly a member of the CSI congregation in Chinna Shivnur, started a church

---

5. This was the late Pastor Sanjeevi's church.

Studying and Restudying Village Christians

that he later turned over to Pastor Satyanandam, who is there now. This had included some members of the already long-neglected CSI congregation. One of its leaders had donated a piece of his land on which to build a church. Some other CSI members had contributed their labor for a church building that could hold fifty people, as well as a separate two-room parsonage. While construction was underway, three young men from the landholding Reddy caste tried to prevent the church's completion, verbally abusing the pastor's wife and threatening to blow up the building if the pastor and his wife did not leave the village. Six members of the CSI congregation had defended the independent pastor and helped him complete the building.

At first, many of the CSI Christians had attended services and supported the new independent church, which included members of both Dalit castes and seven other castes.[6] After some time, however, many of the CSI Christians had stopped attending these services, explaining that the pastor "did not love little children" and "did not tolerate elderly people." During visits in 2008, they had again pleaded with visiting CSI pastors to help them reclaim the church land and build a new church and parsonage. More recently, an energetic student minister helped them to get the land back and build a worship shed. During the year that he was responsible for this congregation, he tried to come every Sunday to conduct worship.

The situation in Achampet illustrates several developments in the pastorate. During the thirty years prior to 2008, what was once the most active of CSI congregations had not been provided with pastoral care. Its members had then helped to start a new independent church, whose pastor was trained in a Pentecostal seminary in Hyderabad; but later, many had had a falling out with this pastor. They clearly preferred to reconstitute their old congregation, which had included all the members of a single Dalit caste. If regular pastoral visits were to resume, restoration of the old might yet happen; but it seemed unlikely that they would get what they really wanted: a pastor and his family living in their midst. In the meantime, the independent church, only one hundred yards down the road, continues to thrive, drawing together thirty members from this village and another thirty from nearby villages. Yet, only a few Madiga families from the former (and perhaps future) CSI congregation remained in this new church.

Later chapters examine more closely the three types of churches now present in an area where fifty years ago there were only CSI congregations. In ad-

---

6. Both Madigas and Malas, as well as individuals or families from the following castes: Kapu-Reddy (landholders), Mudhiraj (small farmers), Sakali (washermen), Kammari (smiths), Wadla (carpenters), Golla (herders), and Kummari (potters).

dition to these older congregations, not all of which are still functioning, there are many new independent churches. There is now also a third type: a few new CSI congregations that share certain features in common with the independent churches. All of these churches exist within the same political, social, and religious environment of rural Telangana (and more generally, of rural South India).

Principal Discoveries

The original study made two discoveries, which might seem to point in opposite directions. On the one hand, there was widespread participation by Christians in village Hindu rituals. On the other hand, during 1959 and 1960 a small number of Hindus chose to become Christians and join these congregations. Many of them said that they had been healed by the power of Lord Jesus, some at the healing services of the lay Christian preacher Sadhu Joseph, a few because Jesus appeared in a dream and healed them. Both developments, however, suggest a porous boundary between Christians and Hindus in these villages, a situation quite different from the social and religious separation present in the lives of educated urban Christians.

Our current study, begun in May 2008, can report three noteworthy developments. First, the number of functioning CSI congregations in the pastorate has decreased, and the membership in the still functioning congregations has also decreased. Some congregations without a resident pastor have no Christian worship, except on the rare occasions of a visit by a pastor from another village.

In 1959 an ordained presbyter was in charge of the thirty congregations in the Wadiaram pastorate. He was assisted by unordained pastors called "evangelists." The ideal in the early days of the British Methodist Mission was to have a teacher-pastor living in the midst of each congregation in a house that served both as parsonage and, with its veranda, as a worship hall. That ideal slipped further and further away since the number of evangelists did not keep pace with the growing number of congregations.[7] By 1959, six of the nine congregations in the Jangarai section of the pastorate still normally had an evangelist in residence. The other three were called "second village" congregations. Although they were only a few miles from the villages where evangelists lived, they were

---

7. There was a rise in salaries because of inflation during World War II and the reallocation of some mission funds to other countries. These changes made a reduction in the number of evangelists inevitable, even though contributions from the city churches were increasing.

Studying and Restudying Village Christians

rarely visited. These congregations did not meet for worship on their own, and the groups who considered themselves Christians grew smaller and smaller. Since 1959, the number of evangelists has further decreased, and pastoral neglect has increased. In 2008, only two of the CSI congregations in this part of the pastorate had a pastor in residence.

Efforts to train lay leaders for congregations without pastors have only occasionally succeeded, and those congregations are often not regularly visited by the CSI pastors in other villages. In the villages without resident pastors, the number of persons in the old congregation who retain some sense of their Christian identity has often sharply decreased. Even in the older congregations where there still is a pastor, the membership has declined. One reason for this is the prevalence of intermarriage between Christian and Hindu families. Since a wife generally moves to her husband's village, the number of Hindu girls marrying into a Christian congregation should equal the number of Christian girls leaving the congregation and joining their husbands' Hindu families. Inadequate pastoral care, however, has meant that many of the women from Hindu families are never fully integrated into the in-law Christian families and therefore do not always raise their children as Christians.

The first significant development, then, is the decline of the older congregations. The second development, equally significant and perhaps more surprising, is very different. Since 1985, many new independent churches have been started, some in villages with an older CSI congregation and some in villages where there were previously no Christians. While almost all members of the CSI congregations belong to the two Dalit castes, the Malas and the Madigas, more than half of the newer churches have a majority of members belonging to the "higher" non-Dalit castes.

Almost all of these Pentecostal, independent Baptist, and other kinds of evangelical churches have their own pastors. These pastors have often had less education and briefer theological training than the CSI pastors, but they have been diligent pastors and effective evangelists. Many of the new converts testify to being miraculously healed. The converts' experience of Jesus as healer is one theme continuous with the situation during the earlier study, fifty years ago.

There has also been a third development: some lay initiatives that have brought new Christians into CSI congregations. Most notable has been the evangelistic effort of a retired nurse from Hyderabad, Mrs. Deevenamma, who belongs to a CSI church there. This has led to one active new congregation and a number of conversions in other villages. Her prayers for healing from illness and from the effects of witchcraft have led many to witness to their having been healed by the power of Jesus.

Issues Important in the Original Study and Issues Important Today

The final chapter of *Village Christians* noted a variety of challenges to Christians living in villages and their responses to these challenges. The first was the challenge of inferior social status. At the beginning of the study in 1959, all the members of those congregations were either Madigas or Malas, the two caste communities that constitute most of that one-fifth of the population that the government of India calls the "Scheduled Castes" — also known as "outcastes," "untouchables," "Harijans,"[8] or (more recently) "Dalits." Fifty years ago the majority were landless laborers bound to their landlords, often forced to perform "unclean" tasks for the rest of the village and despised for doing so. The chief Christian response had been to pursue education. This did not, by itself, bring them better occupations or greater dignity in the village but did increase the chance of their children securing better jobs and higher social status in the city.

Closely related to lower status was the challenge of poverty, which some Christians were addressing either by leaving the village or by acquiring land from the government. Some land grants and scholarships were designated for "Harijans," a category from which Christians were excluded by government order, a policy that led some Dalit Christians to register for the census as Hindus. This was one challenge of Hindu nationalism, other forms of which included the arguments of the Arya Samaj and the intimidation by Hindu young men and "higher-caste" landholders. In 1959 the most evident challenge to the integrity of the Christian community may have been the village religion surrounding it. Other challenges from modern culture were then just on the horizon. In the five decades since, they have become more significant: the beginning of democratic government, bringing political parties to these villages, and the growing impact of urban lifestyles and secularization.[9]

All these challenges from the social and religious environment have con-

---

8. Gandhi introduced a new collective name for "untouchable" castes, calling them Harijans, "children of Vishnu (God)." While he sharply criticized the exclusion of Harijans from Hindu temples and the whole Brahmanic ideology that considered them impure, he insisted that they were and must remain part of the larger Hindu community. He therefore vigorously opposed Ambedkar's view that Harijans (Dalits) could choose to leave the Hindu community; he also opposed Christian efforts to convert Harijans. He was particularly critical of Bishop Azariah, the first Indian bishop in the Anglican Church, in charge of the Dornakal Diocese bordering the British Methodist Mission in Hyderabad State, who sharply criticized caste consciousness in Indian society and in the Christian church, and who led an expanding Christian community in his diocese composed largely of Harijans. Azariah believed that he was securing a practical liberation of Malas and Madigas, while Gandhi's view of the Harijans' future in a reformed Hindu society was only an unproven theory (Harper, *In the Shadow of the Mahatma*, 291-351).

9. Luke and Carman, *Village Christians*, chapter 11.

tinued down to the present, but the importance of each challenge has varied from village to village and from family to family. The same is true of the internal obstacles that Christians have faced in responding to these challenges. These include the persistence of material motives and the inadequacy of pastoral care in the older congregations, along with the lack of lay leadership.

Of the six village congregations with resident evangelists fifty years ago, only one now has a pastor in residence, and, at the start of this 2008 restudy, only two others continued to have regular Sunday worship. In all these congregations the number of Christian individuals and families has declined, but the number has also decreased markedly in the one congregation where an evangelist or pastor has been continuously stationed. Moreover, in this congregation, the oldest and largest in the pastorate, the participation of many of its members in some village rituals seems to have continued down to the present.

While the CSI churches in the cities have grown in numbers and financial commitment during the past fifty years, the older village congregations struggle to survive. Because almost all their members are Dalits, they may choose to deny or at least disguise their Christian identity in order to receive government benefits of free land. Later chapters take up the consequences of this government policy and also discuss the erosive influence on fragile Christian families of the surrounding religious culture, especially when they marry their children to Hindu relatives.

As noted above, while older CSI congregations have been declining, new independent churches have started and grown. The total Christian population in this area may therefore have increased, both in numbers and in vitality. This development, however, brings with it new problems as well as new opportunities. Fifty years ago, all the Christians in these villages belonged to the Church of South India. Now they belong to a variety of churches, having members from many different castes. We explore this situation in more detail in chapter 6 and come back to the questions it raises, both theological and practical, in chapters 11 and 112.

The discovery of so many new churches has altered and complicated this study, making it no longer simply an updating of information about the congregations existing fifty years ago. With respect to all the newer congregations, this has become not a "restudy" but an entirely new study, one that we have been able only to begin.

Explaining the Order of Chapters in This Study

The first part of this book presents three dimensions of the environment surrounding these Christians. Chapter 2 recounts the political and social history of the Telangana region, especially since Indian independence in 1947 and the end of the Nizam's rule in 1948. It briefly describes the traditional social and economic system and notes some recent changes, many related to the introduction of democratic government in the villages and the closer connection between the villages and the cities, especially the metropolis of Hyderabad, the state capital of Andhra Pradesh.

Chapter 3 starts with a brief sketch of earlier developments in the history of Christianity in India and goes on to describe the Hyderabad Methodist Mission, the Medak Diocese in the Church of South India, and the recent spread of Pentecostal and other independent churches.

Chapter 4 describes the village Hindu environment surrounding the small Christian minorities in these villages. It relies heavily on the description and analysis of village religion given in *Village Christians,* but it focuses primarily on the village rituals in which many Christians continue to participate. This dual participation was a major and controversial discovery of the 1959 study. One feature to which we give more attention is black magic or witchcraft, which seems to have increased in the past fifty years. Healing from the effects of such sorcery is a major reason given by those who have decided to become Christians.

The central part of the book is divided into three "stories." Chapter 5 considers what has happened to the CSI congregations studied fifty years ago. The story differs considerably for each of three types of older churches. (1) The two large congregations (Bandaposanipally and Shankarraj Kondapur) seem to have continued with the least change, while (2) six others have seriously declined[10] or even disappeared.[11] There is also (3) one congregation[12] that has lost most of its erstwhile members but has reconstituted itself because of unusual lay leadership and timely help from the presbyter in charge of the Wadiaram pastorate. While their circumstances differ, all of these older congregations share important features because they are under the same system of pastoral supervision. They also participate in the same system of inter-village marriage arrangements. With the exception of Ambajipet, they have not succeeded in developing lay leaders and have therefore been seriously damaged, in the absence of a resident evangelist, by the lack of regular visits from evangelists or pastors from other villages. With the same exception, all their members come from one or both of the two Dalit castes.

Chapter 6 focuses on the independent churches, whose presence has trans-

---

10. Achampet, Jangarai, Gawalapally, and Eduapally.
11. Chettipally and Mirzapally.
12. Ambajipet.

Studying and Restudying Village Christians

formed the Christian landscape of this area. Because they came to our attention after the short period of fieldwork had begun, we were not able to gather nearly as much information as we would have liked, about either the history of these churches or their present activities. We faced the further difficulty that they were outside the network of CSI pastors and congregations that provided our initial connection with Christians in this region. Nevertheless, we can report on a number of the new beginnings that these independent churches represent, thanks to the cordial welcome extended by several independent pastors. We remember with special gratitude the generous spirit and personal assistance of the late Pastor Sanjeevi of Chegunta, whose death in May 2011 came shortly after he had arranged and shared in interviews with five women in his congregation.

The special case at the end of chapter 6 is outside the area of the Wadiaram pastorate, but the healing ministry of Mrs. Tharamma of Medak has had great impact on a number of people in the area studied. Her own dramatic healing and the healings of many others for which she fervently prayed disturbed her neighbors in the CSI cathedral compound in Medak. Their opposition influenced her decision to start her own independent church. How her distinctive ministry should be related to the official pastoral ministry of the Church of South India remains controversial. This controversy illustrates some current tensions between the Medak Diocese and the independent churches.

Chapter 7 describes newer congregations affiliated with the CSI Wadiaram pastorate that in varying respects resemble the independent churches. Much of the chapter is about Mrs. Raduva Deevenamma Mithra, a retired nurse from Hyderabad who helped to initiate and support two of the new congregations. The one large congregation began as an independent church that Mrs. Deevenamma later transferred to the Church of South India. Many of the instances that we report about healing by the power of Jesus occurred in response to her evangelism and her fervent prayers.

Chapters 8 and 9 report important facets in the life of the CSI congregations. Chapter 8 is concerned with Christian adaptations of Hindu rituals, village customs, and Indian forms of music and drama. While the participation of village Christians in Hindu rituals involves their following two religious tracks at the same time, adaptations give them the opportunity to find Christian meaning in modified Hindu ceremonies. The Hyderabad Methodist Mission was distinctive among Protestants in the official sanction and leadership it gave to such adaptations, notably in conducting a "pilgrimage" modeled on a regional Hindu *jathara* in many pastorates at Christmas or Easter. This practice has continued and been expanded in the CSI Medak Diocese.

Chapter 9 deals with the distinctive Christian beliefs of CSI Christians. Here we see "adaptation" — or the lack of it — on the part of individual Christians in the verbal formulation of the beliefs taught by earlier generations of Indian pastors and British Methodist missionaries. We summarize both P. Y. Luke's presentation of the distinctive beliefs he encountered fifty years ago and the recent answers given by a small number of respondents to questions we posed. The sampling is much too small to assume that the responses are representative, but they certainly are of great interest. The statements are often quite elaborate and relatively "orthodox," reflecting much that was learned from past and present generations of pastors and teachers, but the respondents also relate some of their beliefs to their own life experiences. The importance of divine protection and blessing is very clear.

Chapter 10 considers the phenomena of healing and conversion in all three types of churches we discuss. We begin by noting some of the different understandings of "conversion," which has been important, both as a concept and a practice, throughout Christian history. It has also been a controversial topic in India. Healing ascribed to the power of Jesus has likewise been important in all of Christian history, though perhaps much more so in some times and places than in others. This report may contribute to current discussion about the nature of conversion and the significance of praying for both physical and spiritual healing.

Because this book represents an initial study of a few congregations and is based on limited data, the outcome of the study is presented in the form of questions arising from the challenges rather than sweeping conclusions. The questions in chapter 11, in particular, take up challenges facing the congregations in the CSI Medak Diocese, which was the host of the 1959 study and our generous and cooperative partner for the study that began in 2008.

Chapter 12 considers questions that arise from the complicated situation that was discovered: the recent development of an enlarged but divided church. The Church of South India began as an effort to bring all Protestant Christians in South India together in a single visible body. It did not succeed in this, but in many Protestant mission areas, all Christians in the villages belonged to the same denomination — in this case, that of the British Methodists who became one of the uniting partners in the Church of South India. Fifty years ago, all the Christians in these villages belonged to the CSI Medak Diocese. Now the CSI village congregations are only one of several Protestant churches, and there are also a few Roman Catholic churches not far away. Thus here, as in many other places in India and around the world, the Christian church is divided by disparate traditions and social connections, and also by competing strategies.

Our specific questions arise from the divisions between the CSI congregations and the independent churches in the same vicinity. Both those within a church and those studying it find it hard to determine who are to be counted

Studying and Restudying Village Christians

as Christians and how "good Christians" are to be evaluated. This is our first question. The second question recognizes the importance of caste for Indian Christians, both in strengthening the bonds within a single-caste congregation and in weakening the unity within a multi-caste church. We therefore ask: how strong is the unity in multi-caste congregations? The third question concerns those Christians who belong to what they and other villagers consider castes that are higher than the Dalits. What is the impact on them, if any, of Dalit theology?

The final section takes up several questions that are part of a larger question: What are the prospects for these village churches? Will government policies continue to inhibit the growth of largely Dalit congregations, most of them part of the CSI Medak Diocese? Will the continuing growth of the independent churches change their relation with the Church of South India? Will all these churches cooperate in matters of mutual concern, and will they recognize one another as part of a larger Christian community? Their members have inherited many Christian traditions, now understood with a village mindset that emphasizes material blessings from God but also leaves open the possibility of a close devotional relationship. These traditions come together for them in the powerful presence of Jesus the healer.

CHAPTER 2

A Brief History of Developments in Telangana

Telangana: A Region in North-Central Deccan

What and where is Telangana? It does not yet appear on maps of India; it is the part of Andhra Pradesh that was formerly the Telugu-speaking part (and by far the largest part) of the princely state of Hyderabad. It is an ancient region with enough sense of separate identity that some political parties have agitated for its separation from the rest of Andhra Pradesh to form a new state with Hyderabad as its capital. That agitation has finally been successful. Both the state legislature and the national parliament have voted to enact this separation.[1]

Geographically, Telangana is the north-central part of the Deccan plateau in South India, bounded by two great rivers, the Godavari to the north and east and the Krishna to the south. The plateau slopes downward from northwest to southeast, falling from two thousand feet above sea level to a few hundred feet, not far from where the two rivers enter the huge delta of Coastal Andhra and empty into the Bay of Bengal. The countryside is rolling rather than flat and is dotted by bare rock hills, looking like gigantic rock piles or single huge boulders. The elevations and depressions in the landscape make it easier for many villages to have reservoirs ("tanks" in Indian English), which are quite essential, for most of the rainfall comes in the first monsoon, between June and October, when there is a southwest wind off the Indian Ocean. Very little

---

1. On February 18, 2014, the Lok Sabha, the Lower House of India's Parliament, unanimously passed a bill creating a new state of Telangana. The Upper House of Parliament ratified this decision a few days later. For ten years the present capital of Hyderabad, while well within the boundaries of Telangana, will continue to be the capital of both states.

rain can be counted on in the second monsoon, from October to December, which comes from the northeast off the Bay of Bengal, in often violent storms, and provides most of the rain for the southeast coast of India. The reservoirs and rivers, along with some wells, provide the irrigation necessary for growing rice, which is the preferred staple, though many poor people have to make do with the crops that depend on rain falling on the fields during the monsoons. This is the so-called dry crop, which includes millet, corn, and a dark brown grain called *ragi*. This description of the land begins with rain and the food it makes possible because that is so vital for the villages. The unpredictability of the rains is closely connected to the unpredictable divine blessings for which people pray.

Hyderabad and Telangana before 1948

Prior to 1948, Hyderabad State was one of the two largest princely states in India. Such states were not ruled directly by the British but were under the control of princely families, though always under the watchful eye of a British political officer (the "resident"). In the case of Hyderabad State, there was some semblance of sovereignty and independent rule, including the issuing of its own coins and stamps, but a contingent of British-Indian troops was stationed in the city of Secunderabad, adjoining the capital city of Hyderabad. The resident was regularly consulted on matters of importance, especially those concerned with relations between Hyderabad State and other parts of India.

Twenty-four hundred years ago, the present territory of Andhra Pradesh came into the expanded Mauryan Empire of Ashoka, the greatest king of ancient India, who later in his reign regretted his bloody victories and became a Buddhist. Among the inscriptions he set up on pillars all over his kingdom was one in Nellore, in the southeast corner of the Telugu country. After Ashoka's death, his empire fell apart, and the Andhras ruled much of South India during the reign of the Buddhist Satavahana dynasty for more than four centuries. Another Buddhist kingdom followed briefly in the third century C.E., and after that came four Hindu kingdoms. The last of these was ruled by the Kakatiyas from their capital, Warangal, ninety miles northeast of Hyderabad City, from 1081 to 1323 C.E.

After the rule of the Kakatiyas was ended by the army of Muhammad bin Tughlak, Telangana was ruled by two Muslim dynasties. The second began its rule from the hill fortress of Golkonda and later established a new capital nearby. This became the present city of Hyderabad. At its height, the Qutb

Shahi sultans ruled most of the Telugu-speaking area of South India, but the Golkonda kingdom fell in 1687 to the armies of the last powerful Mughal emperor. Aurungzeb appointed one of his generals, Asaf Jah, as viceroy of the region. Asaf Jah became the first Nizam. By 1724, he was able to establish his rule, and before he died in 1748, Hyderabad's dominions had become virtually independent. By that time, however, the British and French were competing for influence in various royal courts and ultimately for control of India. Claimants supported by the French gained the throne (first a grandson of Asaf Jah, who was succeeded by his uncle). Thirteen years later a candidate supported by the British won out; the line of rulers called "the Nizam" lasted until 1948. The Nizam's government supported British rule during the Indian Uprising in 1857 (also called the "Great Mutiny") and again during both World Wars.[2]

The Nizams acquired enormous wealth and so did the powerful noble families, both Muslim and Hindu, who supported them.[3] Loyal service was rewarded with large tracts of land encompassing many villages. Such feudal domains were called *jagirs*. They were of different kinds, but all of them extracted much in taxation and provided very few services. By the end of the Nizams' rule, about two-fifths of the state's land area and one-third of the inhabitants were in some form of *jagirdari* rule. Beneath the noble *jagirdars* were Hindu *zamindars* and below them were hereditary village lords, whose landless tenants had to struggle to subsist. Even people in areas remaining more directly under the Nizams' control received neither educational and medical services nor police protection comparable to those in parts of India that were under direct British rule.[4]

Up to 1948, about 10 percent of the Hyderabad State population was Muslim. Most Muslims lived in the capital city of Hyderabad or in the smaller cities and large towns. Their language was Urdu: this combined many Arabic, Persian, and Turkic words with the North Indian language of Hindi, and was written in a modified Perso-Arabic script. Urdu was the official language of the state. It was used for all official government activities, which were conducted largely by Muslim and Hindu officials. The 90 percent of the population who were not Muslims spoke one of three other languages. The majority spoke Telugu, the Dravidian language spoken in the northeastern quadrant of South India. Those in the southwestern districts spoke Kannada, another Dravidian language. In the northwest, Marathi, a North Indian language derived from Sanskrit, prevailed. The districts of Hyderabad State where most people spoke Telugu came

---

2. Wiebe, *Heirs and Joint Heirs*, 38-43; George, Alacoque, and Colaco, *Medak District*, 1-2; Luke and Carman, *Village Christians*, 1-3.

3. The Nizams' wealth came from the taxes they collected and from the diamond mines at Golkonda.

4. Wiebe, *Heirs and Joint Heirs*, 43-50.

to be known as Telangana, but this area had no separate political status. All this changed after the ending of the Nizams' rule and, only a few years later, of Hyderabad State itself.

Indian Independence and the End of Hyderabad State

The entire subcontinent of South Asia is bounded by mountains from the northwest to northeast, by the Arabian Sea in the southwest and by the Bay of Bengal in the southeast. Before British rule was established, the entire area had never been united into a single political system. Though much territory had come under the rule of previous empires, most notably the Mauryan Empire of Ashoka and the Mughal Empire at its furthest extent, the whole had never been politically unified. Throughout most of its history, the subcontinent has been divided into many kingdoms, which were often further subdivided into vassal states. The ascendency of European power, after commercial gain was achieved, came by taking advantage of the local wars and shifting alliances among these many kingdoms. As happened in Hyderabad, colonial powers exploited situations where there were rival claimants to various vacant thrones. The English East India Company gradually gained power over these kingdoms, with whom "favorable" agreements and treaties were negotiated. In 1858 the Company was abolished and direct rule over the Indian Empire was assumed by the British Crown.

The popular movement toward independence in the twentieth century involved the parts of India under direct British rule. The parties that negotiated the terms of India's independence largely ignored the wishes of 566 princely states. The British made separate agreements with each of these states, both large and small, and would not assign them to either India or Pakistan. Each state was free to decide whether to join India or Pakistan, or to remain independent. In fact, within a few days, all but two princely states were pressured to accede to one of these new nations.

The Hindu prince who ruled Jammu and Kashmir, with its overwhelmingly Muslim population, delayed his decision but then asked the Indian government to send troops to defend the state against armed intruders. India promptly did so, while Pakistan allowed more "volunteers" to cross the border to help liberate what it regarded as Muslim territory. The result has been a divided state right down to the present that has repeatedly involved India and Pakistan in a state of war that, despite cease-fires, still exists.

Hyderabad presented a situation that was the opposite of that of Kashmir: a Muslim ruler in a state with a largely Hindu population. The Nizam opted for independence, claiming that the state had enough strength to become an independent country. The government of India refused to accept the Nizam's decision. At the end of 1947, it concluded a Standstill Agreement with the Nizam's government. After the Nizam built up arms supplies and allowed militant gangs, the Razakars, to terrorize the non-Muslim population, the Indian army moved into the state and quickly ended the Nizam's rule.[5]

In 1956, when many of the Indian states were reorganized to approximate the areas where different languages were spoken, the Telugu-speaking part of Hyderabad State was added to the state of Andhra to the south and east, and the capital of the combined state was established in Hyderabad City. The new state of Andhra Pradesh has existed since then, and for the first time a democratic system of local government has been introduced in Telangana. Because Telangana was economically less developed at the time of the merger, many wealthy families from elsewhere in the state moved to Hyderabad and other cities in Telangana and established new industries. There have been complaints from Telangana residents that most of the new jobs have gone to people from outside the region. Efforts by the state government to respond to these complaints have not lessened the criticism and the repeated calls for a separate state, which is now scheduled to become a reality.[6]

Village Social Structure and the Position of Dalits

One English word, "caste," is commonly used to stand for two Indian words and concepts. Our word "caste" comes from a Portuguese word meaning "(pure) race" or "breed." The Sanskrit word *varna* originally meant "color." The idea of "four castes" comes from the concept of "four *varnas*," which is what almost every western introduction to Hinduism describes. In this scheme developed by the Brahmins, the four *varnas* are four different categories of people, each with its own distinctive nature, including a different "color" or hue. They are ranked in the order of their ritual purity. Priests come first, warriors come second, and merchants are third, but they are all "twice-born" castes because adolescent boys receive a sacred thread to wear the rest of their lives and thus become officially

---

5. See Bawa, *The Last Nizam*.
6. The "Gentlemen's Agreement" of Andhra Pradesh (1956), signed between Telangana and Andhra leaders before the new state was established, promised safeguards to prevent discrimination against Telangana peoples by the government of Andhra Pradesh. Violations of this agreement, against "*mulki* [native] peoples," lie behind ongoing demands for separate statehood for Telangana (communication from R. E. Frykenberg). For historical context, see his "The Genesis of the Andhra Movement."

A Brief History of Developments in Telangana

"twice born." Brahmins have considered members of the fourth *varna*, called Shudras, to have a lower status, for in this view they were intended to be the servants of the upper castes. Shudras have often contested their lower ranking, and most of them object to the name Shudra *(Śūdra)*.

Those following a modern western approach to ancient Indian history hold that the three higher *varnas* represent the very early division of Indo-European society into three groups: priests, rulers, and commoners. The Aryan tribes that entered India after 2000 B.C.E. retained this division but added a fourth: those previous residents of the Indian subcontinent whom they conquered or in some fashion incorporated into their society. Foreigners, tribal people, and some slaves were "outside" or "below" this four-*varna* structure.

The second word translated as "caste" is *jati* (called *kulam* in these villages). This is the community into which one is born, the network of more and less distant relatives from which comes one's partner in marriage, and normally one's dinner companions, since one usually eats only within one's own caste. One may accept water or food from someone of another caste, provided it is a higher caste than one's own. Many *jatis* have the names of a particular occupation, though people in the same *jati* may in fact have different occupations. In this book, when we speak of a caste, we mean a *jati*, which is the meaning much closer to social reality.

In South India there is scarcely a twice-born warrior *varna*, though there are often *jatis* who claim that they were once high-caste warriors and rulers. In the villages there are only a few high-caste merchants who claim to belong to the third *varna*. There are Brahmins of various ranks and kinds, but in South Indian villages, they usually do not constitute more than 4 percent of the population. About three-quarters of the village people are in *jatis* or *kulams* that in the *varna* system are all considered Shudras, but these *jatis* are also ranked, though there is not always agreement as to the order. The landholding *jatis* rank highest, and then come various artisan castes, some of whom consider themselves as high as the Brahmins (including the rather low-ranking barbers). In centuries past there was another division, between right-handed castes, consisting of Brahmins, landholders. and their servants, and left-handed castes, including many of the artisans — and *their* servants.

There is more agreement about the rank of those at the top and at the bottom than about those in the middle. In terms of power relations in the village, it is very often the landholders who are the "rulers."[7] The 15 to 20 percent at the

---

7. The Brahmanical division of castes into four *varnas* makes little sense in a South Indian village, where only the few families of Brahmins and merchants (*komatis, baniyas,* or *vaishyas*) can claim to belong to the higher "twice-born" *(dvija)* castes. The Brahmanical ranking of castes

bottom of this social ranking have often been called "outcastes" because they are outside and below the *varna* system, but they are themselves divided into at least two *jatis* who do not intermarry or eat together and who regularly dispute who is higher and who is lower. Throughout the Telugu-speaking area there are two main outcaste castes, the Malas and the Madigas. Up to a few generations

---

(kulams or *jatis)*, according to greater or lesser purity, however, does govern a rough consensus, which varies somewhat from region to region. The order in a particular village can be determined by seeing which castes do or do not accept food from other castes. This indicates which are ranked equal or higher, or conversely, lower or less ritually pure. There is ongoing dispute among some castes about their precise ranking.

Most of those who live in the main part of the village belong to castes that Brahmins call *shudras*, a term that many in other castes reject because it implies that they are servants of the three higher categories of castes *(varnas)*. We therefore will not use this collective term. Among those castes, the landholding *jatis* are the most powerful and generally rank highest (the Kapu, Reddi, Deshmukh, Velema, and Kamma). Not all of these are present in any one village. There are also other landholders who have almost as high a status, including the Muthirasi or Mudhiraj, some of whom have recently become Christians.

Among the many occupational castes, the potters (Kummari) and herders (Golla) claim equal ritual rank with the landholders. After them come the weavers (Sale) and toddy-tappers (Gaondla), then the washermen (Sakali) and barbers (Mangali). Still lower are the stone-workers (Vaddari) and hunters (Erkala), who also make mats. There are also castes that are not present in every village, including fishermen (Bestha) and tailors (Darzi).

There are five groups of craftsmen who do intermarry and therefore constitute a single caste (Pancha Bramha or Viswa Bramha). They are the carpenters (Wadla), blacksmiths (Kammari), goldsmiths (Amsula or Kamsali), coppersmiths (Kasi), and sculptors who carve divine images (Kancheri). They do not recognize the superiority of Brahmins and will accept food from no other castes, but no other caste (except recently some Madigas) will accept food from them. It is possible that they once belonged to a religious sect that rejected Brahmin authority, such as the Lingayats, Jains, or Buddhists. Interestingly, the Baljas, exclusive worshipers of Shiva, who may have once been part of the Lingayat movement of protest against the Brahmins, do have a high ritual ranking (above the merchants, though below the Brahmins).

All these castes consider themselves far superior to the Malas and Madigas, who live in separate hamlets at the edge of the village. They are "outside" the Brahmin system of four castes, even though their services are essential to the village economy and also to village religion. They are distinct from one another. They do not intermarry. The Malas consider themselves superior to the Madigas, a claim that the Madigas reject. Each caste has had traditional degrading duties: the Malas in connection with funerals and the disposal of dead animals, the Madigas in the skinning of dead cattle and the tanning of their hides. Some Malas have had a traditional role in sacrificing pigs to a village goddess, while the Madiga headman had to sacrifice buffalo. Madigas were leather workers and the servants of village officials. Until recently, they did not own any land and were close to being domestic servants or serfs. Now many have small landholdings, whose produce supplements their earnings as farm laborers. The other groups, who live outside the villages and/or migrate from place to place are called "Scheduled Tribes," which are described separately. See Luke and Carman, *Village Christians*, 8; Dube, *Indian Village*, 19-20, 36-40; Wiebe, "Religious Change in South India"; also incorporated in Wiebe, *Christians in Andra Pradesh*, 176.

ago, many were virtual slaves or serfs working for families of what was considered a higher caste. Some were obligated to do the dirty work of the village, that is, that which is ritually polluting. The theoretical ranking of the four-*varna* system and the more practical ranking of the *jati* system, which is largely based on wealth and political power, share the same ideological principle: ritual purity. If some castes are more pure or clean, others must be less so. The castes at the bottom were referred to in English as "untouchables" because their touch was defiling to "higher-caste" Hindus. Even the shadow of an untouchable crossing a Brahmin's path might require a Brahmin to take a ritual bath. While the more extreme signs of their low status are no longer enforced in these villages, a crucial marker remains. The outcaste groups live in a hamlet often separated from the main village by a road or even an entire field. The recent expansion of many villages has lessened the physical separation between the two parts of the village, but often not the social distance between them.

Mahatma Gandhi tried to raise the status of these untouchables by calling them Harijans, "Children of God." The government of independent India has outlawed untouchability, and various efforts have been made by the government and private agencies to lift outcastes out of poverty and illiteracy. Gandhi challenged the ranking according to degrees of purity, but he defended the system of separate caste communities. So far the basic structure of social life in these villages has only slightly weakened a ranking based on ritual purity as well as on political and economic power. We might say that the Brahmins supply the theory and the wealthy families (often the big landholders) exercise the power to keep the traditional system functioning. After Dr. Ambedkar led a half million members of his outcaste group, the Mahars (with more to follow after his death), to convert to his new form of Buddhism, a new name for all outcastes came into use: Dalit, which means the "crushed" or "oppressed."[8] Most of the Christians described in *Village Christians,* as well as their Hindu relatives and neighbors, were Dalits.

Some of the individuals and families who have recently become Christians come from other castes living in the main part of the village; some belong to groups that are considered by the government to be not "castes," but "tribes." While in other parts of India, "tribes" are often those who live far away from Hindu villages in jungles or mountains, here "tribes" are those groups who live

---

8. Bhimrao Ramji Ambedkar was born in 1891 and grew up in the Mahar outcaste community and in Maharashtra (north of Telangana) but received an extensive education, including a Ph.D. in political science from Columbia University and advanced studies at the London School of Economics. He became a spokesman for all Indian outcastes, whom he called Dalits, and tried unsuccessfully to secure a separate electorate for Dalits, comparable to what the British colonial government had granted to Muslims (Viswanathan, *Outside the Fold,* 211).

at the edge of or outside villages and often move from place to place. One group, the Lambadas, are related to Gypsies (Banjaras) in other parts of India and have their own distinct language and customs. Another group, the Budagajangalu, are traveling minstrels who often settle near a village and also work as day laborers.

Changes in Society during the Past Fifty Years

Several changes have taken place in the past fifty years in the Jangarai section and in the Wadiaram pastorate as a whole. Previously, the resident evangelist in a village was the pastor, teacher, doctor, and guide to members of the congregation and to others in the Dalit hamlet; he often exercised a certain amount of authority. This combination of roles was gradually reduced by various developments in the region.

The government of Andhra Pradesh has started a program to improve the educational system. The goal is for every village to have a primary school, and for there to be a middle school for every three to four villages. High schools and junior colleges have been established in the administrative centers, and degree-granting colleges have opened in the district headquarters and in other towns in the district. Education has been made compulsory. Free bus passes are issued to Dalit students to make affordable their transportation to the schools and colleges. Parents are counseled and considered to have committed an offense if they do not send their children to school. Another important element of the plan is for each village to be provided with preschool facilities. Ultimately, there should be no child in any village who does not attend school and become literate.

Medical facilities are also being improved. Increasingly, villages are visited by health workers who counsel women about bearing children and prenatal care. Primary health care centers are being set up close to surrounding villages. These centers also provide information regarding family planning, leprosy, tuberculosis, AIDS, and other diseases that recur every year. The state government (now led by the Congress Party) has introduced a plan by which poor people who hold a "white ration card" are to be treated free of cost in government and private hospitals. Emergency care is also generally available.

Village infrastructure is also being developed. Many villages now have roads connecting them to main roads. Public transportation is provided by government buses connecting villages to larger towns and cities. Many village families today own at least a bicycle, and some even have motorcycles or scooters. Instead of only one telephone in the village at the headman's house, today almost every family has at least one cell phone, which gives them greater independence.

A Brief History of Developments in Telangana

The government's goal is to electrify every village. While there was formerly one radio per village, today many homes have television, giving them greater access to the outside world.

The government housing program for Dalits made it possible for many Dalit families to move out of thatch-roofed mud huts and to build houses with roofs of more durable Mangalore tiles. With recent government help, some houses have concrete roofs. Living conditions have improved in other respects as well. The government has constructed community halls for the "upper castes" as well as for Dalits in the midst of their respective parts of the village, thereby encouraging increased community life. Where there are no church buildings for worship, both upper-caste Christians (in the independent churches) and Dalits (in CSI congregations) are using their own particular community halls for Sunday worship services.

There is also a drastic change in the appearance of the countryside. Factories can be seen along the roadsides, especially along the road from Wadiaram to Medak, on or near which are many of the congregations in the Jangarai section. Iron foundries, factories manufacturing foam and recycled paper, and other factories have unfortunately polluted the air with constant gas emissions and polluted village reservoirs with effluents. The region has attracted migrants from far-off places. The factory owners have often brought employees from their own part of North India, thus depriving local villagers of some employment opportunities.

Political Systems in Andhra Pradesh

The political situation has changed drastically since the end of the Nizam's rule in 1948, before which the districts and other administrative units were largely under the control of Muslim government officials or of families who ruled groups of villages called *jagirs*. Within each village, however, the local village councils *(panchayats)* were usually dominated by the Hindu landholding castes and the village Brahmins. After Hyderabad State joined India, a democratic system of government was instituted. Henceforth all adults could vote for council members at the village, subdistrict, and district levels, as well as for representatives to the state legislative assembly and the national parliament. The same political parties could compete at all levels.

Now, like the national government of India, Andhra Pradesh has a parliamentary system with two houses, the legislative assembly and the legislative council, with 288 members and 90 members, respectively. General elections choosing members of the assembly are held every five years, and the leader of the largest party or coalition of parties becomes the chief minister, assisted by a cabinet called the council of ministers. The governor is appointed by the president of India, and like the president, has both ceremonial and political functions, not least in making appointments. The day-to-day administration is the responsibility of various non-elected officials, some at the state level and some for each district, with its district collector and district magistrate. Other officials head the smaller units within the district. In addition to the police, there are officials supervising development projects, teachers at every level in a vast educational system, as well as medical personnel in hospitals and clinics.

There are elected representatives, not only to the national assembly and the state legislature, but also to municipal councils in the cities and towns, a council for each circle of villages, and another council for the district as a whole. In the early years after independence, the Congress Party candidates usually won, with some opposition from the Communist Party. Gradually, other parties gained in strength and sometimes defeated the Congress Party at the state or local level. Often members of certain caste groups all vote for the same candidate, though the affiliation of a particular caste with a particular political party has varied somewhat from district to district and from one election to another. In the post-independence political system in India, a certain number of seats are reserved for minorities, including Muslims, "Scheduled Castes," and "Backward Classes." The chairmanship of village and regional councils rotates among the various constituencies, so minority groups who are lower in the traditional social ranking get their turn at leadership. The actual control of the councils often depends on alliances between castes, as well as on the impact of forceful personalities. Some of the council members are women.

For Dalits, who previously had no political voice, this change is particularly important. For Christians belonging to Dalit castes, however, the positive effect of this change has been blunted by the Presidential Order of 1950 defining "Scheduled Castes" as restricted to Hindus. Later on, first Sikhs and then Buddhists of Dalit background were added, but Muslims and Christians from the groups traditionally considered "outcastes" are still excluded, despite many protests. In August 2009 the Andhra Pradesh state assembly "adopted a resolution urging the Central Government to extend the benefits of Scheduled Castes (SC) to Christians and Muslims of Dalit origin."[9] So far the Indian government

---

9. On August 25, 2009, the State Assembly of Andhra Pradesh passed a resolution urging the central government of India to "extend the benefits of Scheduled Castes to Christians and Muslims of Dalit origin." The vote was nearly unanimous. Only the three members of Hindu nationalist parties voted against it. (This information was sent in an e-mail by the Rev. Raj Bharath Patta of the National Council of Churches in India.) Andhra Pradesh was the third state to pass such a resolution. The central government, however, has taken no action in response.

has not responded to this resolution, though its minister of minorities, himself a Muslim, has stated his agreement. (Unfortunately, Dr. Y. S. Rajashekar Reddy, the chief minister who moved this resolution and who was himself a Christian, was killed in a helicopter crash a few months later.) Under the present regulations, Christians who register as Christians are not considered to belong to the Scheduled Castes but are counted in one of the Backward Class constituencies. Christians who register themselves as Hindus, however, are considered to be part of the Scheduled Castes. Thus, some of the Dalit Christians are no longer officially Christians, while other Christians are not officially Dalits, even though they still live in the Dalit section of the village and are considered by everyone else in the village, as well by themselves, to be Dalit Malas or Madigas. The examples given in "Participation of Some Village Christians in Politics" below show that Dalit Christians in the Wadiaram pastorate have sometimes been able to win political offices reserved for members of the Scheduled Castes.

There may be many in these villages for whom the Indian government's official position — that registered Christians are not members of the Scheduled Castes — makes no sense. It contradicts the continuing social reality and unjustly deprives Christians of the special benefits and reservations available to other Dalits. The fact that the state legislature passed a resolution to end this discrimination against both Christians and Muslims from Dalit backgrounds suggests that public opinion is turning in this direction, perhaps especially in South India, where Christians are a larger minority. In the meantime, churches are often not providing evidence as to who officially belongs to their membership. In some cases in another part of the state, pastors are even asked to write letters saying that certain members of their congregation are really not Christians![10] Since the Hindu nationalist party (Bharatiya Janata Party, or BJP) and its legislative allies, which are stronger in many states than in Andhra Pradesh, as well as in the central government, support the present law, no change is likely in the near future. Because of their good standing in the community at large, however, some Dalit Christians may be able to contest seats, at least in local elections, that are reserved for candidates from the Scheduled Castes.

Opinions may differ as to whether educated Christians with good jobs in the cities should continue to have reservations in the legislature and special benefits because of their Dalit background, but Dalit Christians in the villages are in a very different position. Despite the ending of legal servitude, greater educational opportunities, and the weakening of the most blatant forms of caste prejudice, they still must live in a hamlet at the edge of the main village, many of whose residents continue to look down on them. Even their Christian religion

---

10. Source withheld in order to protect the persons concerned.

is scorned by being connected with their caste names; it is known in the main village as "the religion of Malas and Madigas." It remains to be seen whether the new independent churches, with many members living in the main village, will be able to change the way that all Christians are regarded throughout the village. The few who have been successful in local and regional politics, whether or not they are officially Christians, show that some attitudes are changing. It is not accidental that all these persons have lived in or nearby larger villages and towns, where urban attitudes are making an impact and enterprising individuals can forge ahead regardless of their background. One indication of this change is greater toleration of inter-caste marriages than in the more remote villages.

New Urban Connections of Village Christians

The city of Hyderabad is continuing to grow rapidly and is expanding, not only in population, but also in geographical spread, a spread that brings more and more of the surrounding towns and villages into the urban complex. The road running between Hyderabad and Wadiaram, a distance of about forty-five miles, has been widened to become part of a national highway going north all the way to New Delhi. Now factories and tall apartment buildings are springing up more than halfway north to Wadiaram. The town of Toopran, at the southern end of the Wadiaram pastorate, is now a small city of more than 50,000. There is frequent bus service to the capital city along the main highway, with less frequent buses providing connections to Hyderabad from what were formerly remote villages. Many people in Toopran commute to work in the metropolis; and from most villages, Hyderabad is only two hours away.

In 1832 Charles Metcalfe, then the British resident in Hyderabad and the chief "adviser" to the Nizam's court, wrote that the villages were "little republics, having nearly everything they want within themselves."[11] While these villages were never completely self-sufficient, they were parts of relatively small regional networks with little interaction with the wider world outside the network. Fifty years ago, only a decade after the end of the Nizam's rule, the situation was just beginning to change. Now, since 2010, there is much more than better transportation to link the villages to the city. Cell phones unite villagers to friends and relatives who have moved to the city, and television connects every village to the entire Telugu-speaking area and, less directly, to the rest of India and the whole world.

---

11. Wiebe, *Christians in Andhra Pradesh*, 62. Metcalfe borrowed the concept from Sir Thomas Munro's 1806 report on the subject (communication from R. E. Frykenberg).

A Brief History of Developments in Telangana

It is now much easier not just to visit Hyderabad for a day, but to move there permanently, returning to a home village only for visits. This is true for most caste groups in the village. Our limited information is only about two all-Dalit congregations, the largest ones in this part of the pastorate. Ten Christian families moved from Kondapur to get factory jobs or day labor in Hyderabad. Fifteen young people have left Bandaposanipally to start college courses and/or to find jobs in the city. One of them has completed a college degree and found a position in the Life Insurance Corporation. Three are studying for a bachelor of arts degree, two for a bachelor of education, and one is in an intermediate (junior college) program. All but two of the remaining young people had finished their secondary education. (Three had passed their tenth standard exam while three had failed it.) It is not surprising that only two of the fifteen are women since most young women their age have already married and moved away to their husbands' villages. It is more surprising that all the migrants from one congregation sought jobs, while half of those from a rather similar congregation were continuing their education to the college level. A more detailed and extensive survey in the other congregations would reveal further differences and alternative pathways, and it is too early to say whether some individuals or families will return, perhaps even after retirement, to their home villages.

Most of the Christian young people and at least some of the families return home for Christmas. The young people returning have led the local youth in such innovations as decorating the church and singing carols, but so far they have not lessened the tight hold of the older men on congregational affairs. We were told that those who have left after failing their tenth standard exam sometimes boast about their success in urban life, showing off electronic gadgets and talking about their love affairs. Some of the migrants say they are attending a CSI church in the city, while others are going to independent churches. How many no longer have any church connection is not known. Whether or not they keep a Christian connection may only be determined in the future, especially by their partners in marriage.

Looking at the urban connection in terms of the city churches' connection to the villages is also instructive. Because of migration from so many villages, CSI churches in Hyderabad have grown considerably, and new pastorates have been established. Many urban church members now enjoy an income many times that of their relatives in the villages. Some city Christians have started to tithe; all in CSI churches are supposed to pay a monthly membership fee, and some make liberal offerings. All the CSI urban pastorates normally contribute 75 percent of the offerings they receive to the diocesan central pool. The remainder provide their pastor with various allowances and a festival gift. Funds in the diocesan central pool pay a large fraction of the salaries of all the rural pastors.

The CSI rural congregations are therefore dependent on the city churches to pay for their pastoral care. This is still another "urban connection" for village churches, replacing their former dependence on the Methodist Missionary Society in Great Britain.

Despite the closer connection between city and village, there are many continuing differences between forms of urban and rural life, and more specific differences in the patterns of Christian life. This study is concerned with village Christians, but it is also necessarily concerned with pastoral care. Many CSI pastors, even if they began their lives in a village, have had much of their education in an urban setting. Many of their expectations are those of the urban middle class, and their seminary education is urban, even though great efforts are made to keep students connected with village churches. It is not surprising, therefore, that assignments to remote rural pastorates are often unwelcome and that moving back to the city is considered a promotion. One of the advantages that some independent pastors have is that they feel more at home in a village setting than do CSI pastors. The challenge for all pastors is to bridge the gap between village and city, both in lifestyle and in theology, for that is what the members of their congregations will increasingly have to do.

Participation of Some Village Christians in Politics

Returning to an area where the political involvement of a few individuals was noted fifty years ago has given us an unusual opportunity to learn of developments in succeeding generations. A paragraph in *Village Christians* refers to Daniel of Rayelli village, in the southern part of the pastorate, who was elected chairman of the new village board *(panchayat)* and was also elected vice chairman of the congregation.[12] Daniel's grandmother had become a Christian after her husband died. Daniel was the eldest son of her son, Papaiah, all six of whose children were married to Hindus. Daniel's wife was converted after their marriage; she stopped drinking and was taught to read by the evangelist for the congregation. She and Daniel had eight sons and two daughters, all of whom were married to Christians and lived as Christians. (The eldest son's marriage was performed by the late P. Y. Luke, co-author of *Village Christians*.) Three of Daniel's great-grandsons have had "love marriages" — with decisions made by the couple, rather than by their parents — one to a Hindu girl of the Reddy caste, one to a Brahmin who became a Christian, and one to a Marathi Christian.

---

12. Luke and Carman, *Village Christians*, 135.

A Brief History of Developments in Telangana

Daniel's third son, Samuel, continued his father's political legacy. (Samuel's three children have all had Christian marriages.) He was elected a member of the village council *(panchayat)* in 1980 and was on the state electricity board; he also held various other offices, including vice chairman of the Cooperative Society in the large town of Toopran. In 1984 and 1989 he ran, unsuccessfully, for the national parliament as an independent candidate, and also ran once, unsuccessfully, for the state legislative assembly. After that, he joined the Hindu nationalist party (BJP) and held many offices in the party as well as representing labor unions. He served as general secretary of the Sawmill and Timber Merchants Association, and he also represented the Wadiaram pastorate for two terms on the Medak District Church Council. Someone lodged a complaint that since he was a Christian, he should not be allowed to be a candidate for a seat reserved for a member of the Scheduled Castes. Samuel responded by asserting his patriotism for India as a whole and his support for a separate Telangana state, whereupon the opposition to his candidacy subsided. He hopes to run again for the state legislature or for parliament. He is now recovering from a paralytic stroke. His income is secured by the sawmill he owns and his vast farmlands. Samuel's youngest son, Emmanuel, has also entered politics, winning a place on the village council on the BJP ticket.

Another of Daniel's grandsons (the son of his eldest son, David) has also entered politics, but he is affiliated with the Telugu Desam Party. He has served for five years as the vice chairman of the village council. Another of Daniel's grandsons has worked for the central government's telephone department as a line inspector and has been elected general secretary of the Telephone Workers' Union.

The role of women from Dalit Christian families in local politics deserves notice. One is Krishnaveni, a Dalit woman with Christian parents, who moved from her village to Wadiaram. She was first helped by the CSI presbyter and then started attending the independent church of Pastor Nehemiah. While working in a factory, she fell in love with Asif, a young Muslim, and married him. Both continued their previous religious practices. She once gave a dinner in her husband's honor; there, she related that at one time her husband's heart had stopped beating, but that she prayed over him and he recovered. Asif then testified that Jesus Christ appeared to him in a dream with a bright light and told him to testify that Jesus had rescued him from death. Krishnaveni then testified how Christians in Wadiaram had helped her to become literate. She has been elected as the Mandal president, and her husband has supported her in her political career. She now comes to the CSI church occasionally for prayers and when invited for special occasions. She is considered a political leader in good standing.

Another woman politician, Prathiba, is the current president of the Wadiaram village council. She married a Christian Dalit in a Christian marriage ceremony. Her husband had earned bachelor's and master's degrees; he became an inspector of schools, appointed to a position reserved for a member of the Scheduled Castes. He then established a high school bearing his wife's name in Chegunta, the town adjoining Wadiaram. He lived in the Dalit hamlet, but Prathiba built a house on the other side of the village, close to the Backward Class community, including the fisher caste and some other caste groups. In 2005 the post of *sarpanch* (head, president, or chairperson) of the village council was reserved for a Scheduled Caste member. Because of where she was living, Prathiba was able to gain the support of both the Scheduled Castes and the Backward Class community. Running as the candidate of a party pressing for a separate Telangana state, she won the election.

Both women competed for the position of chairperson of the Wadiaram village council, and both raised questions about the Christian family connections of the other candidate without affecting the outcome, so one now chairs the village council and the other chairs the mandal (subdistrict) council.

Mrs. Sunchu Balamma Devadass holds the same position of chairperson of the village council *(panchayat)* in Chinna Shivnur. She is a member of the local CSI church and the wife of Pastor Devadass, also originally from that church, who became a Pentecostal minister and started the independent church in Achampet, which was discussed in chapter 1. They returned to their home village so that she could run for the council *(panchayat)* chairmanship, which that year was reserved for a Scheduled Caste candidate. She won easily, running as an independent candidate with the support of the whole village. After the election, she joined a party advocating a separate Telangana state. It is well known that Mrs. Devadass is a Christian, but that did not deter people from voting for her to hold a Scheduled Caste position, and no one seems to have objected.

CHAPTER 3

Christianity in India and Telangana

Thomas Christians and Roman Catholic Missions

Early in Christian history, churches were established in India. Most Indian Christians believe that the apostle Thomas arrived in southwest India (the present state of Kerala) in 52 C.E. and several years later was martyred outside the city of Mailapur (now part of metropolitan Chennai), on a hill now called St. Thomas Mount. According to a tradition that was passed down for centuries in song and verse, St. Thomas came from Arabia by sea and landed near an ancient seaport that was important in the coastal trade, which then extended from the Mediterranean to China.[1] The "Song of Thomas" recounts his founding of churches in seven nearby towns, his journeys to Mailapur, and one journey all the way to China. These Christians used Syriac in their liturgy, just as the Jews who had already settled in these towns used Hebrew for their prayers and as the Muslims who came a few centuries later used Arabic. Many Syrian Christian families trace their lineage back to the apostle Thomas's original converts, all coming from high-caste Hindu families. There are also traditions that at least twice the Christian community was joined by refugees from Mesopotamia and Persia, the first fleeing persecution by Sassanian-Zoroastrian rule, the second escaping from Muslim rule.

Like many later churches, the Syrian churches show evidence of their foreign origin but also of adaptation of their religious and social practices to the local culture. The "Song of Thomas" lists thousands of converts in each of the

---

1. Churches in the Middle East also celebrate the life of the apostle Thomas in a history that highlights his journey to a king in Bactria but also includes his later journey to South India.

Brahmanical four *varnas,* but no aboriginals or "untouchables." The number of those miraculously healed was also listed: more than two hundred each from leprosy, paralysis, and blindness, as well as "ninety-four souls delivered from death."[2] The linking of Syrian Christians with the higher *varnas* has continued to be central to these Christians' sense of their own place in a largely Hindu society, and the kinds of healings catalogued are remarkably similar to those we describe in later chapters of this book.

Until the modern period most Syrian Christians continued to live only in southwest India, where they were a highly ranked minority, equivalent to the upper castes. Since the coming of the Portuguese in 1498, their history has been intertwined with that of Roman Catholics. During the 150 years of Portuguese military dominance, the affiliation of Syrian Christians was forcibly shifted from the Church of the East to Roman Catholicism. After that, part of the community of Thomas Christians renounced its allegiance to Rome but linked itself to a different patriarch in the Middle East (Monophysite instead of Diophysite or Nestorian) while retaining most of its ancient Syriac liturgy. Since then, Syrian Christians have been split into a variety of denominations, which since the nineteenth century has included a reformed group of churches (Mar Thoma) influenced by Protestant missionaries and an Anglican community now part of the Church of South India.

Two large groups of Syrian Christians are affiliated with Rome, one retaining the Syriac liturgy, the other following the ritual in Latin and, since Vatican II, in modern Indian languages. Other Roman Catholic groups include many Hindu converts in the formerly Portuguese territory of Goa, and two large caste communities of fishermen who made a collective decision to become Catholic Christians in response to the missionary efforts of the pioneer Jesuit St. Francis Xavier. Various Roman Catholic orders started missions outside of Portuguese territory. Perhaps the most notable were the two simultaneous Jesuit missions in the Tamil city of Madurai. The one directed to low-caste Hindus was kept separate from the other directed exclusively to Brahmins and other high-caste Hindus. The latter was conducted by the Italian Jesuit Roberto de Nobili, who adopted the lifestyle of a Brahmin ascetic and learned to speak and write in both Sanskrit and Tamil in order to argue for the truth of Catholic teaching against Hindu scholars. In the first generation both missions were successful in gaining converts and in developing a form of Christianity more adapted to Hindu culture. They were hampered, however, by the opposition of other Catholic orders that thought this adaptation was going too far. A century later, when the Jesuit order was suppressed by papal decree, many Catholic converts in South India

---

2. Frykenberg, *Christianity in India,* 100.

were left without pastoral guidance. This led some to return to their previous Hindu connection and others to join the new Protestant churches.

In the nineteenth century the Jesuit order was restored and enabled to resume its missions in India, and many other Catholic missions multiplied. For the first time, many Indians became priests. The number of Roman Catholics quadrupled by 1900. Since then, their numbers have further multiplied, and Catholic missions have expanded in many parts of India, especially in establishing schools and colleges. They form the largest Christian community in India as a whole.

Roman Catholics have generally been more willing than Protestants to continue caste distinctions, and they generally have a larger proportion of members belonging to the higher and middle castes than do Protestant denominations. Catholic Christians have also made closer connections with Hindu traditions than have most Protestants. Their celibate priests share some of the respect that Hindus accord to their own ascetics; Catholic scholars have explored many Hindu scriptures and philosophical traditions; and popular Catholic rituals such as the procession of saints' images have often attracted many Hindus.[3]

One of the earliest Catholic missionaries in India, the Franciscan friar Luis de Salvador, visited the powerful Hindu kingdom of Vijayanagar, which included the southwestern section of the Telugu country, now in Andhra Pradesh. Though opposed by the Brahmins, he eventually won the king's favor and was granted permission to preach and establish churches. A generation later, around 1530, another Franciscan, Antonio de Padrao, continued the mission and gained converts among the weaver, herder, and toddy-tapper castes.[4] This mission was not sustained, and a Jesuit mission after 1550 was also largely unsuccessful, both in Vijayanagar and in the Islamic kingdom of Bijapur to the north.

In 1622 the papacy established a new body, the Propaganda Fide (Sacred Congregation for the Propagation of the Faith), to supervise Roman Catholic missions, one that was outside the control of the Portuguese government and church, known as the Padroado. By that time, Indian rulers were treating many Catholic priests as agents of the Portuguese government. Under the supervision of the new Congregation in Rome, a missionary went to the kingdom of Golkonda in 1645, followed by priests from several Catholic orders. By 1735, however, missionary work in the Telugu area came to a standstill, and the churches declined. A severe famine and local wars contributed to the decline, as did

---

3. Frykenberg, *Christianity in India*, 116-41.
4. Their hereditary occupation was to climb palm trees and tap their sap, which was used to make the strong alcoholic drink called "toddy" in Indian English, *kalu* in Telugu, and *arrack* in both Arabic and Urdu.

the lack of Indian clergy.[5] In the nineteenth century, Catholic missions were revived, and the number of Telugu Catholics has greatly increased (610,000 in 1970), but they are still fewer than the number of Protestants in Andhra Pradesh. While the number of Indian priests has multiplied in the past one hundred years, the corps of priests coming from the Telugu-speaking area is still small.[6]

A survey in the 1970s found that the number of Catholics in the entire Medak District was fewer than 2000. Some of them are families that migrated northward from Coastal Andhra during a severe famine there between 1896 and 1900. Out of 1260 villages in the Medak District, there were 200 Catholic families in 25 villages. All those in the rural areas belonged to the landholding Reddy and Thogata castes. (There were no Catholics from the Dalit castes.) Until 1972, there were only 2 priests, and the 8 sisters were all working in the one urban parish. Then the Society of the Divine Word took over responsibility, increasing the clerical leadership to 4 priests, 3 lay brothers, and 13 sisters.[7]

Earliest Protestants and Dalit "Mass Movements"

The first Protestant *(Evangelische)* missionaries in India were two Lutheran Pietists from Germany, appointed by King Frederick IV of Denmark.[8] In 1706 Bartholomaeus Ziegenbalg and Heinrich Plutschau arrived in Tranquebar, a Danish seaport on the southeast coast of India, in what is now Tamil Nadu. Ziegenbalg set himself to learning both classical and spoken Tamil as quickly as possible, first sitting with school children and later listening to Tamil texts even while he ate. Within a year he was able to write and preach in Tamil, and within two years he composed two Tamil dictionaries and a grammar. His primary objective was to translate the entire Bible into Tamil. He lived only until 1719, long enough to complete the New Testament and see it published on a printing press sent from Europe. He learned about and sent to Europe descriptions of

---

5. An exception to the decline is the village of Faringipuram, near Guntur in central, or coastal, Andhra, which since the seventeenth or eighteenth century has been ruled by Catholics belonging to the landholding Kamma caste (communication from R. E. Frykenberg).

6. George, Alacoque, and Colaco, *Medak District*, 29-37.

7. George, Alacoque, and Colaco, *Medak District*, 69-75.

8. In the previous century, two Dutch Reformed chaplains in the service of the Dutch East India Company (Rogerius and Baldaeus) had written about "East Indian paganism" during their stay in South India and Ceylon. Baldaeus tried to convert Roman Catholics in Jaffna to the Reformed faith, but Dutch chaplains did not think of themselves primarily as bringing the gospel to Hindus. See Hudson, *Protestant Origins in India*, 5-9, and Frykenberg, *Christianity in India*, 145-46.

every phase of Tamil culture, and at the same time he started a school in which children of any caste could learn arithmetic as well as reading and writing. By the time that he died, he had completed building the New Jerusalem Church. The first Indian catechist was a captain in the palace guard of the king of Thanjāvur. In 1733 a member of the landholding and literate Vellala caste with the Christian name of Aaron became the first ordained Tamil minister to work in that kingdom.[9]

The small number of German missionaries in the generations that followed trained a significant number of Tamil teacher-pastors, who spread the new type of schools and the "Evangelical" churches to many cities and towns in the Tamil country. These churches included individuals and families from various castes, with the leadership coming from the Vellalas. Those in the castes considered lower would accept their leadership, but Vellalas would not accept a pastor from a lower caste, especially one from a Dalit caste. In the very first congregation, Ziegenbalg wrote back to Germany that those dressed in European clothes "sit on benches and stools," but those in Indian clothes "sit on mats and down on the paved floor." "Heathens and Muslims stand at the four windows and doors."[10] Divisions in seating arrangements between Europeans, high-caste Tamils, and low-caste Tamils persisted for a long time, and they reflected social distinctions that are still present within the Christian community in India. These early Lutheran Christians were "sitting together, separately" in the same building for a common act of worship, and there was room around the edges for Hindu and Muslim onlookers. Another division in seating that has continued is between women and men: women sit on one side of the church or worship hall, while men sit on the other.

By the beginning of the nineteenth century, another kind of Protestant congregation was gaining strength. In the extreme south of the Tamil country, members of the toddy-tapper caste, then known as Shanars, were a significant fraction of the population, often living in their own settlements at some distance from other villages. When they started to become Christians in large numbers, they often formed congregations consisting only of members of their own caste. While they were considered "untouchables" by "higher-caste" Hindus, they themselves began to claim a higher status, saying that they had once been "lords" *(nadars)* belonging to the second or "warrior" *varna* and thus originally outranked their present masters, the landholding Vellalas. In this claim they

---

9. Frykenberg, *Christianity in India*, 146-52; Hudson, *Protestant Origins in India*, 10-34.
10. Hudson, *Protestant Origins in India*, 50, quoting Ziegenbalg 1957: 90. Other sources also mention that the lowest-caste Christians sat on unpaved ground without a mat (communication from R. E. Frykenberg).

were joined by others of the same caste who remained Hindu. They all are now called Nadars. Thus, an entire caste community succeeded in raising its caste ranking. While not considered "rulers," they are now considered higher than the outcaste communities (Dalits), and their economic position has greatly improved. They form a cohesive caste community, whether they are Christians or Hindus.

The Nadar Christians soon considerably outnumbered the Vellala Christians, but the latter, initially with greater wealth and more education, continued their leadership in many congregations and mission institutions. As Christians, many of them continued some aspects of their century-old attempt to follow a Brahmanical lifestyle, being strict vegetarians and spending time in devotional exercises and family prayers. Many Christian Vellalas have also continued their social relations with their Hindu relatives.

There were also many in the early Protestant churches who belonged to the lowest castes, now called Dalits. Yet, it was only after the middle of the nineteenth century that Dalits became the large majority of Protestant Christians. In Telugu-speaking areas, now equivalent to Andhra Pradesh, a very high proportion of them are Dalits.

During the nineteenth century, the number of British and American missionaries in India greatly increased, and many Christian schools and colleges were started. There were still only a small number of individual converts, many of whom were rejected by their families and often lived within a mission community. In many places, Protestant missionaries insisted that those seeking baptism move to the town where the missionary lived, receive Christian instruction for several months, and demonstrate that they had abandoned all their previous Hindu practices. That pattern changed when new converts were baptized in their own villages and continued to live there. This practice began among the Nadars by 1800. The first instance in the Telugu country may have begun about 1860 when the Mala headman Venkayya and fifteen others were baptized in their home village by the Anglican missionary T. Y. Darling. Their relatives in other villages also started to become Christians.[11] About five years later a husband and wife (Yerragantla Periah and Nagamma) from the other major Dalit caste, the Madigas, were baptized one hundred miles further south. Soon thereafter Periah persuaded John Clough, the new American Baptist missionary in Ongole, located near the coast, to allow several of his relatives and other Madigas in his village to be baptized and to remain in their home village, rather than come to the town where the missionary was living. Within a few months there were more new Telugu converts than there had been in thirty-

---

11. Oddie, "Christian Conversion in Telugu Country, 1860-1900."

one years of missionary activity, and in the following decade their numbers increased to thousands more.

Thus began the "mass movements" among both outcaste groups in the Telugu-speaking area, the Malas and the Madigas. The same new style of rural churches led by local pastors with minimal education, supervised by foreign missionaries responsible for a large numbers of villages, was followed in other Protestant missions in adjoining districts. In the areas of greatest expansion by the American Baptist mission, most of the new Christians were Madigas. In the adjoining and sometimes overlapping areas of the American (United) Lutheran mission, however, it was Mala communities that became Christians. Thus, in some parts of Guntur District, there are still two churches within the same village, one Baptist and one Lutheran, each consisting of a single caste group.

Yerragantla Periah: Pioneer Dalit Christian Leader

Yerragantla Periah was John Everett Clough's partner in starting the first major conversion movement among Madigas. His leadership owed much to his unusual religious background. He grew up taking part in the Madiga worship of village goddesses; but, from his grandfather's time, his family members were lay disciples of a guru *(acharya)* of the devotional community worshiping Vishnu as the supreme deity, following the tradition of the twelfth-century teacher Ramanuja.[12] As an adult, Periah was initiated by a woman guru into the yoga tradition of a devotee of Shiva named Veerabrahmam. This gave Periah an even higher standing among Madigas. From then on, he spent an hour a day in meditation and became a guru with disciples in many villages. After becoming a Christian and for the rest of his life, he kept a staff that marked him as a guru. He persuaded many of his disciples, as well as many members of the Ramanuja sect, to become Christians. In his old age, he said, "What the teacher of Yoga told me was good. But nothing satisfied my soul till I heard of Jesus Christ."[13]

When Periah and his wife, Nagamma, first met Clough's colleague, Dr. Lyman Jewett, the older missionary was so impressed by the sincerity of their faith that he was ready to baptize them immediately. Half a year later, when Clough asked Periah to bring the thirty or more new believers to Ongole (in coastal Guntur District) for instruction before baptism, Periah objected. After some

---

12. Clough, *Social Christianity in the Orient*, 93. See also Rauschenbusch-Clough, *While Sewing Sandals*, and Downie, *The Lone Star*.
13. Clough, *Social Christianity in the Orient*, 95.

discussion, he convinced Clough that it would be better to come to his village, forty miles away, where Clough could give several days of instruction and then baptize those he considered to be sincere. Clough decided that Periah's way was appropriate since many of the new converts had been Periah's disciples and since this approach would be in accord with "New Testament methods." In Periah's village, five days later, Clough baptized twenty-eight people from various villages, almost as many as the thirty-eight who had been baptized by the American Baptist Mission during the previous thirty-one years!

More than ten thousand Madigas became Christians in the following twelve years. A large number of these had been influenced by disciples of a Muslim sufi who had established a reformed Hindu sect centered in yoga. He was known as Yogi Nasriah. Many of the "Nasriah people" became Christians.[14]

Clough and Periah had an unusual partnership that lasted from the time they met in 1866, when Periah was almost fifty years old and Clough was thirty, until Periah's death in 1897. For the first ten years, Periah and his wife, Nagamma, preached to fellow Madigas in a widening area around Ongole. Though he was illiterate, Periah was respected by his fellow Madigas. Clough considered him a person of dignity and integrity and said that Periah had taken "more distinct steps in his religious experience" than had most western Christians.[15] He went from village goddess worship through two forms of popular devotion and at least one yogic practice to an emotional commitment to Lord Jesus and an unwavering allegiance to his Christian teacher, John Clough. The earlier steps were not simply left behind. The indefatigable evangelist and prudent counselor remained the dignified yoga teacher. His former disciples and their relatives became the nucleus of a rapidly multiplying Christian community. There was a dramatic increase ten years later, after a terrible famine; this was particularly marked in the villages where Periah and his fellow preachers had worked. If Clough had not broken with previous mission policy by acceding to Periah's urging that new Christians remain in their own villages, this remarkable movement of Madigas to Christianity might never have started, or it might have developed very differently.

British Methodists in Hyderabad State

The work of the Wesleyan Methodist Mission in Hyderabad City began in 1879, with the first worship service in Telugu held in the home of a Telugu Christian

---

14. Clough, *Social Christianity in the Orient*, 142.
15. Clough, *Social Christianity in the Orient*, 92-93.

who had migrated from Madras. By the end of 1880, there were three churches in the twin cities of Hyderabad and Secunderabad: a Telugu congregation, a Tamil congregation of migrants from the Tamil-speaking area to the south, and a Wesleyan group among the British and Indian troops stationed in a suburb of Secunderabad. By 1884, three church buildings had been completed and a girls' boarding school had been started.

The earliest evangelists' preaching was to educated Muslims and Hindus in the two cities. Preaching in surrounding villages was to the artisan castes. The first converts were weavers; but when they found that the Malas were equally welcome, they renounced Christianity in a ceremony in which their tongues were branded. After that, the mission directed its efforts in the villages to the Malas. In many villages Malas responded with group decisions. The "mass movement" gradually spread, with many Malas responding during the famine years (1896-1900). By 1917, ten new mission stations had been established, each with boarding schools and some also with hospitals or clinics.

In 1906 one missionary started preaching to the Madigas. After some hesitation, other missionaries followed suit, drawing an increasing response. This led to the entire Madiga community in some villages becoming Christians. Many of the older Christians, who were Malas, objected. They opposed the baptizing of Madigas, letting them join their congregations, or allowing them to take part in the Lord's Supper. Their objections peaked when Madiga boys were admitted to a boarding school. The Hindu relatives of the Mala Christians also voiced objections. A bitter struggle ensued before the Madigas were accepted into the same village congregations as Malas. In the following decades, however, fewer Mala groups chose to become Christian.

Because there were not enough evangelists to provide one for each village congregation, the mission in 1910 stopped baptizing new groups. In 1916, however, baptisms of village groups were resumed, and missionary work continued among other castes. In 1926 and 1930 summer schools were conducted for inquirers from the upper castes. Some of these inquirers later decided to become Christians. The number of such converts slowly increased until 1940. Thereafter, conversions declined. Evangelistic work among Muslims pursued the original mission agenda, but very few Muslims ever became Christians.

At first, all the educated Indian leaders in the Hyderabad Methodist District were Malas. While the new Madiga Christians generally accepted the pastoral care of Christian Malas, the reverse was not always the case. Moreover, expansion of the Christian community among non-Christian Malas declined because some Malas did not want to remain within the same congregations with Madigas, whom they considered to be of lower caste ranking.

Some of these trends are reflected in the founding of the congregations studied in 1959.[16] The oldest congregation in the pastorate was started in 1912 with all twenty-nine Mala families in the village, and a few years later, eight Madiga families joined them. The same sequence started two years later in another village nearby, with all the Mala families making a group decision in 1914 to become Christians. In 1920 all the Madiga families in the village decided to be baptized and join the congregation. Thus in 1959, all the outcaste (Dalit) families in the village, except for four families of Mala priests, were part of the Christian congregation. Another congregation was founded in 1917, with both Malas and Madigas joining from the outset, and still another a few years later. The three most recent congregations before 1959 (begun in 1927, 1932, and 1950, respectively), however, started and continued with only Madiga families. All these group decisions to become Christians were preceded and accompanied by the preaching of Indian pastors and sometimes by British missionaries. In many cases, one enthusiastic proponent or a small number of influential leaders played a major role in each group's decision to become Christians. In at least one case, a British missionary had intervened to stop the Dalits from being persecuted by the large landholders in the village. Often the new converts expected continued protection and opportunities to educate their children.

It is difficult to ascertain the importance that village Christians gave to such spiritual motives as the yearning for salvation from sin. There was and still is a strong desire for dignity on the part of those who have long suffered from great indignities from the rest of the village. They want dignity for each individual and respect from the rest of the village for the Christian community as a whole. This dignity was often symbolized for these families by the presence of a resident evangelist and in the house in which he and his family lived, the veranda and courtyard of which also served as the place where their children could be taught (especially in the time before there were government schools) and where the congregation could come together for worship.[17]

When a new area was evangelized, a team of ministers and evangelists would travel to the district headquarters and then set up a camp outside of a larger village, where they would stay for a week, during which they would also visit the Dalit hamlets attached to other nearby villages. In times of famine and other crises, when villagers flocked to the cities in search of work, the mission established colonies in the cities for Christian migrants. Through its system of pastoral care for each congregation and its special programs, the Christian

16. This is described in the first part of chapter 4 in Luke and Carman, *Village Christians*, 62-69.

17. The ambiguity of individual and group motives seems particularly striking in the 1950 group decision of Yesudas and his Madiga community to become Christians. See Luke and Carman, *Village Christians*, 66-69.

community continued to expand. The number of baptisms each year rose to a peak of ten thousand in 1937, after which the number of persons baptized annually started to drop. At the time of its merger with the Church of South India in 1947, the Methodist District was the largest Protestant communion in Hyderabad State, with 136,000 baptized members.

Pastoral leaders were first recruited by sending the brightest students from the boarding schools to the Theological Institution in Medak for three years, where they were trained to lead worship and provide primary education. There were also courses for their wives, to prepare them to assist in teaching and pastoral care. The Wesleyan Methodist Mission had from the beginning adopted a policy of training more Indian ministers to be on a par with Methodist ministers from Britain, each of whom would be in charge of about thirty village congregations. Some students were picked from among those graduating from the Wesley Boys' High School in Secunderabad and sent to the United Theological College in Bangalore to study in English for a bachelor of divinity degree. For those without a B.A. (the majority), their study included three years of lower-level theological training in Medak, two years working in village congregations, and four years in Bangalore. Those who graduated were ordained, but the total number of Indian and British ordained ministers was never enough to supervise all the circuits, so some senior evangelists were given annual licenses to preach and administer the sacraments, as well as to supervise the junior evangelists in charge of the congregations. The total number of evangelists rose to almost eight hundred in 1943, but after that started a sharp decline.[18]

C. W. Posnett and the Medak Cathedral

In the Wesleyan Methodist Mission, the groups of village congregations around each mission station were organized into "circuits" in the Methodist pattern. (These later became "pastorates" in the Church of South India.) While British missionaries and Indian ministers had considerable latitude in their own circuits, policies concerning the mission as a whole were decided at an annual two-week meeting every January, where the district chairman had a major voice.

The best remembered chairman was Charles Walker Posnett, who served in this position from 1916 until his retirement and return to England in 1939. When he arrived in Hyderabad in 1895, he first served as chaplain to the British soldiers stationed outside the city, but he was impatient to spread the gospel in the villages. The following year he went out to the market town of Medak, fifty

---

18. This section is a summary of Luke and Carman, *Village Christians*, 16-23.

miles to the north, and built a mission bungalow. He sought to preach the gospel in all the surrounding villages. When a group responded and were baptized, he followed the mission's policy of placing in every congregation an evangelist who would teach children to read and lead the new Christians in worship. Posnett also started a boarding school in Medak for children in the higher grades and encouraged setting up a dispensary.

During several serious famines, Posnett first distributed food to those who were starving and later devised for them a "food for work" program. That helped to construct several buildings in Medak, most notably the cathedral, which took ten years to complete (1916-26). It was opened on Christmas Day, 1924. He raised the substantial funds required from friends and supporters in Great Britain, and he spent as much time as possible supervising the details of construction. Although only a small town, Medak became increasingly the center of the Hyderabad Methodist District. Posnett's work as an evangelistic missionary was noteworthy, as was his supervision of a growing network of congregations and village evangelists, and then for many years of the entire district. Still more remarkable was the cathedral, whose construction he supervised, both in its size and its workmanship, and, ultimately, in its impact on the entire population of the surrounding area. The "Big Temple" is a Gothic cathedral. There are three stained glass windows, floor tiles in six colors brought from England, and Italian marble on the chancel floor. "The tower is 173 feet high, with four pinnacles which can be seen for miles around. The seating capacity of the cathedral is nearly five thousand."[19] After church union, this imposing church did become officially a cathedral, for it is the seat of the CSI bishop in Medak. While most of the administration of the diocese now takes place in Hyderabad, the cathedral has increased in importance. It has become a tourist attraction, and the state Department of Tourism recently paid for constructing a hostel for pilgrims.[20] Especially during Christian festivals it is visited by many Hindus and Muslims, as well as by Christians. It is considered sacred space favorable for prayers, especially for healing from serious diseases and from the effects of witchcraft. In the vestry hangs a large portrait of C. W. Posnett. He was a giant of a man, and his memory lingers in this sacred space.

That memory, we discovered, also remains in village congregations that Posnett is believed to have visited. *Village Christians* includes the account heard in 1959 by Mr. and Mrs. Luke about the beginning of the Methodist congregation in the village of Jangarai, where the entire Madiga community became Christians in 1927. In those days the Madigas were forced to work part of the time

---

19. Vasantha Rao, *Heads and Tales*, 32. See also Sackett, *Posnett of Medak*, 44-47.
20. Vasantha Rao, *Heads and Tales*, 32.

without pay for their landlords or the police, following the widespread practice known as *yeti*. When the Madigas sought help from the nearest Christian evangelist, he took them to Posnett, who "through his personal influence and letters to higher officials had the police chief brought to trial and punished."[21] The Madigas considered Posnett to be their champion; they asked the evangelist to visit them regularly and prepare them for baptism.

In 2008 our research interviewer was told approximately the same story, but he heard that Posnett had rescued them from persecution after they had become Christians. "The villagers recount that when Rev. Posnett came to their village, as people faintly remember, it was either on horseback or on a camel's back. He preached the gospel to all the people, including the upper-caste people. He had a compassionate heart, caring not only for Christians, but for all the people."[22] They remember the name of the offensive police official and the specific ways in which he and other upper-caste people demeaned them and made them work in the fields without paying them. They also remember P. Y. Luke's visit years later, when he "pitched a tent under a tree on the church premises and served the congregation for one full year."[23] Here their memory has embellished history. The Lukes did indeed pitch a tent, which they had borrowed from the diocese, but they stayed there for only three weeks and spent much of their time gathering information for their study.

We know that at different times, Posnett rode on a horse or on a camel, as well as traveling by cart and later by car.[24] In these Christians' memory he was an extraordinary man, large in body, in energy, and in compassion. What may be more remarkable is that Christians in three other villages nearby claim that he also visited them and played a similar role in establishing their congregations. In one case, as in Jangarai, it was "either on horseback or on a camel." While it is quite possible that he visited all four villages, these other "memories" were not shared with the Lukes in 1959. Even if not historically accurate, they celebrate in collective memory a time when a missionary who was revered as a powerful and saintly seer could protect them against indignity and oppression. In one congregation's version of the story, when the landlords beat the evangelist Posnett had sent, he came with "many missionaries, pastors, and evangelists," and he persuaded the landlords "to beg forgiveness, touching the feet of the evangelist and the Dalit believers." This reversal of the Dalits' traditional groveling at the feet of their landlords is a sweet memory, especially when there are so

21. Luke and Carman, *Village Christians*, 65.
22. Field notes from interview in Jangarai, May 2008.
23. Field notes from interview in Jangarai, May 2008.
24. Sackett, *Posnett of Medak*, photograph of Mr. and Mrs. Posnett on a camel, opposite p. 16; 39-41, 91.

many other memories of persecution, even of men being hung upside down and beaten. Now the forced labor has ended, and beatings are exceptional, but these descendants of the first Christian families still suffer the indignities of those considered polluted; they are still not allowed to live in the main part of the village. There is no longer any human protector of the Christian Dalit communities, but the Christian God is believed to have the power to heal, especially when approached in that gigantic church in Medak, a power that for many is even more evident during the pomp and ceremony of Christian festivals.

Medak Diocese in the Church of South India

The movement toward a union of Protestant churches in South India took a significant step in 1906 with the joining of several Congregational and Reformed (Presbyterian) churches into the South India United Church. This church then began negotiations with the Anglicans (1919) and the British Methodists (1925). The final scheme of union had to be approved by each of the churches. The Methodist Mission agreed in 1943, and in September 1947, just a month after Indian independence, the Church of South India was inaugurated. The Medak Diocese consists of two-thirds of the former Hyderabad Methodist District and the Anglican churches in Hyderabad and Secunderabad. (The other one-third, the Karimnagar group, joined the former Anglican Diocese of Dornakal, but has since become a separate Karimnagar Diocese.) The first bishop in Medak, from 1947 to 1960, was the Rt. Rev. Frank Whittaker, who previously had been the Hyderabad Methodist District chairman.[25] Since union, all the licensed lay pastors have been ordained after a further year of theological training. The Diocesan Council meets every two years to deal with general policies. The diocese also sends six presbyters and eight laymen to the biennial meeting of the CSI Synod.

The diocese is divided into 3 District Church Councils. In 1959 there were 8 urban pastorates and 36 rural pastorates, consisting of 668 village congregations, grouped into 97 sections, with 100 superintending evangelists and 216 junior evangelists, which was less than half the number of evangelists in 1943. In the following decade, the number of evangelists declined still further, partially offset by the increasing number of ordained presbyters.

25. Subsequent bishops have been Eber Priestley, 1961-67; H. D. L. Abraham, 1968-75; B. G. Prasada Rao, 1976-81; P. Victor Premasagar, 1982-92; B. Peter Sugandhar, 1993-2008; and T. S. Kanaka Prasad, 2009-13. Bishop Premasagar and Bishop Sugandhar have each served a term as moderator of the entire Church of South India, and Bishop Sugandhar was also chosen as the first chairman of the Communion of Churches in India, which links the CSI, the Church of North India, and the Mar Thoma Church (Vasantha Rao, *Heads and Tales*, 26-38).

In 2005 there were almost 250,000 Christians in the diocese belonging to nearly 1,100 congregations divided among 71 pastorates. They were served by 205 full-time clergy, including 134 presbyters and 61 evangelists. In 2007 there were 130 presbyters and 63 evangelists in parish work, plus 32 clergy pursuing studies at various levels. The Theological Training Centre in Medak has been revived, and by 2007, 92 students in 3 batches had completed the one-year course and were commissioned as evangelists. Of these, 29 have already been ordained as presbyters and 30 were to be ordained as deacons. The bishop also said that since 1994, 120 presbyters have been ordained. Clearly, some of them were evangelists who were promoted after further training. The number of evangelists was only a small fraction of the 800 in 1943, and all the clergy counted together constitute less than one-quarter of the number of congregations. Since each of the large urban congregations has its own pastor, each of the remaining pastors would have to care for an average of 5 congregations. The studies in the Jangarai section do raise the question of how well, if at all, these pastors could actually do this.

About 150 new church buildings were constructed between 1992 and 2007, with 47 others under construction or planned. Almost all the clergy salaries and other expenses of the diocese now come from the 75 percent of congregational offerings remitted to the diocese, most of it from the much wealthier urban churches. Some of the construction costs of new church buildings have come from foreign sources, including a fund started by members of the Posnett family in England and contributions from the Busan Presbyterian Church in South Korea. The diocese includes more than 150 educational institutions at various levels and has just started a medical college at the site of the old leprosy hospital. These strong institutions and the growing urban churches speak to the vitality of the diocese as a whole, but the hundreds of village congregations without a resident evangelist signal an unsolved problem in pastoral care for the many rural pastorates in the diocese.[26]

Dalit Theology and Its Development

In the fifty years since the original study, Indian Christians have developed their own distinctive form of liberation theology, known as Dalit theology. At present it is the most influential theology in Protestant theological seminaries,

---

26. The information in the preceding paragraphs is taken from Bishop Sugandhar's biennial addresses to the Medak Diocesan Council in November 2005 and November 2007, the last before his retirement.

and it is also important for many Roman Catholics. The following paragraphs are written from Vasantha Rao's perspective as a Dalit theologian.

Adding together all the tribal groups and all the "outcaste" castes, Dalits are the indigenous people of the Indian subcontinent, constituting almost 20 percent of the Indian population, and therefore numbering almost 200 million. More than half of the Christian population of India, quite variously estimated to be between 25 and 60 million, are, in this broadest sense, Dalits. Their leaders believe that they originally belonged to a civilization with egalitarian values, enjoying freedom in life with dignity. They possessed land and property and lived in unity with nature. As time passed, immigrants pushed them to the peripheries, leaving them no social identity; making them politically powerless, culturally deprived, religiously inauthentic, and economically dependent; and ultimately plummeting them to "untouchable" status. All this is the consequence of the way Hindus have understood and applied the principles of purity and pollution. Dalits have, in the course of time, internalized this inferior status and have come to accept being virtual slaves as preordained and inescapable.

Untouchables were called by demeaning names, such as *avarna* (outcaste), *achuta* (untouchable) *mleccha, mala, madiga, mahar, dasa, paraya, pulaya,* and many more. Their present leaders have rejected all these names and called themselves Dalits, indicating they are a people subjected to suffering and pain. The term "Dalit" expresses the brokenness of people deprived of the fullness of life. This term was extensively used by the Dalit movement in the North Indian state of Maharashtra. Their members were known as the Dalit Panthers; they protested against the injustices of the so-called upper castes against the untouchables. The term "Dalit" itself was coined by Jyotirao Phule (1827-90), a social reformer, who portrayed the untouchables as the victims of the Hindu social order, that is, the caste system.

Dalits were deprived of any landholdings and were subjected to servitude and forced to take jobs considered "polluting." They were marginalized from society and made to live outside the village, without access to public roads, water reservoirs, or places of worship. Dehumanized in these ways, they accepted their plight as divinely endorsed fate, based on the Hindu caste system and the theory of *karma*.

Searching for identity, self-respect, dignity, and freedom from oppression, many have accepted a liberating faith that would give them a new life. Some have turned to Buddhism, some to Islam, and some to Christianity. Because some Dalits have been discriminated against by other Christians, they may be "thrice alienated": from the church, from the Hindu majority, and from the state.

Christian precursors to Dalit theology include American black theology, Korean people's theology, and Latin American liberation theology. Along with the influence of these theologies, we also note influences from secular Dalit movements in India. In the 1960s there was much secular Dalit literature that raised attention to their plight. This literature exposed those who were responsible for their deplorable situation and raised their hopes for liberation; it motivated them to fight for their freedom. Dalit literature had a definite anti-caste stance since caste is identified as the sole cause of their predicament, misfortune, and misery. It included folklore, folk songs, community practices, religious symbols, and myths. Through these means, Dalits have been able to rediscover their history, which is important for their self-understanding and liberation, denying the Brahmanic myths that subjugate them to perpetual servitude.

In the 1980s a distinct Dalit Christian theology began to emerge through the initiative of Arvind P. Nirmal, "the father of Dalit theology." His writings opposed both dogmatic theology, considered to be metaphysical speculation, and Indian Christian theology, which he saw as too Brahmanical. He judged both these older theologies as far from the reality of the Dalits in their historical situation, both past and present.

The main emphasis in authentic Dalit theology is on "experience" or "pathos." Pathos becomes the epistemological starting point for theologizing. In this theology, Dalits are the subjects of theologizing and never the objects. The theological goal is the liberation of all Dalits, irrespective of their religious and other affiliations, because it is their "Dalitness" that binds them together in a common struggle.

Although in the initial stages exclusive tendencies dominated Dalit theologians, they are now open to non-Dalits doing Dalit theology on the grounds of Christian solidarity. This has paved the way for Dalit theologians to work with Hindus, Muslims, and peoples of other faiths, as well as with secular thinkers with humanistic ideologies. This tendency opens a new vista for theologians of non-Dalit origin to do Dalit theology.[27]

The Bible provides a strong basis for formulating Dalit theology. A. P. Nirmal relied on the Deuteronomic creed, "A wandering Aramean was my father" (Deut. 26:5), reasoning that it depicts the very nature of Dalit life: a people with no identity becoming God's chosen people. The exodus model used by liberation theologians also had its impact on the theologizing process of Dalit theologians, who reread the Bible through the experience of the victims. This reveals that neither God nor the law of *karma* is responsible for their plight, but that it is the consequence of a deliberate human construct, the caste system.

God taking human form in Jesus Christ is acknowledged as God's initiative to be in solidarity with the oppressed Dalits. God is seen as a Dalit God who

---

27. A concrete example is the work of Clarke, *Dalits and Christianity*.

identifies with the servanthood of Dalits, depicted by the "suffering servant" in the book of Isaiah. The full measure of Christ's sufferings lies in his perfect identification with Dalit pathos. Christ's genealogy and birth into a carpenter's family further reveal his "Dalitness." The Gospels provide an opportunity to learn about Christ's ministry to the outcastes and the broken-hearted. Today, the same ministry continues to Dalits, to whom Jesus presents himself as being the one "thirsty," "hungry," "naked," and "imprisoned," much akin to the experience of a Dalit. On the other hand, the confrontation of Jesus with contemporary power structures of Palestine provides inspiration and hope of liberation to the Dalits. Many folk songs sung in the Medak Diocese explain how Jesus, as the Dalit avatar of God, is liberating them from their present oppression and accompanying them in every part of their life, providing them protection and guidance. The cross depicts the brokenness, or "Dalitness," of Jesus (the term "Dalit" in Marathi means "crushed").

Since Dalits are created in the image of God, Dalit theology strives for the dignity of that image. It combats untouchability and tries to recover the equal status of all, so that no one is upper-caste or lower-caste. Regaining political rights, economic liberation, freedom of faith, and establishment of a just society are priorities in the struggles of Christians of Dalit origin and take precedence in Dalit theology.[28]

Spreading Pentecostal and Other Independent Churches

The many independent churches within the area of the Wadiaram pastorate have all been started since the 1959 study, most of them in the past twenty-five years. Behind them were developments in Indian Christianity that began more than one hundred years ago. These were related to revivals in other parts of the world but also to remarkable new movements in India. Many of these movements can be called "Pentecostal" or "charismatic," but there is one tradition that could better be called "independent Baptist," and other strands of modern evangelicalism are also represented.

Nineteenth-century revivals and holiness movements had their counterparts in India, and participants in the 1906 Azuza Street Revival in Los Angeles considered themselves as part of a worldwide revival. There were similar manifestations in Wales and Korea, and within India in the Khasi Hills and in the Mukti Mission in Maharashtra. The latter was led by Pandita Ramabai, who

---

28. Kurvilla, "Dalit Theology"; Massey, "Movements of Liberation"; Oommen, "The Emerging Dalit Theology."

went through a series of dramatic changes during her spiritual journey. Beginning as a devout and gifted Brahmin scholar taught by her father, she went on to the Unitarian reform of Bengali Hinduism in the Brahmo Samaj. Later, as a young Brahmin widow, she decided to follow Christ. After that came many years of dialogue with Anglican and Methodist forms of British and American Christianity. Her final form of Christian piety was one she developed in the refuge she established for Brahmin widows. While this shows similarities to Pentecostalism, Ramabai later distanced herself from the Pentecostal movement.[29] A number of early Pentecostal leaders visited India, and some remained as missionaries. They persuaded Christians from various denominations, but especially from the Plymouth Brethren, to accept their views and adopt Pentecostal practice. One congregation was established in Kerala. Thomas Christians took leadership, along with that of the American Robert F. Cook. By the 1930s, four Pentecostal denominations had developed, one in Ceylon (now Sri Lanka), the other three in what is now Kerala. After 1945, Pentecostal churches also developed in other parts of South India.[30]

In Telugu country (now Andhra Pradesh), the first active denomination was the Indian Pentecostal Church. Its leaders came from Kerala. Resentment of Telugu pastors to P. M. Samuel's leadership led to their turning to World Missionary Evangelism, an American organization founded in 1958. By the end of the 1960s, the Church of God was also active. The Assemblies of God entered the state only in 1978. Some of the leaders were Indians who had migrated to the United States and later returned to India. Much of their work centered on the capital city of Hyderabad. Several pastors established churches that were independent of the older Pentecostal denominations. One of them was called the Sion Fellowship.[31] The pastors of the independent churches included in this study come from a variety of Protestant denominations, and some have been supported by non-Pentecostal missions with headquarters usually in Hyderabad. Independent Baptist pastors typically favor a system that gives greater independence to local churches than the Church of South India allows. This includes a local church's right to choose its own pastor. These pastors must usually raise their own salary, and they often emphasize tithing as an obligation of Christian families and a necessity for a self-supporting church. The particular history of a few of the independent pastors is told briefly in chapter 6.

---

29. Bergunder, *The South Indian Pentecostal Movement*, 2-11, 23-26; Frykenberg, *Christianity in India*, 382-410, 465-67; Hedlund, ed., *Indian and Christian*. Viswanathan (*Outside the Fold*, 118-52) focuses on the importance of rational choice in conversion, as shown in Ramabai's exchange of letters with the high Anglican Sister Geraldine.

30. Bergunder, *The South Indian Pentecostal Movement*, 26-91.

31. Bergunder, *The South Indian Pentecostal Movement*, 92-106.

Because these independent churches are so new and so frequently change their denominational affiliation, it is hard to predict their future on the basis of their brief past. Pentecostals, if broadly defined, may make up as much as 20 percent of the Protestant population of South India.[32] In the area of our study, the members of the twenty-five independent churches we discovered probably constitute more than half of the present Christian population. Some come from Christian families in CSI congregations, but many come from caste communities that previously have shown little interest in the Christian message. They are now joining churches that include members from several castes, including the Dalit castes.

That this local "history" goes back only thirty years is amazing, especially when similar developments are taking place in many parts of India. We should recognize the popularity in CSI congregations, too, of what might be called a Pentecostal style of worship. Fervent prayers to Lord Jesus for healing and equally enthusiastic expressions of praise and thanksgiving are the most meaningful acts of worship for many of these Christians. The focus of this book is not on the past or the future of these churches, but on their present life. That is often affected, even if not determined, by the village religious environment, which is discussed in the following chapter.

---

32. Bergunder, *The South Indian Pentecostal Movement*, 14-15.

CHAPTER 4

The Village Religion Surrounding Christians

Village Hindu Cultural Environment

The 1959 study considered those challenges of the environment that were crucial for village Christians, including the religious environment. The third chapter of *Village Christians* deals with "Hinduism and Islam in the Village." This restudy is based on the information and interpretation in that chapter, but concentrates on a few specific examples of the present situation, especially those traditional practices in which Christians in the older CSI congregations continue to take part.

The religious environment of village Christians includes the social structure described in chapter 2. Brahmins claim superior status and greater ritual purity as the first of the "twice-born" *varnas,* but political and economic power is often exercised by the leading landholding caste or castes in a particular village. Other farmers and the many castes with names indicating their traditional occupation follow in rank, but with considerable disagreement as to which caste is higher than another with a similar occupation. In theory, the ranking is in the order of ritual purity. Both farmers and artisans fit into the Brahmanical system, and all feel themselves superior to those castes that are outside or below that system. These "outcastes" are the traditional servants or serfs of the "higher" castes. In these villages they are divided into two castes, Malas and Madigas, who have traditionally been considered by all the "higher" castes to be the most impure of the castes, forced to live in a separate section at the edge of the main village, called a *palem* or *basthi*. As discussed in chapter 3, the new collective name favored by the progressive leaders of these and similar castes all over India is Dalit (meaning "crushed" or "oppressed").

Despite this physical separation and their traditional exclusion from worship at the shrines in the main part of the village, Dalits hold many beliefs in common with other villagers. They are often skeptical, however, about the Brahmanical explanation of their oppressed state: that it is the result of bad deeds committed in previous lives. They have their own different version of the village myths that explain how each group reached its present social position. They generally accept the reality of the gods and goddesses, ghosts and demons, that are recognized by most villagers, but each Dalit caste has a special relationship with a particular goddess.

Some worship practices are the same in approaching all deities, but there are also specific rituals appropriate for specific deities. Most of the worship is directed to the goddesses dwelling in a particular village, who are believed to be related to but not identical with goddesses with the same names in other villages, as well as to the major goddesses worshiped all over India. These goddesses may be conceived more philosophically to be local expressions of one great goddess. Different caste groups feel themselves connected to particular goddesses, but in times of crisis all caste groups are expected to join in animal sacrifices to the same goddess, sacrifices in which some Dalits have a special role as sacrificers or as beaters of drums. Worship is also offered to the household deities, at least one of which occupies a wall niche or miniature shrine in each house, and may also be recognized with a sign drawn on the wall, with a diagram outside the door, or by an amulet worn on the body. Even the auspicious red mark on a married woman's forehead (*bottu* or *tilaka*) is a sacred sign. Villagers also recognize powerful deities at regional shrines far away from the village, to which they travel on regional pilgrimages, which will be discussed in chapter 8.

Codes of behavior are somewhat different for each caste (*kulam* or *jati*), including what foods they may eat, but they have much in common, including a strong expectation of loyalty to one's family and caste. In matters of ritual practice, conformity is expected to the rules of one's own caste, but there is a wide degree of tolerance of different sectarian affiliations. If Christians are regarded as a new sect worshiping the new god, Lord Jesus, they are more likely to be tolerated by Hindu villagers than if they are considered to be breaking with their ancestral caste affiliation.

Christians' Participation in Hindu Rituals Fifty Years Ago

Christians' participation in Hindu rituals means both (1) performing or contributing to the performance of these rites and (2) believing in their efficacy and in

The Village Religion Surrounding Christians

the divine or demonic powers to whom or against whom the rites are directed.[1] In the case of all but one of the congregations with resident evangelists and the three without, the majority of families (all the families in the three "second village" congregations) took part in the following kinds of village rituals:

(1) calendar festivals
(2) agricultural festivals
(3) visiting shrines in other villages and at inter-village pilgrimages or religious fairs *(jathara* or *urs)*
(4) worshiping small images of Balamma or Ellamma in their homes
(5) paying assessments for animal sacrifices to the village goddesses, where the sacrifices are performed by certain Dalit families as a traditional duty (with all families, except for Brahmins and other vegetarians, receiving a share of the sacrificed meat)
(6) using amulets, talismans, and other charms to ward off harm
(7) observing domestic lifecycle ceremonies, including naming, marriages, and funerals
(8) women wearing an auspicious red dot or line *(bottu)* on the forehead, and men wearing a long lock of hair *(zuttu)* at the back of the crown.

The few families that observed the church's prohibitions did not take part in many of these rituals. Those who had land observed the agricultural festivals, paid their assessments for the village sacrifices (though they did not eat the sacrificed meat), used amulets, and carried out the lifecycle ceremonies, but they did not give their children Hindu names. The major exception we found in 1959 was in Achampet, where the young men took a firm stand against participating in any of these rituals, except for the lifecycle ceremonies, and even there made some modifications.[2] Most of the families were sufficiently influenced by the young men to give up all the rituals except for paying the sacrificial assessments, using amulets, and observing the lifecycle ceremonies.

There were many factors that contributed to the persistence of these practices, in addition to insufficient Christian teaching and pastoral care. These included social pressures, economic or even physical coercion, and such subtler pressure as the desire of Christians to enjoy themselves and provide their children with a feast and new clothes at the same time they were being enjoyed

---

1. Christians' participation in the general religion of the village is summarized at the beginning of chapter 8 in Luke and Carman, *Village Christians*, 165-68, but the details of the many different rituals are given in appendix A to chapter 3 (44-60).

2. Luke and Carman, *Village Christians*, 184.

by the rest of the village. There was a sense of solidarity with the rest of the village, especially in warding off a threat to everyone. There was also a vague feeling that the village as a whole was bound to certain divine powers, whose reality Christians accepted. The rites that persisted most widely among these Christians were those considered to be fitting or auspicious, many connected to the lifecycle and especially to marriage.[3]

Lifecycle Rituals

The ceremonies and accompanying family celebrations discussed here are described in more detail in the appendix on "Hindu Village Ceremonies" at the end of chapter 3 in *Village Christians*.[4] With some variations, they are still performed by most of the Christian families in the older CSI congregations. The motivation behind these ceremonies is to remove impurity and to maximize auspiciousness. Traditionally, the social structure of the village is based on permanent differences in ritual purity between people born into different castes. If proper distance is not kept or physical contact takes place, a higher-caste person is polluted and must perform a ritual of purification. Similarly, death in the family and, to a lesser degree, being soiled by any bodily emission, calls for purifying rituals, sometimes including being shorn by the barber or taking a bath. The higher one's caste status, the more important it is to perform purification rituals.

There are other rituals, however, that express a different axis of value: that between the auspicious and the inauspicious. Good luck or bad luck can befall anyone, regardless of caste status. What is considered auspicious should be celebrated at the right time and place. This is especially true of weddings, after which married women wear the jewelry and colorful saris signifying their auspiciousness, which is further demonstrated by their bearing children. For higher-caste Hindus, widows are most unlucky and remain so for the rest of their lives. They must give up their jewelry, wear unadorned white saris without blouses *(cholis)*, and stay out of sight. Widows of lower castes are less affected by their unfortunate status and may even remarry. Families of all castes, however, observe many ceremonies marking auspicious times, while seeking to avoid the inauspicious times and removing temporary impurities with the appropriate rituals.[5]

---

3. Luke and Carman, *Village Christians*, 167-68.
4. See chapter 3, Luke and Carman, *Village Christians*, 44-50.
5. Luke and Carman, *Village Christians*, 31-32; Dube, *Indian Village*, 92-93; Srinivas, *Religion and Society Among the Coorgs*, 70-122; Carman and Marglin, eds., *Purity and Auspiciousness*.

The Village Religion Surrounding Christians

The first observance is the cradle ceremony (*purudu* or *thottela*). On the twenty-first day after birth, the mother is purified and the baby is given a name.

The second ceremony is a specifically Christian purification *(shuddhi)* of the mother three months after her delivery, receiving special prayers in the church. This is the old "churching" ceremony of European Christians, marking the mother's first return to the church after her period of impurity.

The third ceremony takes place at home at about the same time. It is called *anna prasa:* giving the baby its first solid food and letting the baby choose among different objects, such as a pen, a knife, or a spoon. The choice is supposed to reveal whether the child will become a scholar, a glutton, or a thief!

The fourth ceremony, when it is distinguished from the second, is a process of naming that depends on the baby's early experiences. For example, if the baby has been ill, that illness may be thought to have been caused by a particular ancestral spirit, who is appeased by giving the child its name.

The fifth ceremony is the first haircut, which takes place sometime within the first two years, after the baby's hair has grown quite long. In its Hindu form, the ceremony takes place at the shrine of a goddess, to whom the hair is presented as an offering. For Christians, the haircut may coincide with the child's baptism or christening, often in the eleventh month, after the hardening of the fontanel. During a church service the pastor baptizes the child with a Christian name that sounds similar to the Hindu name given earlier.

The sixth ceremony is called *onamalu*. This is when a two-year-old is "taught" to write the first letters of the alphabet.

The seventh ceremony is specifically Christian and does not always take place. This is *nirdharana,* which is confirmation by the bishop or by the presbyter in charge of the pastorate, and thereby admission to Holy Communion.

The eighth ceremony consists of all the rituals and festivities associated with the wedding. These include *nischithartham,* an informal meeting at home to confirm the alliance, without a meal; *pradhanam,* the formal engagement, which is celebrated with a meal at home; and *pendli,* the wedding itself, including the marriage ceremony and a feast at home. When a Christian woman marries a Hindu man, the wedding is usually totally Hindu. When a Hindu woman marries a Christian man or when both are from Christian families, there is now more likely to be a Christian liturgy conducted by the pastor. Sometimes this takes place at the church and sometimes in a temporary shed *(pandal)* in front of the home of the bridegroom's parents. Even when the wedding is celebrated at the church, the wedding attire is like that at Hindu weddings.[6]

---

6. Victor, "Meaning and Significance of Rural Dalit Christian Marriage Symbols," 701-3. This article is an extract from "The Meaning and Significance of the Rural Dalit Christian Marriage

A ninth festive occasion, called *srimantham*, marks a married daughter's first pregnancy. It takes place in the seventh or eighth month, when she returns to her parents' home from her husband's village. Her good fortune is celebrated in her parents' home with fruits and flowers.

Finally, there are death rituals, beginning with the burial *(savu)* and continuing with memorial services on the third day after death, the first month remembrance, and the one-year memorial. The funeral procession is described in the following section, and the traditional remembrance of departed elders in the section after that. They are described in this chapter rather than in chapter 8 on Christian adaptations because the Hindu rituals are simply followed, rather than being adapted for Christian use. The few rites of Christian origin remain as they were introduced a few generations ago, and the many village Hindu rituals also are carried out unchanged from their traditional form. The most likely place for future adaptations may be in the Christian wedding service.

Burial Practices Observed by Many Christians

During the period of research in 2008 there were three deaths in the CSI congregations, two in the oldest and largest congregation (Bandaposanipally) and one in a long neglected congregation (Edulapally).

The funeral practices observed for all three persons were about the same. Preparing for the burial begins with making a fire in front of the entrance to the house where the death has occurred. A pot of water is heated over the fire and used to bathe the body, which is then placed on a bamboo-pole stretcher and taken for burial. The major ceremony is the procession from the house to the cemetery. Madigas play the drums leading the procession, but Malas have also learned to play band instruments, so they, too, walk at the front. The son of the deceased follows, carrying a cross made from green tree branches. This cross is a substitute for the firebrand with which, in the Hindu ceremony, the son lights the funeral pyre.

The procession does not go immediately to the burial ground, but proceeds slowly while some villagers dance to the rhythm of the drums. Although Christians sing devotional songs the night before the funeral, there is no singing at this point, only the beating of the drums. The relatives of the deceased throw rice flakes mixed with coins. The Madigas choose one drummer to pick up the

---

Symbols, with Special Reference to Selected Congregations of CSI Medak Diocese," an unpublished B.D. thesis for Serampore University, March 2001, a copy of which resides in the United Theological College Library, Bangalore.

The Village Religion Surrounding Christians

coins that fall in their path. The Malas appoint their trumpeter to pick up the coins that fall close to them. In between the bands are the dancers. While the drumming continues, the one chosen picks up the coins that fall on the flat ground by pressing his forehead onto the coin; when it sticks to his forehead, he lifts it up and puts it in his pocket. If the coin is standing up on its edge, the drummer lifts it up with his eyelid!

Relatives of the deceased may put a currency note in a drummer's mouth or fold the note into a cone shape and fix its sharp base in the ground. The drummer or trumpeter often displays his skill by lifting the note by the tip with his eyelid while playing his instrument, sometimes bending, sometimes kneeling. Viewers never fail to applaud. This display of talent is even more admired when the procession is stuck in rain or drizzle, and the mud, dirt, and slush become a challenge.

Drummers, in particular, manage to keep the procession moving slowly, so that there will be more opportunity to collect money. When the procession takes longer than expected, relatives run to nearby shops and change their rupee notes into coins, which they continue to throw from the back to the front of the procession.

The pastor who accompanies the procession has been seen pleading with the drummers to stop this practice, but without success. Once in Bandaposanipally, the ministerial candidate then in charge of the congregation was vehement in his criticism. He was told by the relatives from Hyderabad that they had brought a lot of coins to throw; they would use them up and did not want to take them home. In Edulapally, when the ministerial candidate explained the proper Christian way of taking a body to the place of burial, the village Christians pleaded that this particular occasion would be "the last time" and asked the pastor not to object to their traditional procession. Any alternative to the traditional way would be considered "the next time." In Bandaposanipally, village Christians told the ministerial candidate that this had always been the practice and that he had no right to stop it.

When a death happens in a Mala family, a particular Madiga family is traditionally expected to clean the house[7] and pave the ground in front of it with water mixed with cow dung. Thus the house is made clean before the family returns home after the funeral. Certain Madiga families are designated to serve certain stipulated Mala families. At the end of the harvest, these Madigas are

---

7. This involves washing all the floors, or, in the case of mud flooring, applying water mixed with cow dung to make a hard surface. Walls, inside and out, are white-washed with a mixture of water and lime, making a smooth surface. The walls are then ready to be smeared with red mud mixed with water, which makes a base coat for decorations in white.

given a measure of the produce for their services. When, on the other hand, a death occurs in a Madiga family, there is no one to provide the same services. The bereaved family must do it for themselves.

The stone tablet on the grave is inscribed with both the Hindu and the Christian names (it is very seldom that a Christian has only one name). Whichever name is more prominent is given first, and the second name is put in brackets. Normally, candles and incense sticks are lit on the grave; a garland is placed, and relatives also leave coins.

The "third day" ritual requires that special food be cooked for the departed, food that he or she liked most while alive. The food is placed on the grave in a ritual called "placing food for the birds." It is expected that the departed soul will come back and eat the food. In order to confirm that this has happened, the family sits down at some distance from the grave to watch. When a bird or a dog sees the food and begins to eat, the family goes back home, satisfied that the spirit has descended in the form of the bird or dog. If the food is not eaten, the same ceremony is repeated on the following odd days, beginning on the fifth day. If even on the ninth day no bird or animal comes, the family ignores the lack of success and observes the memorial day.

On the memorial day, a coconut is broken before a framed photograph of the deceased. Normally, the privilege of breaking the coconut is given to the pastor. If the pastor will not do this, as was the case with the ministerial candidate, an elder of the congregation breaks it. Food is placed in front of the photo and on the grave, after which a meal is served to all those gathered. Food is then kept out overnight for the spirit to enjoy. At times, the food placed before the photo is eaten by an elder in the family.

It was observed in Bandaposanipally that a very prominent church member, along with many of his male family members, shaved his head. The one exception was the dead man's twenty-year-old grandson, a student in junior college and a baptized and confirmed member of the congregation. The family members all went to the grave, and that night they arranged for a performance of *kathakalakshepam* by a team of storytellers from a neighboring village. In presenting the story, Hindu mythology was mixed with the good deeds of the deceased. The family paid the actors about five hundred rupees for their services. The Bandaposanipally ministerial candidate tried his best to organize as an alternative the all-night singing of Christian devotional songs, but he could not do so because the family had already made the arrangements. The family explained that the sisters, married to Hindu men, had come from other villages and organized the program. For this reason, the program was not in the Christians' hands. In many instances, there is no Christian prayer meeting on this memorial day. If there is prayer, it takes place as soon as the family returns from the grave. It is conducted by the pastor, who is given an offering of between twenty and sixty rupees.

The bereaved family purchases a bottle of toddy for each visiting family. When the neighbors come for dinner, they are offered toddy, and the head of the family and other family members drink with them. If the pastor objects, they say something like, "However much we try to avoid drinking, somehow this happens." They blame it on relatives who come from other villages and explain that without serving toddy, the guests would not have been properly honored.

When Vasantha Rao visited one family, they all gathered within their house. The male members, aged six to sixty, with shaved heads, stood for prayer. (The house was then under construction.) Attached to the door posts was a cloth bag full of grain, while opposite to it inside the room, a cross mark had been made with limestone water. A photograph taken at the time depicts the amalgamation of Hindu and Christian practices: men with shaved heads (Hindu practice) are standing for prayer (Christian practice); door posts are tied with a bag of grain (Hindu practice), and the room is marked with a cross of limestone water (Christian practice).

Remembering Departed Elders

Peddala amavasya is the day when the departed elders in a family are remembered in a Hindu ritual observed on the new moon night two weeks before the important festival of *Dasara,* which is usually in October.[8] Members of the oldest CSI congregation, recognizing that this is not a church activity, observe it in semi-secrecy after asking their Hindu neighbors about the right date.

On the proper day, these Christian families observe a very simple ritual. On both sides of the door in the front room of the house are square or rectangular niches. Earthen lamps are placed in these niches; mutton curry and rice are cooked and placed beneath the niches, along with yogurt. Each plate of food placed there commemorates a departed elder in the family. The food is later eaten by the older members of the family. With this simple ritual the departed are remembered and honored.[9]

In Hindu families the ritual is more elaborate. Photographs of the parents and other elders who have died are treated almost like divine images. Saffron and vermilion marks are applied to their foreheads. An elaborate meal is prepared and served along with alcoholic drinks.

---

8. A Christian adaptation of this ritual is described in chapter 8.
9. Described in chapter 8.

Christians Celebrate a Hindu Calendar Festival *(Dasara)*

Christians of the Bandaposanipally CSI congregation celebrated *Dasara* on Friday, October 9, 2008. On the previous day, the men collected one hundred rupees from each family to buy two goats. Early the following morning, the women paved the ground in front of their houses with a mix of water and cow dung, something that they normally do only on Sundays. They also washed and cleaned their houses and bathed their children in preparation for the festival. While the women were busy with the children at home, the men slaughtered the goats at the Scheduled Caste community hall and prepared thirty-nine portions of meat, one for each family, including the pastor. (The pastor, however, would not accept his share.) Each family collected its portion, and the women began cooking the meat, fried rice, and other traditional foods. At 1:00 p.m., the cooking was done, and they ate their festival meal.

At 3:00 p.m., the whole family dressed in new clothes and went to their fields, hoping to catch a glimpse of the kingfisher bird. Once they had seen the bird, they gathered rice sheaves from the fields and then went to the *jambi* tree in the center of the village. There, the Brahmin priest performed a ritual while the Hindus worshiped the tree. The Christians present simply looked on. The priest then sprinkled holy water on the tree and on the worshipers. The Christians considered it a blessing if some of the holy water was sprinkled on them. The Hindus rushed to the *jambi* tree while the Christians waited. Because of their lower caste status, they were not supposed to touch the tree or pluck its leaves before the Hindus did, but after the Hindus had finished, members of the Christian congregation flocked to the tree and plucked their share of leaves. They mixed grains of rice with the *jambi* leaves (symbolic of gold) and wished their friends "happy *Dasara*" by putting the mixture in their friends' pockets and hugging them.

The Christians then visited the village elders and other prominent people. Reverently touching their feet, they wished them good health and success in the coming year. It is customary at this time for the village elders to give them gifts in return. (This practice may have replaced the older custom of landlords making a *dasara* gift to their tenants and servants. *Dasara* is usually also the time when people working in government or private firms get a bonus.)

When the Christians returned home, they attached the sheaves of rice that they had brought from the fields to their front door posts. The older men and women in the house who had not gone out with them were greeted with the *jambi* leaves and rice grains. In the evening, the adult children also brought out toddy for their parents. Although their pastor had not joined them in celebrating *dasara*, someone else fixed sheaves of rice to both sides of the pastor's door posts. The *jambi* leaves were put into the large pots or containers where rice was stored. This practice was thought to bring blessings since the Brahmin priest had blessed the leaves with holy water.

It is customary at *dasara* for parents to invite married daughters, who usually live in their husbands' villages, to return home with husband and children. They are treated with honor and given gifts. Many Christian women from Hindu families went to their parents' homes for the celebration, while the daughters who had married men in other villages came back home to Bandaposanipally for the festival. In the evening some were taken out for a treat, while others cooked special meals at home. Toddy and other forms of alcohol were the main items of hospitality. The evening was also the time when all the women in Christian families gathered with neighboring women to play *batkamma* in their courtyards. While they played, the Christian women sang hymns.

During the visit, the daughters and sons-in-law were presented with new clothes and money for their travel expenses. Since the children had school holidays for only ten days, the guests returned home after a few days, hoping to come back for *Dasara* the following year.[10]

Amulets and Black Spots

Many children have amulets hanging around their necks. The amulets are of different types; some are copper; some are bronze; and some are made of a bundle of cloth. When parents observe that their children are not sleeping soundly or eating properly, or when they are fidgeting, crying without reason, or look sickly, they take them to a traditional Muslim doctor. He writes a verse from the Koran on a piece of paper, folds it, and puts it inside a small copper, bronze, or cloth container. He attaches strings on both sides of the amulet and hangs it around the neck of the child. The parents believe that the child will neither be further affected by the sickness nor suffer any other calamity. Many Hindus as well as many Christians follow this practice of village Muslims.

In Bandaposanipally, a woman came to the church carrying a child wearing an amulet. She was happy to pose for a picture in front of the altar of the church. On the other hand, during a prayer meeting in the Gypsy settlement, when Vasantha Rao saw a child wearing an amulet, the mother tucked the amulet inside the child's shirt before a photo was taken. She was very much aware that wearing an amulet is not a Christian practice, but an imitation of her Muslim

---

10. In one village, even the presbyter's wife left to spend the Dasara holidays in her mother's home.

or Hindu neighbors. In Bandaposanipally, however, amulets can also be seen tied onto the waists of grown men in the Christian congregation.

A similar protection is believed to be afforded by wearing a black spot, which wards off the evil eye of some people as well as the evil inherent in nature. A black paste is made by burning garlic paste over a flame. When the paste has blackened, the powder is collected and mixed with oil to make a new paste. This is used to put a spot on the cheek of a bride or bridegroom, to ward off any evil eye. A spot is also put on any person who will be seen a great deal in public. Young girls have a spot applied to their cheek when they reach puberty to protect them against the evil eye of anyone coming to celebrate their new adult status. Christian children are always seen with this black spot on their foreheads, and their parents do not seem to think of this practice as contrary to Christian custom. When a woman in Bandaposanipally came to the church carrying a child with such a spot, she allowed a photograph to be taken of herself with the child.

Christians Possessed by Village Goddesses

One of the striking features of village religion in South India is spirit possession: a person seems to be invaded by the power of a spirit or local deity, usually in such a way that he or she loses normal consciousness and is believed to speak words originating from the possessing spirit. During the period of such possession, the person, usually a woman, loses her normal identity so completely that, afterward, she remembers nothing of the time when she was possessed. Sometimes a person with a traditional priestly role is frequently possessed by her shrine goddess; sometimes possession marks an unanticipated change from an ordinary existence to one dedicated to a particular goddess. Neither the person possessed nor those who witness the possession consider this experience to be consciously chosen. Rather, it is considered to be something that happens entirely by the choice of a particular spirit or divine being. If the words spoken in a trance are unintelligible, someone else must interpret what listeners consider a divine message. Often the goddess is believed to be announcing her displeasure at the neglect of her offerings and issuing a warning to the whole village.

No instance in which a Christian woman underwent this kind of total possession was observed, but a different kind of possession occurred within a Christian family, one that lasted for several weeks. This did not render the person unconscious, but it altered her behavior and led both her and her neighbors to believe that a goddess had taken control of her life.

In this case, an ant colony came into the family's hut and made a hill on the

The Village Religion Surrounding Christians

mud floor. Such ant hills are considered the temporary home of one particular goddess, and the young wife, though she was a Christian, felt herself to be possessed by the goddess and obligated to worship her as present in the ant hill. She stopped attending Christian worship. Neither she nor her family considered this to be a voluntary decision on her part. It was simply an inevitable consequence of the goddess moving into her home and dwelling in the ant hill.

After several weeks, the ant hill subsided and finally disappeared, and the young woman slowly returned to normal. Yet, she continued to look on from outside the group when Christians gathered for worship. When an ant hill appeared in the adjoining hut of the woman's mother-in-law, a person who had been a Christian for much longer, the older woman showed the same symptoms, altering her behavior and appearance. She believed that she was now, entirely outside her choice, for the time being a worshiper of this particular goddess, obligated to bring her offerings that the goddess prescribed. Both of these possessions were temporary, fading as the ant-hill home of the goddess moved elsewhere. It is not known whether or not this kind of experience permanently altered the lives of the two Christian women.

In another village, a Christian woman showed signs of a similar possession, which forced her to wear her hair long and unkempt. Her brother eventually rescued her, cutting her hair shorter while she slept, after which she felt that the goddess had left her body. In all these cases, possession did not entail a temporary unconscious state but rather a longer period in which the woman concerned felt the goddess controlling her body and mind from within.

Both kinds of goddess-possession are considered to be different from the invasion of an evil spirit, often induced by black magic, though some of the abnormal behavior and trance-like state may appear similar. While the effects of black magic may be reversed by counter-magic — or by the power of Lord Jesus, possession is believed to be entirely in the hands of the goddess, beginning and ending according to her will.

Black Magic (Witchcraft) and Counter-Magic

Whether black magic or witchcraft *(banumathi)* should be considered part of village religion is debatable. What is clear is that it is an important and frightful reality for many villagers. Warding it off or undoing its effects is a major preoccupation for both Hindus and Christians. A large proportion of the healings after fervent prayer to Lord Jesus are healings from witchcraft. It seems worthwhile, therefore, to describe it in some detail.

Much of our information comes from a former magician who says that he gave up his profession twenty years ago when he accepted Christ. As a child he was curious about the magic that his father was performing. His father told him that there were no books; one learns the art by watching others perform it. He learned that there were two kinds of magic (*mantrikam,* derived from *mantra,* a Sanskrit word denoting a sacred word or chant and hence a secret formula; magicians can manipulate the power present in such "sacred words"). One kind of magic is related to darkness, the other to light. It is this second, good kind of magic that he said was chiefly practiced by his own Bainla subcaste, who are the Malas' priests. This good or "light" magic, which provides the antidote against the bad or "dark" magic, is called *bhutavaidyam,* "medicine against the demons."

The "dark" magic is intended to hurt others or even cause them to die. It must be learned from an experienced guru, who teaches a group of three or four persons at a time. They remove their clothes and stand in a village reservoir submerged to their shoulders, holding a cloth stained with menstrual blood between their teeth, with both ashes and mud in their hands. They return home before dawn and later practice the witchcraft on a tree to learn of its effect. If the tree withers, they know that their magic is working. Later on, they may tie something belonging to the intended victim to the tree. If the tree dries up, they believe that the person targeted will also wither away. Another technique is to go to a temple of Hanuman (the monkey god) and, while sitting before the image, recite the sacred chant given by the teacher and throw hot pepper seeds at the image. Hanuman, they say, then retaliates by tormenting the person whose name the magician has uttered.

These techniques and many other ways of hurting a substitute for the victim are well known to most villagers. What is secret is the magic formula, the *mantra,* which this ex-magician did not reveal. Of course, the particular circumstances must remain secret since neither the jealous neighbor who pays for the magic spell nor the magician wants their dangerous activities to be known. Even the suspicion of engaging in such "dark" magic will bring down the wrath of other villagers, who have been known to pull out the suspect's teeth or even kill him (or her). Our informant also talked about the even more powerful magic of some wandering tribal people, who could both kill the victim and later bring him or her back to life. More personally, he described how he himself had been the target of black magic that caused him to swoon on new moon and full moon nights, and to get very thirsty. To escape this torture, he sold his land in his own village and moved to a suburb of Hyderabad, where he grew a beard in Muslim style and found a job in a factory making iron tools.

This ex-magician's major task and that of his caste relatives practicing "light" magic was to undo the effects of "dark" magic, while fending off the suspicions of those who thought that they were engaged in witchcraft. When people came to him suspecting that some spell had been cast on them, he would ask them to bring the traditional provisions: white flour, nine kinds of grain, a hen or goat, and five limes. On the outskirts of the village, any "light" magician would draw on the ground a figure of a person and have the supposed victim sit down on it. After the magician applied sacred ash to the patient's forehead, he would mentally honor his guru and recite the *mantras* his guru taught him. Then he would take the sacrificial animal and turn it above the head of the patient five times before breaking the animal's neck and chopping off its head. Some of the animal's blood would then be applied to the patient's forehead, and an amulet made from words written on paper. A little of the nine kinds of grain and some plant roots are always put in the amulet, which is tied around the patient's arm, leg, or neck. The patient would be told to walk home without looking back. It is not clear whether this former magician believed that his "cure" had real efficacy. First he said that the ceremony would relieve the patient of his suspicion of being a victim, but then he said that what happens to the goat meat — whether it is tasty or spoiled — shows whether the patient has really been cured. In any case, most villagers do believe in the efficacy of both "dark" and "light" magic.

While our informant was living in disguise, far away from his home village, he heard the gospel from a fellow worker, started reading the New Testament, and began to believe that Christ could heal him from the witchcraft that had attacked him. After he had read the New Testament for several weeks, he said, Jesus appeared to him in a dream, dressed as a medical doctor, and that very night he was healed. The same year he went to the independent church in Toopran and was baptized. After that, he visited many churches and heard the testimonies of those who had suffered from black magic and whom Jesus had healed after their pastors' prayers. Sometimes the testimony came from a former black magician. One of them confessed that he had mercilessly killed small children. From one victim's testimony he figured out that the magician who had cast the spell must be his old friend, whom he then tried to persuade to give up his profession. Despite the misery that black magic had caused in his own family, his friend could not break free from being a magician.

Now the former magician is an evangelist to magicians in his area. He has returned to his home village, but people are still afraid of him, so he leaves his village monthly on the new moon day and the full moon day, the days when magicians cast their spells. He says that he used to sleep in a tree when he was away from home, but later he slept in churches. Finally, he began to attend the Pentecostal church in his own village. The villagers now know that he is a Christian who attends church and that he is an upright person who fights for just causes; he, in turn, is bold, fearing nothing and no one. While reading the book of Proverbs, he said, God warned him not to utter the name of a human being, which is what magicians do in casting a spell. He now sees himself as a witness to his fellow Bainlas of Christ's power. He has sent his sons, who are not yet baptized, to Hyderabad so that they will not follow the caste profession. He lives with his two wives,[11] both of whom now believe in Christ; the younger wife has been baptized.

This former magician's whole life story is one of a dramatic transition from an old village tradition of frightening power to a relatively new Christian movement that relies on the superior power of Christ. He has experienced the suffering caused by witchcraft, the paranoia evoking violent retribution against those suspected of black magic, and the courage of Christians who believe that they are emboldened by a divine power that can overcome both dark magic and dark suspicion.

We were told two sad stories about persons falsely accused of engaging in witchcraft. One concerned a man of about sixty named Rajaiah, the only one in a Mala community who, with the help of the village headman, had learned to read. As a young man, he performed street plays and, since he was large and robust, he played the part of the man-lion *avatara*, Narasimhaswami, who tore apart the demon-king in order to protect his devotee. People in his village believed that a person who plays this role must know witchcraft, and they started blaming Rajaiah for every cold or cough, fever or bodyache, that they suffered. They also expected him to use good magic to cure the sick; when he said that he could not do that, they assaulted him. Once he had to stand in the village reservoir and swear before the goddess of the reservoir that he knew nothing about witchcraft, whereupon the village council declared him innocent. After that, he used to stay in his house in the morning, while others were on the streets. At noon, he and his wife would go to work in their fields, returning only after dark when others were off the streets.

One day when his wife was taking part in a women's festival, Rajaiah went by himself to their fields to cut grass. As he was lifting a bundle of grass to carry on his head, some of his neighbors hit him from behind with an axe and, when he fell down, killed him with a large stone. His wife later found his body, hidden in a haystack. She raised a hue and cry, but no action was taken against his murderers. One of his children is a journalist, who still threatens to sue the villagers. The villagers say that if he continues to behave like that, he, too, will someday be killed.

The other person falsely accused of witchcraft was a thirty-nine-year-old woman named Yadamma, also of the Mala caste, but in another village. She worked as a cook at the village hostel and earned three hundred rupees a month.

---

11. Like many other Christian communities in Asia and Africa, the Medak Diocese tolerates such marriages if they began before the members of the family became Christians.

When she heard that someone was in need of a loan, she would find a lender and add 1 percent as her commission. Recently she built a house near the location where the Bainla families live. A neighbor borrowed several bags of cement, but never returned them and only later made a partial payment. Since the Bainlas have a reputation of performing black magic, Yadamma was afraid that they might cast a spell on her house. At a neighbor's suggestion, she hired some magicians from Hyderabad to cast a counter-spell to protect her house. They told her that they needed a special kind of antique bronze plate and went with her to her mother's house to look for one. Her sister-in-law found the plate and gave it to Yadamma, but then called on the neighbors, complaining that Yadamma was planning some mischief against her family. After the resulting quarrel, the villagers drove Yadamma and the magicians away.

Since this incident took place, Yadamma's parents no longer invite her to come home to celebrate Hindu festivals, and the rumor spread to her own village that she was engaging in black magic. Later, the man who still owed her money for cement accused her of casting a spell by sprinkling saffron and vermilion powder in front of his house. She appealed to the (independent) Christian pastor for support. He tried to help her, but to no avail. The village elders made her swear to her innocence before the image of the goddess Durga. After she did so, the elders dismissed the charges, but the village hostel fired her from her job, and she is no longer able to act as an assistant to the money lenders. She has now taken refuge in the Christian God, and to every accusation she responds, "Everything is your will, O Father."

Tharamma of Medak believes herself to have been the victim of witchcraft as well as to have suffered through various serious illnesses.[12] All these life-threatening events, she testifies, she has survived through Lord Jesus' power. She has described the form of black magic that affected her and the means she used to thwart it: first "light" magic and then the effective prayers of various "servants of God." The Christians who have opposed her healing ministry and those who have come to her for help all share her belief that witchcraft is a powerful and deadly force. Jesus, however, is still more powerful, she believes. With her repeated prayers, she has been able to help many sufferers from witchcraft.

The pervasiveness of the belief in black magic is shown by a recent event of a less dangerous kind. About ten years ago, a group of young men from Bandaposanipally decided to put on a dramatic performance with singing and dancing. It was styled on dramas presenting stories from the Hindu scripture, the Bhagavata Purana, but it presented biblical stories centering on the life of Christ. The young men decided who would play which part and ordered cos-

---

12. Her life story is related in chapter 6.

tumes from a drama company. They chose a site midway between three villages so that they could attract as large an audience as possible. They had to construct their own stage, which cost them 15,000 rupees, a huge amount for them. They shared this cost among all the participants.

When the stage was finished and the first performance was drawing near, they learned that some Hindus in their village had hired magicians to put the stage under a spell. Three or four magicians *(mantriks)* came and recited *mantras* that would prevent the actors from performing. As soon as the Christians learned about this, they hired magicians from another village to be present during the performance. These magicians told them to bring along a gunnysack of limes, which they would use for counter-magic. The actors brought the limes and got ready for the performance.

Things did not start well, for when the first actor, playing Jehovah the Creator, stepped out onto the stage, he fell flat on his face. At once, the second set of magicians cut up some limes, took them up on the stage, and scattered them around the head of the fallen actor. At the same time they were muttering their own *mantras*. After they again threw limes in front of the fallen actor, he stood up, performed his part, and made his exit. The next actor was Adam, but he, too, when he came on stage, fell flat. Once again the magicians cut limes and repeated their counter-magic with the same result. Adam got up and said his lines before leaving the stage. The next actor represented Eve, and the same sequence of events followed. The fourth character was the Serpent, played by a very young man named Mark, who still has vivid memories of the ordeal until he fell and blacked out. It was only after the magicians took the spell off the stage, he told us, that he stood up and played his part. Each and every subsequent actor had the same experience as he entered, so the magicians were kept busy until the drama was completed. Both the magic and the counter-magic were quite evidently effective. Presumably both the actors and the audience believed in both kinds of magic, but no one prayed for the intervention of Jesus, even though the drama was entitled "The Life of Christ."

Bhakti in Village Religion

The treatment of village religion in *Village Christians* concluded that in these Telangana villages, "the influence of the *bhakti* (sectarian devotional) movements is rather indirect," with "little exclusive or enthusiastic devotion to the particular personal god recognized by that sect as the Supreme Lord."[13] This

---

13. Luke and Carman, *Village Christians*, 29.

The Village Religion Surrounding Christians

judgment might have been too much influenced by the interpretation of village religion by the Indian anthropologist S. C. Dube. In his extensive study of the village of Shamirpet only fifty or sixty miles from Wadiaram, Dube concluded that while festivals and other ceremonies were regularly observed, daily remembrance of the creator was "postponed for old age," and younger people made little effort to seek "any deep religious experience or thrill."[14]

Dube did not find evidence of religious experience in festivals and ceremonies. His two exceptions to this lack both refer to the excitement of people watching someone in an ecstatic state of "possession," one possessed by the spirit of a Muslim saint, the other by a village goddess.[15] Devotion to some form of Vishnu or Shiva is indeed more common among some Brahmins and some Lingayats than among those in most other castes.[16] There is a much more widespread popular *bhakti*, however, which is evident during festivals and journeys to regional shrines.

Many villagers practice the standard ritual of reverently approaching a deity in image form and offering fruits and vegetables, flowers, or money. They understand that such *puja* may be part of any one of various religious approaches, depending on the worshiper's intention and spiritual capacity. The offering may be in fulfillment of a vow or other religious obligation, or it may be a gift accompanying a request for some favor or blessing. It may also, however, be the physical sign of a spiritual offering of one's inner self to the Lord of the universe, who is believed to be incarnate in the image being worshiped or in the human representative of that Lord. This last approach is understood to be that of *bhakti*, which may take the form of various kinds of human love but may also resemble the defeated warrior's abject surrender to the victor or the servant's total willingness to please his or her master.

Bhakti is often translated as "devotion." In its classical and sectarian forms it is directed to a deity considered to be the supreme Lord of the universe and the bestower of salvation on his (or less frequently her) devotees. *Bhakti* is the

---

14. Dube, *Indian Village*, 89, quoted in Luke and Carman, *Village Christians*, 42-43.

15. Dube, *Indian Village*, 89, quoted in Luke and Carman, *Village Christians*, 42-43.

16. The *lingam* is the central object of worship in most temples of Shiva. It is understood by many to be a phallic symbol representing the sexual union of Lord Shiva with his wife, the goddess Parvati. For worshipers, it also has more spiritual meanings. The Lingayats or Virashaivas are a reformed sect started by Basava in the twelfth century, which originally rejected caste distinctions and temple worship led by Brahmins. They owe their name to the tiny *lingam* in a silver case that they wear on a chain around their necks. The Lingayats are the largest caste, with considerable wealth and political power, in the neighboring state of Karnataka. Their priestly sub-caste, called Jangama, is also present in some of the villages studied in Telengana, where their caste ranking is high, though lower than that of Brahmins (McCormack, "On Lingayat Culture," 175-87).

love of the devotee for the Lord, and sometimes that love is expressed in highly emotional singing and dancing, so emotional that it seems very close to possession by the goddess, but there is an important difference. The possessed person often speaks for the goddess but forgets her own persona; when she comes out of the trance, she does not remember what she has said or done. The devotee *(bhakta),* on the other hand, is vividly aware of the moments when she came closest to God, rejoices in a fleeting experience of union, and bemoans her usual state of separation from God, painfully aware of her unfulfilled passion.

While the single-minded devotion of the great Hindu saints may be rare, strong appeals to the compassion of the deity in making some request are frequent among both Hindus and Christians. Some Hindu theologians consider such prayer a very effective means to gain God's favor, but regard it as a lower form of *bhakti,* whose highest form is not a means to an end, but is identical with the final goal of permanent union with God. It requires such complete surrender to God's will that one does not make any requests to God for one's own physical welfare, or even for the health of one's family. The word is derived from the Sanskrit root meaning "to share," which is interpreted as a sharing of love between the deity and the devotee. For sectarian theologians, this sharing often requires a total commitment on the part of the devotee, for whom the goal of union with God in eternal life is inseparable from the present sharing in divine love.[17]

Devotion, or *bhakti,* in its Hindu forms has seemed to some Christians to be akin to their own love of God, especially to their loving relationship with Jesus. For other Christians, *bhakti* is simply an Indian word that they use to express their love of God. It is also possible to regard both this word and many of its devotional forms as part of the legacy that Indian Christians have received and naturally incorporate into their own religious life. The language of Bible translations owes much to the vocabulary of *bhakti.* Christian poets have written many hymns expressing their love for God in this vocabulary. Village Christians sometimes find such hymns less appealing than choruses closer to the devotional forms of village religion.

Our restudy confirms that the love of God expressed by new Christian converts is often closely related to their gratitude to Jesus Christ for the healing that they have experienced; it is natural for them to express this love in the language of *bhakti.*[18] Such language also fits two ways in which love for God

---

17. Carman, "*Bhakti*"; Carman, "Hindu *Bhakti* as a Middle Way"; Carman, "The Dignity and Indignity of Service"; Ramanujan, *Hymns for the Drowning,* 103-69.

18. See Sundara Rao, *Bhakti in the Telugu Hymnal;* Vasantha Rao, *Heads and Tales,* 20-25; and Joseph, *Bhakti Theology of Purushottam Chowdhari.*

in Christ is recognized by many Hindus. The first is the admiration shown for Indian Christian saints, whom they consider true *bhaktas*. The second is that some Hindus consider themselves followers of Jesus. If Hindus familiar with *bhakti* are attracted by the Christian message or in some other way have a profound encounter with Lord Jesus, they may consider themselves, whether or not they seek baptism or have any connection with the Christian community, to be *Yesu-bhaktas*, "devotees of Jesus."[19] Perhaps even more than other features of the village environment, this form of devotion, whether as an ideal or a present reality, is part of the life experience of many village Christians.

---

19. Verma, *Christbhakti;* also Hoefer's *Churchless Christianity.*

CHAPTER 5

The Older Congregations in the Jangarai Section

Comparing the Situation in 1959 with More Recent Developments

After looking at various facets of their environment and the history behind the village churches, we now turn to the churches themselves. They can be divided into three groups: the older CSI congregations, the independent churches, and the newest congregations within the CSI pastorate. This chapter is concerned with the older congregations that were studied in 1959, when the Wadiaram pastorate was one of forty-nine pastorates in the Medak Diocese, about forty of them in rural areas. In this pastorate there were thirty congregations, divided among three sections. As many congregations as possible had an "evangelist" (Telugu *pantulu*, "teacher") living in their midst, with one evangelist in each section appointed as "senior evangelist." The congregations without an evangelist in residence were called "second village" congregations. An ordained presbyter was in charge of the whole pastorate.

The 1959 study focused on the Jangarai section, which had nine congregations, six of which normally had resident evangelists. While the other three should have been regularly visited by an evangelist from another village and less frequently by the presbyter, in fact all three had long been neglected. These congregations were all located in the "outcaste" (now Dalit) section of the village (called a *palem* or *basti*), and all the Christian families belonged to one or other of the two major Dalit communities, the Malas and the Madigas. The nine villages with Christian congregations were scattered among about thirty other villages where there were no Christians.

Since many adults worked during the day, the resident evangelist was expected to lead the congregation in a worship service Sunday evening that in-

The Older Congregations in the Jangarai Section

cluded hymns and prayers, scripture readings, and a sermon. On other nights he would conduct prayers at the usual place of worship, which was the broad veranda of the parsonage, or in one of the Christian homes. The latter was usually when a birthday or other auspicious occasion was being celebrated, or alternatively, when someone in the family was ill. Attendance at these different forms of worship varied considerably. The number of women usually exceeded the number of men, who were often exhausted from a hard day's work in the fields and sometimes affected by their evening drink of toddy. Attendance usually increased at the time of the presbyter's visits, when he would often conduct a communion service. The frequency of these visits varied with the weather, the distance of the village from the main road, and the energy of the presbyter.

The two largest congregations were better off economically than the other congregations, with many families owning a small plot of farmland and able to put a tile roof on their homes. Poorer families (in some congregations, all the families) had to work as day laborers; they lived in small huts with mud walls and thatch roofs, and they sometimes had to share the space with one or two other families (often part of a larger joint family). Although the evangelists and the presbyter emphasized the importance of supporting the church with regular and special offerings, even the wealthier congregations contributed only a small part of the evangelist's salary. The rest, as well as the presbyter's salary, had to come from the central funds of the diocese.

The previous study began less than twelve years after India gained its independence and only ten years after the princely state headed by the Nizam of Hyderabad came to an end. Under the Nizam's rule, villages in Telangana received fewer services than those under British rule. Especially in education there was a marked difference. The Nizam did not provide government schools in the villages, so only the wealthier children, who went to private schools, learned to read and write. One of the original duties of the Christian evangelists was to provide the rudiments of education, especially to the children in the congregation. Members of one congregation remembered that it was the prospect of having their children educated that led their ancestors to become Christians. The actual results were mixed. Not only did the evangelists' skill as teachers vary a great deal, but families also differed in their willingness to send their children to school instead of out to work. There can be no doubt, however, about the importance of education for Dalit groups, who for thousands of years had been deliberately denied that privilege. Some Christian children who did learn to read in the village went on to boarding schools in the towns and cities, often leaving their village homes permanently.[1]

---

1. Luke and Carman, *Village Christians*, 70-82.

Fifty years ago the situation was already beginning to change, with the government establishing more and more schools and offering some scholarships for secondary education. Christians sometimes but not always missed out on scholarships that were reserved for Dalits who registered as Hindus. Finally, in 2006, the government of Andhra Pradesh extended scholarship aid to children in all categories of Backward Classes and Scheduled Castes. Most villages have primary schools that all children are obliged to attend. The goal is for children to continue in school through "tenth standard" (i.e., to finish high school); some scholarships are even available for college.

The number of evangelists had already started to decrease fifty years ago, and their role as primary school teachers was vanishing. Now the very category of "evangelist" has been discontinued, replaced by various ranks of pastors: theological students in training, deacons, junior presbyters, and presbyters in charge of a pastorate, above whom is the bishop. This new arrangement brings some changes in pastoral care, which we discuss later. It also means that sharing a pastor among several congregations is now the rule rather than the exception, but it is not one with which church members are happy. Many would probably agree with the sentiment expressed by their grandparents in 1959: "A congregation without an evangelist is like a temple without a god [divine image]."

The number of congregations in the Wadiaram pastorate has decreased from thirty in 1959 to about twenty-two in 2009, in part because a few were split off to form a new pastorate centered in the town of Medchal. While the number of literate Christians has increased, and more are able to take part in church affairs, most of these CSI congregations seem unable, or perhaps never have been taught, to conduct worship without the presence of a pastor.

In chapter 2 we noted improvements in technology. There are now roads to all these villages that auto-rickshaws and buses can use, as well as bicycles and motorcycles. This makes it much easier not only to visit nearby villages, but also to go to the towns of Medak and Toopran. Government programs have increased average family income. Many Christians share in the economic improvement, though they are still poor by urban standards. More families have land to farm, and day laborers earn better wages. There are more homes with tiled roofs and some with brick walls. Those built with a government subsidy generally have cement-block walls and a cement slab for the roof. Some of the increased income is spent on cigarettes and toddy, but many families are better fed and clothed than their grandparents were fifty years ago. So far this greater prosperity has not significantly changed the giving habits of members of the CSI congregations. Their offerings, unlike those given in the independent churches, are not enough to support their own pastors.

The twenty-two congregations in the present pastorate are now divided into

The Older Congregations in the Jangarai Section

five sections, each the responsibility of an ordained presbyter or one on the way to ordination. It happens, however, that of the six congregations studied fifty years ago that normally had an evangelist and his family in residence, only one now has a resident pastor. Two of the others have maintained regular services conducted by a CSI pastor, but their membership has dropped considerably. The other three have experienced more drastic decline and some recent renewal. Two of the three are in villages where there is now an independent church. (We discuss the new CSI congregations in chapter 9.)

We have only a little information about developments between the 1959 study and our current project. In June 1977 four professors from the Andhra Christian Theological College in Hyderabad visited four of the village congregations included in the 1959 study as a deliberate reflection on that study after almost twenty years. They reported that the number of families in each of the congregations had remained the same. Most were from the Mala and Madiga communities. They found that communal antagonism among Christians had lessened. One congregation had had no Sunday services since the previous evangelist left fifteen years before, and no services at all since the previous Christmas. In two villages there were regular worship services on Sunday night, but with an attendance of ten. The attendance was better in the village where the pastor lived, and the offering was eight times larger. They noted that pastoral visits had declined and that local leadership had not been developed. Christians complained that the clergy were not interested in their problems and did not perform lifecycle ceremonies, even marriage, so traditional ceremonies continued. Regarding other participation by Christians in Hindu rituals, they received a variety of responses.[2]

This brief study generally corresponds with what was discovered in 1959,

---

2. This survey was conducted in June 1977. The four-page report was dated February 2, 1978, and signed by B. David Raju, who was in charge of an outreach program of the seminary in another part of the Wadiaram pastorate. The other committee members were P. Victor Premasagar (later bishop of the Medak Diocese), R. Yesurathanam (later principal of ACTC), and G. Sampurna Rao. The report was based on interviews with several lay members of four congregations and inspection of the church rolls. The congregations were Ambajipet, Gawallapally, Jangarai, and Bandaposanipally. The report gives the number of families in each congregation, while *Village Christians* lists the numbers in terms of individuals. Therefore, it is impossible to verify the committee's report that the number of Christians was the same in 1977 as in 1959. The committee's conclusions were more negative than those in *Village Christians*. They found that the one pastor made few visits to the three congregations without a pastor, that there were no baptisms or confirmations, and that there were no regular worship or communion services. Nor did they find any Christian nurture or literacy work. The final observation was quite emphatic: "There is no cultural adaptation at all. Jesus is one of the village deities. For lack of any serious attempt to help, Christians are left to do whatever they can. Often the life of the congregation and its worship is only Christian in name."

but it provides little that would indicate emerging trends. Formerly the church rolls kept in each congregation would have helped with this, but about 1980 the village congregations stopped recording this information, presumably to deny officials or politicians the knowledge of who was or was not a baptized Christian. At some point, the diocese seems to have stopped keeping exact statistics about all the pastorates and about the total number of baptized and confirmed Christians.

Sustaining the Old Pattern in the Two Large Congregations

There continue to be two large congregations in what used to be the Jangarai section of the Wadiaram pastorate. They have maintained the old pattern of pastoral care even though only one now has a resident pastor. The congregation in Bandaposanipally is the larger of the two; it still has fifty families.[3] A church roll is no longer kept. This is the only one of the older CSI congregations studied to have had an evangelist or pastor continuously in residence. In 2008, when a ministerial candidate was there for a year, attendance at the Sunday service had dropped to twenty, mostly women and children. More recently the average attendance has risen to almost fifty. Many of the older men do not come to worship, but more than forty of them gather once a month at the place of worship for *chitti*, a meeting at which each man contributes a specified amount of money, most of which goes to the winner in the casting of lots. Some of the men are addicted to alcohol, and many are inclined to press their opinions on the pastor, especially if he is young and inexperienced. Even if they do not attend Sunday worship, they insist that the pastor should come to their homes on special occasions to pray for their families and bless them.

All the families now own some land, some received as a government grant.[4] Most of these are "dry lands," watered only by monsoon rains and occasional showers and used to grow corn and sunflowers. Each family also has a small piece of irrigated "wet land" on which it grows rice. Family members work in their own fields and as day laborers in one another's fields. They can also take advantage of the government's "food for work" program. In 2008 they could earn eighty to one hundred rupees a day for up to one hundred days a year. This

---

3. In 1959 there were 167 baptized Christians, including 41 baptized children under 14, but only 36 communicants. Luke and Carman, *Village Christians*, 70.

4. Strictly speaking, according to Robert Frykenberg, land in India has been "held" rather than "owned." See introductions in his *Land Control and Social Structure in Indian History* and *Land Tenure and Peasant in South Asia*, where this subject is closely analyzed.

program is intended to encourage villagers to stay in their own village, rather than migrating to other places paying higher wages for seasonal labor.

Unlike the situation fifty years ago, when only a few people in the congregation could read, all of the children and young people are literate. In addition to a primary school, there is now a government high school in Bandaposanipally. Fifteen young people have recently migrated to Hyderabad, some to find work and some to continue their studies. They return home only on festival occasions.

The congregation in Bandaposanipally is divided by two issues, which in this village do not coincide. Since the beginning of democratic elections, the votes of Christians have been eagerly sought by three political parties: the all-India Congress Party, the regional Telugu Desam Party, and the more recently founded party pushing for a separate Telangana state. Families and caste groups are wooed with promises of gifts or improved facilities. Here all three parties have won the support of some families in both castes in the congregation. Many of the families are proud to display their allegiance to the party they support.

The other division is caste. A few years after the congregation was established with the baptism of all the Mala families, all the Madiga families joined them.[5] The Malas have continued to be in the majority, and the parsonage is located between the parts of the Dalit hamlet where the two caste groups live. The Madigas are generally poorer than the Malas, and the Malas complain that the Madiga families do not contribute to the cost of whitewashing the church before Christmas and that they did not make donations themselves or raise funds from others for constructing the new church on the hill. While they do not object to sitting together for worship or taking communion together, the two caste groups tend to separate on social occasions. Each group attends the family celebrations in its own caste community, but usually not those of the other caste, and sometimes there are quarrels between the two castes. More friendship may be shown between those in the two castes when their members go together to a meeting at the pastorate headquarters, twelve miles away.

A recent cause of much acrimony was a love affair between a Mala boy and a Madiga girl. All castes make it mandatory to find a marriage partner in the same caste. In this case, however, the girl's parents approved of the couple getting married since they thought it would be impossible to find her a husband in their own Madiga community. The boy's family did not agree; they refused to give their consent. The Madiga family then got the support of the police and had the young couple married in the police station. A daughter was born, and

---

5. According to Luke and Carman, *Village Christians,* 64, the first baptisms in the Jangarai section took place on June 9, 1912. No date is given for the Madigas joining the Christian community, but in 1959 there were twenty-nine Mala families and eight Madiga families in the congregation.

the young husband and wife were living happily together. Their parents, however, began to quarrel so much that the church elders had to come and try to reconcile them. Eventually, the boy's family arranged for a divorce, losing their daughter-in-law and their granddaughter, by paying a 50,000 rupee fine. After that, they arranged for their son to marry a Mala girl from a neighboring village.

In this CSI congregation, most families seek marriage alliances with Christian families in other villages, and most families observe various Christian customs. Even though the congregation is almost a century old, however, many Christians continue to observe some Hindu practices, especially those connected with lifecycle rituals. These include the funeral customs and death anniversaries described in chapter 4, as well as some domestic rituals.

Directly behind the Christian houses is a hill owned by the government. After Hindus and Muslims were given land to construct a temple and a mosque, respectively, Christians asked for land to build a proper church building. They were given five acres. The new church has now been completed, supported in part by a diocesan fund for this purpose, to which the Posnett family in England has contributed. The church is an attractive white building located on the bare rock at the top of the hill. So far, however, it has been used only for weddings and worship services on special occasions. Although the church is only a few hundred yards walk up a low hill, Christians seem to prefer the familiar space on the parsonage veranda, especially for meetings at night, when snakes might lurk beside the path. When a Hindu pilgrimage takes place on the hill in February, many Christians participate. Some Hindus and Muslims would also attend a Christian pilgrimage, if the Mala and Madiga Christians could agree as to when and how it should be held.

The other large congregation is nearby, in the very large village called Shankarraj Kondapur, with a population of about 4,000. The congregation was established about 1920. Malas and Madigas were baptized at the same time, and they have lived together more harmoniously than in some other Dalit congregations. In 1950 there were 54 Christian families. At the time it was the largest congregation in the Jangarai section. In 1959 it was almost as large as the Bandaposanipally congregation, having 150 baptized Christians.[6] Now there are only 34 families, and about 40 children have not been baptized. In one family, all 3 sons were given Hindu names in order to make it easier for them later on to obtain government grants specially for Dalits. At present, only 6 families are Malas. A few years ago, 6 other Mala families that had been part of the congregation moved to nearby villages to secure better lands. Another 10 families have migrated to Hyderabad; we do not know to which castes they belong.

---

6. Luke and Carman, *Village Christians*, 70.

This congregation has maintained its church roll, so there is some information about all the present families. All of them own some dry land; most have one or two acres. Most of the parents have had Christian marriage ceremonies. Half of the wives are from Christian families. The other half have come from Hindu families; all but one were baptized and joined the congregation.

All the families have been able to get bank loans, secured by their lands. About ten years ago their crops failed because of poor monsoon rains. The state government persuaded the banks to waive payments on the loans made to Dalits. Since all the families in the congregation received this benefit, it is possible that many of them had registered as Hindus, thus qualifying for "Scheduled Caste" status. On the other hand, it is also possible that either the state government or some local official had simply ignored the national policy, recognizing the obvious social fact that these Christians were considered by villagers of all castes to be Dalits. In any case, the registration of some of these Christians as Hindus seems to have little to do with their loyalty to the Christian congregation or their participation in Christian worship. There are some exceptions: for example, some parents of unbaptized children do not attend worship and consider themselves Hindus. Most of those in the congregation, however, do think of themselves as Christians. Despite the absence of an evangelist or pastor since 2000, sixty to seventy come to worship (including fifteen to twenty children), which is conducted every Sunday by the CSI pastor coming from Bandaposanipally. There are four lay leaders who assist with worship; they are able to sing the hymns in the old hymnbook. Sometimes girls read the scripture lessons. Younger members can read and sing the hymns in the new hymnbook.

In this congregation, there is a striking contrast between the illiteracy of many older members and the education of the younger ones. All the children learn to read, and many go on from primary school to high school and junior college. There is an upper primary school in the village, and a dozen children live in a government hostel in Chinna Shankarampet, seven miles away, while they go to a high school there. They spend their weekends there but do not go to church. They do attend Sunday worship when they come home on holidays. Almost all marriages are solemnized with a Christian service. Most homes are kept neat. Some have a table and chairs, and a black-and-white television set. The speech of Christians in this village is changing from the colloquial village Telugu of Telangana to a more refined language, whether because children watch television, listen to their teachers, some of whom are from Coastal Andhra, or learn to read classical Telugu in school.

The ten families who have migrated to Hyderabad for factory jobs come back to visit relatives. Their children go to school in the city, and some parents go to church there. The size of Shankarraj Kondapur and improved transportation also contribute to the urban influences. While this congregation is relatively strong, members do complain about the effects of being without a resident pastor. The visiting pastors rarely conduct family prayers in their homes. Christians say that this has weakened their faith and led them to forget Christian traditions, especially rituals connected with the lifecycle. We do not know to what extent Christians here continue to take part in Hindu rituals. Unlike the situation in five other villages in the section, where there are or once were CSI congregations, here no independent church has yet been started. Pastor Anandam does come regularly from his independent church in Ambajipet to visit four families.

These two large congregations are relatively stable, but they continue to live with an old pattern that leads them to expect pastoral care of a kind that the diocese can no longer provide. Both congregations are larger than some nearby independent churches that manage to support their own pastors. The Kondapur congregation has been without a resident pastor for more than ten years. The Bandaposanipally congregation does have its own pastor, but he has to spend much of his time visiting several other congregations. Later in this chapter we return to this problem and the efforts to solve it.

Worship and Preaching

The pattern of worship fifty years ago is described in *Village Christians*. The Sunday night service "normally follows the first order of service from the Telugu Book of Services, while on the other nights he (the evangelist) abbreviates the service as he thinks best." A lyric or hymn generally both preceded and followed the reading of a scripture passage, "often a miracle story or a parable." Finally, there was a prayer by the evangelist that ended with everyone joining in the Lord's Prayer.

Attendance was highest in the hot season, when villagers had little work, but even then averaged less than 20 percent on weeknights and from 14 to 31 percent on Sunday nights. Attendance was considerably higher on the rare occasions of the presbyter's visits. The most regular attendees were the young men and the children.

Whenever the presbyter came, he led a service of Holy Communion, following the Methodist order of service. Many considered his words to be a powerful ritual formula *(mantram)* comparable to the words recited by a Brahmin priest, and they regarded the communion elements to be a Christian equivalent of the Hindu *prasadam,* the consecrated food distributed to worshipers. While the evangelist would generally read the scripture lesson himself, the presbyter when present would ask one of the literate young men to read.

The Older Congregations in the Jangarai Section

Only a few of the lyrics sung were from the hymnbook. The rest were songs learned at revival meetings or taken from the lay healer Sadhu Joseph's book of lyrics. There were also "parable action songs." Both parables and miracles were retold in songs set to folk tunes.

The "family prayers" were those conducted by the evangelist or presbyter when visiting a home; they were largely intercessory prayers for the health of the family and especially for anyone who was ill. Only one or two families in a congregation would say their own prayer after the evening meal.[7]

The same general pattern of worship has continued, but the weeknight prayers may be less regular because the pastor needs to visit congregations in other villages during the week. The Sunday service is more elaborate now, following the Church of South India's second order of service, and on the first and third Sundays of every month, the pastor or a visiting presbyter conducts the communion service. This follows the first order of worship in the CSI liturgy, in which the preparation includes a number of prayers from the Anglican liturgy and many responses to be repeated after the presbyter. If there is not much time, there is a free worship service plus a short "Liturgy for the Breaking of the Bread," following the Methodist tradition.

These CSI services often have several hymns or lyrics as people gather, and the hymn singing may go on for a half hour before the more formal service begins. Some of the literate members of the congregation have their own hymnbooks, and many others know the more familiar hymns by heart. A service at the pastorate headquarters started with three hymns from the hymnbook: "Keep Praising God," "Since Ages, Since Ages, God Is Only One," and a Telugu version of "The Church's One Foundation Is Jesus Christ Her Lord."

The final section of the hymnbook contains newer hymns, many of them more lively and less formal. Sometimes other shorter collections are used, including, at one of the services observed, hymns and lyrics prepared for a preaching tour by students at the Andhra Christian Theological College. Some children bring a notebook in which they write down the songs that they have learned. They sing these songs before worship begins or during the worship service, according to the pastor's request. Sometimes the pastor or a lay worship leader teaches the congregation a new song, which the pastor and his wife sing first, accompanying themselves on a small drum or harmonium. (In one congregation the pastor's young son would accompany many hymns with a rapid and very skillful drum beat.) Many find it easier to follow the beat than to keep on the same pitch, so the pastor needs to be able to sing well.

The second order of the CSI liturgy includes a call to worship, a prayer of

---

7. Luke and Carman, *Village Christians*, 70-73.

thanksgiving, and the confession of sins and absolution, which is followed by a hymn of confession. After that comes the reading of the four lessons in the common Protestant lectionary for that Sunday. These are an Old Testament reading; a psalm, often read responsively; a reading from the New Testament Epistles; and a reading from the Gospels. If at all possible, lay members of the congregation read the lessons. On "Youth Sunday," a layman read the first lesson; he was followed by a ten-year-old girl and the pastor's teenage son and daughter. At another service on the same Sunday, two young men and two young women read the lessons.

The scripture readings are followed by a hymn of preparation before the sermon. In one service this was a newer hymn from the final section of the hymnbook: "I Have Decided to Follow Jesus Today." In another service the pastor and his wife together sang a hymn with a similar theme. In CSI sermons, the text or texts are taken from one or more of the scripture lessons, and there is an announced theme. After "Youth Sunday," the following week's theme was "Christian character."

Following the sermon, everyone reads together the Apostles' Creed, which many know by heart. Then the pastor leads in the intercessory prayers from the service book or prays in his own words. While the offering is being taken, a favorite lyric or hymn is sung. After the offertory comes the concluding prayer, which ends with everyone joining in the Lord's Prayer. Then the pastor pronounces the benediction.

The one communion service observed began with the hymn "Come to the Food of Life," with the congregation standing. The pastor, an ordained presbyter, then followed the CSI order of service. After blessing the communion elements, he started the "passing of the peace" for the men, who were standing on one side of the church, while his wife did the same for the women, who were standing on the other side. After a prayer and another hymn, he invited communicant members to come forward and receive communion. While some came forward, others sang hymns. After taking communion, each person returned to his or her place and prayed silently. The pastor then said the prayers in the order of service and pronounced the benediction, which was followed by some of the women singing one stanza of a hymn.

After the long service ends people usually go to their homes, which are often close by, but are sometimes in a village a few miles away. Since many people come from a distance to the Sunday service at the new church in Chinna Shankarampet, that service is normally held Sunday morning. Services where everyone lives close by are usually held Sunday evening, while many congregations without a resident pastor hold their services at the end of the working day on whatever evening the visiting pastor can arrange to come. There is generally less effort than in many independent churches to provide refreshments, or even a whole meal, after the service. In the older CSI congregations most people know one another, and many are related, whereas in many of the independent churches, people belong to different castes and may come from different villages.

The first study took place at a time when the former two-tier system of pastoral care was still working, though with some difficulties. The evangelists were unordained teacher-pastors living in houses whose veranda and courtyard served as the place for teaching children, leading night prayers, and conducting the Sunday evening service. Their preaching to Hindus and teaching of catechumens involved the singing of Bible stories, including the creation and fall, and events in the life of Jesus. Preaching to the congregation, on the other hand, consisted of comments on a passage of scripture. Favorite passages included the Christmas story, miracle stories in the Gospels and Acts, heroic episodes in the Old Testament, and moral exhortations in the Epistles.[8] The sermon summaries in *Village Christians*[9] show some of the evangelists' efforts to relate their preaching to current affairs, and to use words that were familiar in a village Hindu environment.

The upper tier of ministers consisted of the ordained presbyters. Only they could perform baptisms and celebrate Holy Communion, but there was only one presbyter in each pastorate. Much of his time was taken up supervising the evangelists. Since the presbyter usually visited a village congregation only for baptism and communion, his sermons were usually focused on one or other of the two sacraments. Very few other texts or topics were addressed in his preaching. One other theme was the necessity of giving. Special services at Christmas and Easter gave both evangelists and their presbyter the opportunity to preach on Christ's birth and resurrection. The presbyter's educated language and lack of connection to village life, however, sometimes made it difficult for villagers to understand his preaching.[10]

Now, there is no longer a lower tier of unordained teacher-preachers. At present, there are five presbyters or deacons who will become presbyters. They share the care of more than twenty congregations. Sermons summarized (in the appendices) are too few to give a representative sample of current preaching, but they reveal two changes from fifty years ago: the use of the common lectionary and the setting of a distinct topic for each Sunday. Both changes tend to prevent pastors from too frequently returning to their own favorite themes

---

8. Luke and Carman, *Village Christians*, 127-28.
9. Luke and Carman, *Village Christians*, 139-41.
10. Luke and Carman, *Village Christians*, 126-29.

and texts. There are four scripture lessons each Sunday, and the sermon text does not have to be from one of the assigned lessons. The two sermons that we have summarized on each set of texts (from two successive Sundays) vary a great deal, and the background of the preachers varies at least as much. As it happened, two were experienced pastors who had first been evangelists; one was a minister in training who was preaching a "trial sermon," and one was a laywoman who is a lecturer at a nearby engineering college.

All four sermons tried to address the assigned topic for that Sunday. The first was designated as "Youth Sunday." The sermon given by an ordained presbyter commented on many biblical passages, including all four scripture lessons, starting with the apostle Paul's instructions to his former assistant, Timothy, and quoting, "Let no one despise you because of your youth." After lifting up as an example David's playing the harp to relieve King Saul's depression, he discussed the Gospel passage, which was Jesus' conversation with the rich young man. The last scriptural reference was to the psalm reading: "Your youth is renewed like the eagle's."

The college teacher's sermon began with a quotation ascribed to Martin Luther: "Darkness will not be removed by darkness." She then discussed the fear of parents that their daughters might fall in love when they go away to school or college. She described an incident that took place at her college six years before: an inter-caste love affair that ended with the young man's attempted suicide because the young woman, from a Dalit caste, would not marry him. She followed this story with several pieces of advice to young people on meeting moral challenges. At the end of the sermon, she discussed Paul's teaching to Timothy and Jesus' words to the rich young man, "Go and sell all that you have . . ."

The other two sermons had the assigned theme of "Christian character." The sermon by the pastor-in-training began with a text outside the scripture lesson, 1 Peter 2:12. He then proceeded to a saying in English, afterward translated into Telugu, which ends with the line: "When character is lost, everything is lost." He then discussed the difference in meaning of five Telugu words referring to character and illustrated the meaning of character by noting the good conduct certificates issued by Indian schools. He also explored two of the scripture lessons, Ephesians 6:10 and 1 Samuel 24:1-18. The latter describes how David, who was being hunted by King Saul, proved himself an exemplary model for Christians by not killing the king when he had the opportunity because he recognized Saul's divine appointment as king. The application to Christians from David's example was that they should forgive others and speak the truth, avoiding hurting others, stealing, and doing any injustice. Jesus exemplified good character by his life and by his teaching that his followers are to be the "salt of the earth" and the "light of the world."

The Older Congregations in the Jangarai Section

The second sermon, by an ordained deacon who had been an evangelist, started with a brief definition of Christian character, without which, he declared, we are a disgrace to God. He then moved to the Old Testament lesson mentioned above: David's restraining himself from killing King Saul, which he considered an exemplary model. His advice to young people, and to the whole congregation, was to follow Christ and to share their experience of salvation. This led him to Jesus' metaphors, salt and light.

The preachers all tried to give illustrations that the congregation could relate to, based on their hearers' experience. One was the actual incident of the college love affair and attempted suicide. One related to a story about Queen Victoria, who went out in disguise, the preacher said, and had to beg for an umbrella from a reluctant donor. The queen later berated her ministers for the conditions in which she found her poor subjects. The example in another sermon was of a sculptor who insisted on starting over after finding a minor blemish in his carving. No one would notice it, he was told, and it would be a waste of his time and energy to begin again. He replied, "People might not recognize the scar, but I would know it is there. Even if my time and energy is wasted, I don't want to present an imperfect figure."

Also important is the relation between the pastor's sermon and his or her prayers. It is not only the words, but whether they are said in a way that assures the congregation of the pastor's sincerity.

Disintegration of Congregations without a Resident Pastor

The Achampet congregation described in chapter 1 may provide the most graphic illustration of this disintegration. In 1959 it was considered the most active congregation in the Wadiaram pastorate and the most self-consciously Christian, with large crosses painted on the outside walls of some houses. Because its young men were so firm in their faith and so articulate, the presbyter thought that the congregation could manage on its own, without one of the dwindling number of evangelists. The experiment failed, in part because the new lay leaders were given so little help by the presbyter and by the evangelists in nearby villages. In some respects, however, Achampet is not the most extreme example of the consequences of pastoral neglect, perhaps because all of the Madiga families (and none of the Malas) had become Christians at the same time (1932), so the congregation expressed their caste solidarity as well as their Christian faith. They maintained their church roll all through the years of neglect and took their children to the CSI cathedral in Medak for baptism. Some of their leaders say that their faith never diminished, and now regular worship has been restored.

In 1959 three of the nine village congregations in the Jangarai section had already been long neglected, so much so that only a few even remembered the Christian names that they were given at baptism. In one of the three villages (Chettipally), there is now an independent church with an active pastor in residence. In a second (Mirzapally), a new congregation was started in 1989 by a Christian laywoman named Shanthamma. She came from the Hebron Church in Hyderabad founded by the Bakht Singh group. Although she built a church, the congregation shrank from seventeen families to five once she stopped coming to preach and lead prayers. In the third village (Edulapally), there is no new congregation, but there has been a recent effort (during the period of this study) to revive the old CSI congregation.

Two other congregations (in Jangarai and Gawallapally) had resident evangelists fifty years ago but have now been without for many years. In Gawallapally the church-parsonage is still standing, but the building in Jangarai is now in ruins.[11] Like Achampet, both were single-caste Madiga congregations in which caste solidarity reinforced their Christian commitment, but their poverty left them subject to pressure from their landlords. The Jangarai congregation has lost some members to a small independent church consisting largely of Mudhiraj caste converts. When a CSI pastor visits, the congregation gathers in the Dalit community hall. Christians in Jangarai feel free to attend services at different churches. The Gawallapally worship hall has been repaired with the financial assistance of Mrs. Deevenamma from Hyderabad. (Her work is discussed in chapter 7.) When the CSI pastor visits, some Christians attend the worship he conducts. If he does not come or is delayed, they go to independent churches. Some families in the old Gawallapally congregation now generally attend the large Pentecostal church in Ambajipet, which is a few miles away.

Intermarriage and Its Consequences

It is not surprising that new converts to Christianity should continue much of their former religious life, especially if they joined the church as part of a group decision, but not a group large enough or sufficiently well taught to pull away from the customs of their Hindu relatives and neighbors. They have therefore not formed communities as distinctive and separate as those of many urban Christians in India. It may be more surprising to urban Christian church leaders if the situation in village congregations does not change from one generation to the next. The weakness of Christian teaching and pastoral care observed fifty

---

11. In May 2014, a new church was under construction. See the photo section.

years ago may be partly responsible, along with the fact that in every generation more than half of the Christians growing up in these congregations are marrying non-Christians of the same caste. To understand why this is the case, we need to look at the structure of Hindu marriage in South Indian villages.

For almost all castes in South India, the family line runs from father to son. If there are no sons, the husband of one of the daughters may move into the household and become the heir (a practice called *illutam*). Thus, sons generally stay in the same village with their parents and often in the same house. They do not often marry within the same village, where many of their fathers' relatives live, but marry a girl in another village, who then leaves her home village and joins her husband's family (marriage with close maternal relatives is acceptable). Most marriages in the villages are arranged (sometimes for adolescents, even though they fall below the legal age limit for both Hindus and Christians). Important factors in the parents' choice of a daughter-in-law or son-in-law include wealth, previous acquaintance with their parents' family, and blood relationship. For most families in the older CSI congregations, it is not important whether the spouse is a Christian or not. He or she must be of the same caste and usually from another village. Marriages between Christians occur somewhat by chance, but the smaller the number of Christians in the group of nearby villages, the greater the chance that a Christian will marry a non-Christian.

If the number of sons and daughters in all the families taken together is equal, intermarriage would leave the size of the congregation the same. The same number of Christian girls would marry Hindu boys and move away to their villages as the number of Hindu girls coming into Christian families as they marry the Christian sons. It is generally assumed that the bride will accept and follow her husband's religious practice. This is a village assumption, whereas the official position of the Church of South India and of other denominations is that the Christian girl should remain Christian while the Hindu girl married into a Christian family does not become a Christian automatically. She needs to be instructed in the Christian faith and decide to be baptized. In these older congregations, village custom triumphs. Christian girls entering Hindu families join more or less completely, and more or less willingly, in Hindu practice. A Hindu girl entering a Christian household joins in Christian worship with little or no instruction. She also, however, often continues many of her Hindu practices and later involves her children in those practices. Unless the Christian girls moving away retain their church connection, the exchange is therefore only numerically 50-50. The qualitative exchange is not equal, for the Hindu girls joining the Christian congregation are more likely to maintain their Hindu connections and less likely to become fully participating Christians, and the number of active Christians in the congregation is likely to diminish.

While marriage between Christians and Hindus rarely occurs among urban Christians, such intermarriage is common in these villages. If it is against official church policy, that rule is ignored in the congregations studied. Not only do the wives from Hindu families tend to continue their Hindu practices, but they also tend to bring up their children to observe Hindu customs.

Addressing Problems in Pastoral Care

For the first half of the twentieth century, the Methodist Mission sought to encourage and care for a constantly expanding number of Christian congregations made up in large part of the poorest villagers, most of them illiterate. Placing a teacher-catechist in every village congregation was at the core of the mission's strategy, but so was the support system behind each junior evangelist: a senior evangelist for each section of the pastorate and at least a junior minister in charge of each pastorate, who was in turn supervised by a more senior Indian minister or a British missionary. The schools in mission centers, especially in Medak and Hyderabad, were needed to continue the education of some Christians, who might decide to become evangelists or even to go on to college and higher theological education.

The system never worked perfectly, for the number of village congregations kept outstripping the number of evangelists, as well as the capacity of the supervising ministers. The number of evangelists continued to increase, reaching a peak of almost eight hundred in 1943, most of them largely supported by funds from Great Britain. This peak occurred four years after Posnett's retirement and during World War II, when the number of British missionaries had started to decrease.

Inflation during the war decreased the value of evangelists' salaries. Raising them as part of a general salary adjustment eased one problem but meant that there was money for fewer evangelists. The budget for these salaries was further cut by an agreement between the Medak Diocese and the Methodist Mission to begin a phased reduction of funds from abroad. This change was supposed to be matched by an increase in giving by the village congregations. When a congregation did not contribute the stipulated amount, the rest was deducted from the evangelist's monthly salary, which understandably left the evangelists very dismayed. The 1959 study brought this situation to light, and as a result the policy was changed: evangelists were required to forward only the offerings actually received from their congregations. The mission provided a temporary "cushion" to make this change possible, but in the long run, there was still a negative effect. Reducing outside support without increased local contributions led to a radical decrease in the number of evangelists and also affected their morale; many of them were unwilling to visit congregations in other villages. The "New Pattern" adopted by the diocese officially made all the evangelists in each section of a pastorate jointly responsible for all the congregations, but at least in the one section surveyed in 1959, this official policy made no difference in practice.

By 1959, the three congregations in the Jangarai section of the pastorate that had long had no resident evangelist had practically disappeared. They had seldom or never been visited by evangelists living only a few miles away. Since the number of evangelists in the diocese as a whole was continuing to decline, more congregations were likely to disappear unless evangelists effectively extended their care to other villages or lay leaders were trained and enabled to care for congregations without evangelists. This was one reason for the concern voiced in the 1959 study about the future of all these CSI village congregations.

As it has turned out, many of the congregations without evangelists have not maintained regular worship. Many formerly Christian families have lost any connection with a Christian congregation and have returned completely to their Hindu practices. We did not try to determine how many families that still participate in Christian worship have registered with the government as Hindus. (In other parts of Andhra Pradesh, there have been many who have done just that.) All these developments have led to a decline in the number of Christian families in still functioning congregations and in the number of those congregations. The precise nature and extent of the decline varies greatly from one congregation to another.

The Medak Diocese did not succeed in persuading most village congregations to increase their giving so that they could support their own resident evangelist. The program to train voluntary church workers to assist the evangelists and lead worship in congregations without an evangelist began with high hopes but was finally unsuccessful. Not enough people agreed to take the training, and many of those who did found that the evangelists were unwilling to share leadership with them. In the decade after the 1959 study, the number of evangelists plummeted to less than one hundred. This meant that a much smaller total number of evangelists and presbyters had to provide pastoral care for three or four times as many village congregations. They were unable to do this adequately, so many village congregations were partially or totally abandoned. The congregations that did have resident pastors kept their strong sense of Christian identity, even when most families observed a hybrid religion including both Christian and Hindu practices and beliefs.

It was already clear fifty years ago that pastoral care was inadequate and that the situation was likely to get worse. After the 1959 study, P. Y. Luke tried to make some improvements, especially when he was chairman of the Medak District Church Council. In 1959 those congregations with resident evangelists had regular worship and some community solidarity, but in the following decade, with the decreasing number of evangelists, more and more congregations were without a pastor in residence.

As noted in previous chapters, the Medak Diocese has changed in the past fifty years from the system of pastoral care just described to one in which there are no longer unordained "evangelists" serving as village pastor-teachers. Instead, there are presbyters who are already ordained and deacons who will be ordained in due course. Each one is responsible for the village or town in which he lives and also for several other CSI congregations in nearby villages. Some of these pastors began their service as evangelists and have been ordained as deacons or presbyters after some additional study.

The remarkable increase in the number of independent pastors, many supervising both a church and several satellite congregations, provides a contrasting model of pastoral care, which is largely self-supporting. This model has its own weaknesses, but it does pose a continuing challenge to the Church of South India. Can the better educated CSI presbyters match the zeal and practical skills of the independent pastors, both as congregational leaders and as outgoing evangelists? There is certainly no answer to this question at this time, but failure to meet this challenge could bring further decline in the CSI rural pastorates.

The present CSI model of pastoral care requires many pastors to visit several congregations every week. One pastor during 2008-9 demonstrated how this could be done. While still a theological student, Nithin Kumar was placed in charge of one of the largest congregations, Bandaposanipally, where attendance at worship had seriously declined. He was able to persuade a larger number to join in Sunday worship, and he enlisted a few young men to accompany him in visiting long neglected congregations. He set up a weekly schedule, starting with an 8:00-9:00 a.m. Sunday School and a 9:00-11:00 a.m. worship service in his home congregation. Then he conducted prayers for the six Christian families in the Gypsy settlement and, after that, went on to one of the neglected congregations to lead a service from 11:30 to 1:00. In that village, the son of a former evangelist had seized the church property. Nithin Kumar was able to reclaim it and to start building a new church. After returning home for lunch and a rest, he visited two congregations in another direction and held two one-hour services each Sunday evening. On Tuesday evening, he led worship in another neglected village where there are still ten Christian families, and there he built a small shed for worship. On Thursday evening, he went to the more distant village of Achampet, described in chapter 1, where the congregation had not gathered for worship for several years. He was able to reclaim the church land

The Older Congregations in the Jangarai Section

from the families that had built a cattle shed there, and he started building a new worship shed. In this previously all-Madiga congregation, he was able to persuade some Mala families to join in worship. Once or twice a month, he also visited a village across a nearby river where there were three Christian families. Every Monday, Wednesday, and Saturday he visited two Christian families in his home village.

After finishing his theological studies, the Rev. Nithin Kumar has been put in charge of a congregation elsewhere in the same pastorate that was previously poorly cared for. He is now responsible for four congregations and also visits other villages. He has started two annual festivals in his home congregation, and he is trying to start a weekly fellowship lunch after the Sunday morning service. (This custom has thus far been more frequent in independent churches than in the CSI.) The town where he is now stationed, which is located on the national highway going south to Hyderabad, has grown to a small city of 50,000 in which there are many independent churches. Just a few months after coming there, he was asked to speak at a Christian festival organized by an independent church, and he has also visited the independent Baptist Bible College.

This report reveals an energy and dedication to ministry like that of some independent pastors, as well as the skill to direct that energy in helpful ways. Nithin Kumar has been able to enlist several lay assistants to help him revive neglected congregations by visiting multiple villages. This young pastor's efforts represent the best that can be expected in the old pattern. His present charge of four congregations is difficult enough, especially if he expands his main congregation in a growing city. His successor in Bandaposanipally will find it even more difficult to keep visiting seven congregations every week besides his home congregation.

Even if that pastor's responsibilities were reduced by a more equal distribution, the pleas of many congregations for their own pastor would not be met. Providing so many additional CSI pastors is presently impossible. There are not enough funds, and there are not nearly enough candidates who have felt the call to full-time ministry and are securing even the lower level of ministerial training. The alternative of training voluntary church workers failed largely because evangelists were not willing or able to train lay assistants to take over significant pastoral responsibilities. There are now far more literate members of these congregations than there were fifty years ago, but neither the pastors nor the congregations may be willing to accept the service of those without the standard ecclesiastic and academic credentials. There is, however, one area in which the equal status of at least a few laypersons has been recognized: the power of their prayers. We turn in the final section of this chapter to a congregation sustained by its response to prayers for healing and by the leadership of those offering those prayers.

Ambajipet: Lay Leadership in a Diminished Congregation

As noted in chapter 3, the CSI Christians in Ambajipet now credit C. W. Posnett with starting their congregation. In 1959, however, an older member of the congregation told Mr. and Mrs. Luke that a Christian father in another village was willing for his daughter to marry a young man in Ambajipet if the man would become a Christian. "The boy, Prakasham, finally agreed to be baptized, not alone, but along with his family, and later this family persuaded all the other Mala families to be baptized. This was in 1914, and in 1920 the Madiga families in the village were baptized and joined the Congregation."[12] In 1959 there were 102 baptized Christians, including children, with 31 communicant members. Only four members were literate, and only one owned a Bible. A retired evangelist was then in charge of the congregation. He was allowed to live in the evangelist's house, but he was paid no salary. For that reason, he did not feel obligated to provide much pastoral care. While this was one of the least active congregations at that time, it was here that two non-Dalit families and a young man became Christians during the 1959 study, partly in response to Mr. Luke's preaching and partly because one couple had dreams of Christ healing them.

When the delegation from Hyderabad visited the congregation eighteen years later (1977), they were told that no Sunday services had been held since the evangelist left fifteen years before, and that the last service held in the church was the previous Christmas. Christians in Ambajipet remembered the service of Holy Communion conducted by Mr. Luke in 1959. They said that their children had grown up without being baptized. The delegation reported that these Christians considered baptism to be only a naming ceremony and thought that "the Lord's Supper is a gift of God to his people to cure all their diseases."[13]

By 2008, the number of families had shrunk from twenty to twelve, and of these only eight were active; two families had moved away to an area paying higher wages because many of the residents there had gotten jobs in the Middle East. One reason given for the decline in the congregation was the absence of a resident evangelist for so many years. A second reason was that the presbyter from Wadiaram, though he came every week to conduct services, would leave immediately afterward without visiting Christians in their homes. In addition, at some point, the evangelist's house and worship space had collapsed, after which there were no longer Sunday services. In 2003, however, the Rev. E. Samuel, then the presbyter in charge of the Wadiaram pastorate, took the initiative in constructing a new church building with a partial contribution from a South

---

12. Luke and Carman, *Village Christians*, 64.
13. B. David Raju's Memorandum, 1-2.

The Older Congregations in the Jangarai Section

Korean church. Since then the presbyter regularly comes on Sundays to conduct worship for the small congregation in their new church. (On May 23, 2010, there were eighteen women, twelve men, and eight children.) There are two additional reasons for the decline in numbers. Several Dalit families moved into new houses built by the government for (non-Christian) Dalits, after which they stopped attending church services. There is now also a Christian competitor: several families who were formerly members of this CSI congregation now attend Pastor Anandam's large independent church.[14]

It is remarkable that a congregation that until 1959 consisted only of Dalits (both Malas and Madigas) should now have only three Dalit families, but also nine families from five other castes (potter, toddy-tapper, washerman, herder, and farmer). The fathers in the potter caste family and one of the toddy-tapper caste families are the sons of the two couples that were baptized and joined the congregation during P. Y. Luke's stay. Two years later, four from other castes were baptized,[15] but none of their descendants are now part of the congregation.

Someone in each of five families in the present congregation was healed from an illness or the effects of black magic after repeated prayers to Christ in the church or in their homes. In all these cases, it was because of the healing that the individual or family joined the church, most of them within the past ten years. Sometimes these were prayers by the presbyter, but more often they were offered by one or more of three laypeople in the congregation. We introduce them here, along with a description of these healings after prayer to Christ.

Kurma Tharamma, a widow in Ambajipet, lives with her married son; they belong to the Kapu landholding caste. Because her fingers were clamped together permanently in a tight fist, she consulted magicians in Mirzapally who prescribed traditional medicines. As these did not help, she went to Medak cathedral and slept overnight in the pilgrims' center, before attending the daily morning service. She did this one night every month until she was cured. Thereafter, out of gratitude, she went to the Sunday morning service once a month, wrapping her Bible in a gunny sack so that her neighbors would not know where she was going. When the purpose of her trips was discovered, she was accused of verbally abusing some of her neighbors, and the village elders levied a fine of three thousand rupees. To pay this large sum, she had to pawn her gold chain. Once she had paid the fine, she testified openly about her new faith in Jesus Christ and how he had healed her. Now she would go, she said, not only once a month to the church in Medak, but also on all other Sundays to the CSI church in her home village. Then she went to the cathedral and was baptized. At

14. See chapter 6.
15. Luke and Carman, *Village Christians*, 154-57.

first she was shunned by many villagers, but after hearing her repeatedly affirm her faith in Jesus Christ, the villagers respect her and relate to her as they did before they knew that she was attending a Christian church.

Dr. Mahima Paranjyothi, who is now retired and living in Hyderabad, practiced homeopathic medicine in Ambajipet and the surrounding villages for many years and was a mainstay of the local CSI congregation. Her father, Mr. Malaga Sanjeeva Rao, who came from a local family, spent his life as an evangelist in the Medak Diocese. After he retired in 1986, he came to live with his daughter, and in 1991, he started a new congregation in the nearby village of Sangaipally.

When Dr. Paranjyothi began her practice, she found that black magic was rampant. In many homes, an affected person's shouts could be heard by the neighbors, especially after sunset. When people came to her for treatment, she would also share the gospel with them. At one point, she stopped her medical practice in order to accompany her father in his evangelistic and pastoral visits to Sangaipally. After her father's death, she resumed her practice, and people from Sangaipally came to her for treatment. She formed an evangelistic team with four others in her home congregation to visit every house in the Dalit section of Ambajipet, Sangaipally, and other nearby villages at the festival seasons of Christmas and Easter. At the time there were still no buses going to many of these villages.

Paranjyothi and Kummari Dass were able to construct a new church building, assisted financially by Mrs. Deevenamma and a church in South Korea, as well as by the CSI presbyter in Wadiaram, the Rev. E. Samuel, who himself came every Sunday to conduct worship. The new church served as the place of worship, not only for the Ambajipet congregation, but also for two families from the no longer functioning church in Sangaipally.

When Kummari Dass was born, his Hindu parents in the potter caste had already experienced the death of their first two sons, so they put him unclothed on the village trash heap without performing the usual ceremonies for the newborn. A Christian watchman saw what was happening and asked why the baby was treated in this way. When he heard the explanation, he called his wife, who cleaned and clothed the baby, took him in her arms, and named him Dass.[16] After that, Dass's own father shifted from making pots to farming, and the family began to attend Christian worship services in Ambajipet. Dass played with the children of the evangelist Laxmiah and learned Christian practices, including

16. The baby was put on the trash heap to reverse the family's bad fortune, following the death of two sons on whom they had lavished care. This public display of lack of interest in the new baby's fate is a ritual, not an abandonment. It is potentially harmful to the infant, however, which is why the Christian watchman was moved to pick up the baby and turn him over to his wife to clean up before returning the newborn to his parents.

The Older Congregations in the Jangarai Section

singing and praying. He also walked all the way to Chinna Shankarampet with the evangelist's children to attend the primary school, where he studied up to fifth grade. Then, because his father was becoming old and weak, Dass stopped going to school in order to help his father with farming.

When Dass grew up, he married a Hindu woman named Laxmi in a Hindu ceremony, but a year later, she was baptized with his mother's name of Rajavva. From childhood, Dass was a committed Christian. Once when he was visiting relatives, he met a woman possessed by a demon. After he prayed for her, she was healed. Another relative had spent 30,000 rupees on medicines in vain attempts to regain her health. After Dass prayed for her in her own village, she came to Ambajipet, where Dass and Paranjyothi prayed for her on five consecutive Sundays. She was healed of her illness and was later baptized in the Chinna Shankarampet church led by Deevenamma. Now the woman attends Sunday worship in her own village.

Dass has a neighbor, Kurma Durgaiah, who was never healthy. He believed that all his pains were the result of black magic. Dass repeatedly told him about the healing power of Jesus, and Durgaiah finally professed faith in Jesus. He was afraid, however, of what his fellow caste members would do if he were to be baptized. Dass encouraged him, saying, "It never bothered them when you were sick. Why should they be bothered when you are healed?" Durgaiah was convinced and was baptized in the Horeb Prayer Church in Chinna Shankarampet. Dass also met Sakali Lachaiah of the washerman caste, whose story is given below.

Dass is a good friend of Paranjyothi. One night when they went to Sangaipally for a prayer meeting, they learned that a woman named Sathamma was on her deathbed. They asked her family to bring her to Sunday worship in Ambajipet. She came for five Sundays in a row and was healed after prayers offered by Dass, Paranjyothi, and the whole congregation. After Sathamma was healed, the two of them walked with Deevenamma to Sangaipally, where they conducted a thanksgiving prayer meeting in Sathamma's home, after first removing the talismans, idols, and other charms. Four neighboring families then invited the trio to visit their homes and pray for them. Later all four families became disciples of Christ; they now attend Pastor Sanjeevi's independent church in Chegunta. Sathamma attends Sunday worship in the Chinna Shankarampet church.

Dass supports every minister who comes to his village and accompanies each one to other villages. Once he hosted a large group of evangelists from Every Home Crusade. One of them, who came from Ongole in Coastal Andhra, married a local girl and became the pastor of the independent church he started in Chettipally. As previously noted, Dass and his family helped build the new church building for the congregation in Ambajipet.

Unlike laypeople who have lived or were educated in an urban setting, Dass had to leave school after five years to help his father with farming. He exemplifies the kind of village-based lay leadership that will be necessary if CSI congregations without resident pastors are to survive. What is striking in his story is his teamwork with Paranjyothi and Deevenamma, not just for a single event, but for a spiritual partnership lasting more than fifteen years. Their work together was even more significant because it was centered in a congregation that had seriously declined. Fifty years ago it was the first congregation in the Jangarai section to incorporate a few non-Dalit families, but in more recent years, many families have dropped out. This is in part because of efforts by local officials to get Dalits to register for benefits available to Hindu Dalits, and in part because of the attraction of two independent churches in the village and others a few miles away. These lay Christian efforts, along with regular visits by the presbyter in charge of the Wadiaram pastorate, have kept the congregation going, now meeting in a new church building.

There is another dimension of Dass's Christian witness. His Hindu relatives and neighbors want to include him in family and caste gatherings, so much so that they avoid any Hindu ritual to consecrate the food they serve and instead ask him to offer a Christian blessing.

Perhaps the clearest testimony to the corporate ministry of prayer for healing in which Mr. Dass and others have participated comes, not from Dass's own words, but from the testimony of Sakali Lachaiah, who believes that he was healed from leprosy:

> My children and I used to worship Lord Hanuman (the monkey god), but white patches appeared on my skin, and I gradually developed leprosy. I had no money to go to the doctor; my wife supported us with her earnings as a day laborer in the fields. Because of my leprosy, my children were afraid of me. No medicines helped. I went to traditional doctors, and I drank juices made from tree sap, but my disease kept getting worse. After three months, I could not even stand up. One day, Kummari Dass, Dr. Paranjyothi, and some young people were singing in the CSI church. One line of a song caught my attention: "Jesus touched the lame and the lepers, and healed them." It struck me that I might be healed if I worshiped Jesus. Some time before, it had been Dass who told me about Jesus and his healing power when we were walking to the fields and working there. He used to say to me, "Brother Lachaiah, if we pray to Jesus, diseases subside," but I never heeded his words. However, when I was bedridden and began to soil my clothes, Kummari Dass's words were ringing in my ears and I thought it would be good to ask him to pray for me. My son

Ramulu brought Dass to my house, and after he had prayed for me for a month and a half, I began to experience healing. Then I went with my wife and children to the Big Church in Medak and made an offering of five hundred rupees. The pastor there prayed for me. We bought a picture of Jesus Christ and took it home. That same Sunday we asked Dass and Paranjyothi to pray for us in our home, and with their prayers we installed Jesus Christ in our home. We are all going to the CSI church here in Ambajipet every Sunday, and we are all living happily.[17]

Conclusion

The older CSI congregations are all part of the same Wadiaram pastorate, but their fortunes have varied considerably because of different circumstances when they were established, different degrees of pastoral care, and different kinds of lay leadership. Even the three congregations that were so neglected fifty years ago have had quite different histories. Two (Chettipaly and Mirzapally) disappeared as CSI congregations, but some of the former CSI members or their descendants now attend the independent church in their village. In the third congregation (Edulapally), however, a few families have maintained their CSI connection and are now attending a recently reestablished Sunday service.

Three other congregations without a resident evangelist also have distinct histories. Two that are fairly close together and closer to the main road (Jangarai and Gawalapally) have had intermittent pastoral care and have maintained something of a congregational life. The number of families has markedly decreased, however, because of government pressure and the attraction of nearby independent churches. The complicated history of the Achampet congregation has been told in chapter 1. Despite its strong community identity and the enthusiasm of its young men, the congregation was unable to maintain its worship life during decades of pastoral neglect. All three congregations consist only of Madigas.

The two large CSI congregations (Bandaposanipally and Shankarraj Kondapur) have retained most of their former families. One has had an evangelist or pastor in residence almost continuously for the past one hundred years. The other had an evangelist most of the time until ten years ago. Both congregations include most of the members of both Dalit castes, the Malas and the Madigas. That gives them a larger and more secure base, but the two caste communities have remained very separate social units, especially in the older

---

17. Based on field notes from Vasantha Rao and students.

congregation; they do not mingle on festive occasions. While more families in these congregations seek Christian spouses for their children than in some other CSI congregations, many families still engage in some village Hindu practices, and many older men do not come to Sunday worship.

The roadside village of Ambajipet has experienced the most radical decline in numbers but has maintained its congregational life and, with the help of the presbyter, built a new church. The stories of its unusually dedicated lay leaders have just been told. Their primary leadership has not been in conducting formal worship, for the presbyter comes every Sunday from Wadiaram. It is rather their concern for the sick and their unabated intercessory prayers. For Dr. Paranjyothi, this ministry of prayer has in some cases accompanied her homeopathic medical practice. In the case of Mr. Kummari Dass, his ministry has been a lifetime of Christian witness and powerful prayer. For several years, both of them worked together with the retired Christian nurse from Hyderabad, Mrs. Deevenamma Mithra, whose extraordinary evangelism will be described in chapter 7. What will happen now that Paranjyothi has retired to Hyderabad, we do not know. Dass's leadership has not been primarily of the kind that was envisioned in the training program of the diocese in previous decades, substituting for a full-time evangelist or pastor, but he has helped greatly to keep this small congregation alive.

In chapter 11 we return to the question of lay leadership and the future of these older CSI congregations. In the following chapter we describe the independent churches, which have started more recently and developed rather differently from the older congregations, often with greater participation by their lay members.

CHAPTER 6

The Independent Churches

Twenty-Five New Churches in Twenty-Five Years

When the 1959 study in the Wadiaram pastorate ended, it seemed uncertain whether the congregations we had studied would decline in numbers and vitality or revive, aided by new members from other castes. As it has turned out, there has been a marked decline in several of those congregations, some of which are no longer functioning.

What was not anticipated was that new independent churches would spring up that were not connected with the Church of South India, though some of the pastors and lay leaders whose efforts led to this development had been or still are members of the older CSI congregations. Most of the pastors and lay evangelists involved have received brief theological training and sometimes financial support from Indian churches and mission organizations in Hyderabad or other urban centers. These missions are Pentecostal, independent Baptist, or other evangelical Protestant in background. Financial support for these churches comes from local, regional, national, and international churches.

Discovering these new churches has led us to expand our study beyond our initial aim, a restudy of the older congregations. We have learned the names of many independent pastors, the villages in which they have organized churches or conduct worship services for a few Christian families, and, in many cases, the number of individuals and families who have been baptized. A few of these churches are in villages with functioning CSI congregations, several are in villages where an older CSI congregation has partially or completely dissolved, and many are in villages where there have never been Christian families. Several of these villages are some distance away from the CSI congregations in the old Jangarai section.

Within the whole area of the pastorate we have thus far found 25 independent churches, whose pastors also conduct visits and hold worship services in another 20 to 30 villages. In contrast, there are now only 5 CSI pastors responsible for the 22 congregations in the Wadiaram pastorate (now 18 with regular worship).

Concerning 10 of the independent churches, we have some approximate statistics. They are located in the area of the former Jangarai section and the adjacent towns of Chegunta and Wadiaram. Three churches are located in villages where there were previously no Christian families (Ramaipally, Paidigummela, and Sooraram), and 2 are in villages where the old CSI congregation has long since disappeared (Chettipally and Mirzapally). Three are in villages that still have the remnants of an old congregation, but where there has been no resident CSI evangelist or pastor for many years (Ambajipet, Achampet, and Jangarai).[1] The 9th and 10th independent churches are 2 of the 6 new churches in the adjoining market towns of Chegunta and Wadiaram. We have very little information about the other 15 independent churches elsewhere in the area of the Wadiaram pastorate.

The smallest of the 10 churches now has only 5 families out of the original 17, declining after the laywoman who founded the congregation stopped visiting. The largest church claims 400 members. There are 2 churches with about 30 members in 10 to 12 families, 4 churches with between 50 and 75 members, and 2 with about 200, including a few families in several nearby villages.

One striking difference between the independent churches and the older CSI congregations is in their caste composition. Up to 1959, all the Christians in the Jangarai section were Dalits (Malas or Madigas). During the period of the first study a very small number of new members from other castes joined the CSI congregations. Of the 10 new churches, all founded after 1980, 2 consist only of Dalits. In 5, Dalits are in a minority. In one independent church, 21 of 25 families belong to a tribal group; the other 4 are from a landholding caste (Mudhiraj). One of the smaller churches has 5 Mudhiraj families and 5 Dalit families. Two other churches include members from 3 castes. The largest church brings together members from 7 castes, and the 2 other churches have 9 castes represented.

Whether such multi-caste congregations can continue to live in harmony is an important question for the future. Another question is whether Dalit Christians can adjust to being only a small part of a larger Christian fellowship, especially if they view it as a subordinate part. We return to these ques-

---

1. In addition to Anandam's independent church, there is a new "Pentecostal Mission" in Ambajipet.

tions in chapter 12. There are two more immediate questions. First, can the CSI congregations and the independent churches cooperate on matters of mutual interest? Second, will the newest CSI congregation, the Horeb Prayer Church, which started as an independent church, continue to accept the more formal CSI framework?[2]

Anticipation of Current Trends: Sadhu Joseph's Healing Ministry

Fifty years ago there were no independent churches in the area of the Wadiaram pastorate, but there were signs of new developments that would lead to a new type of church and a new emphasis. These signs were reported in *Village Christians* without the authors knowing where these developments would lead. Jesus was experienced as a divine power who appeared in the dreams of Hindu villagers and healed them of various diseases. A few of them decided to become Christians.

When Narayana Gowd (of the toddy-tapper caste) was a child, he attended the primary school run by the Christian evangelist in Ambajipet, but his family had no connection with the evangelist's all-Dalit congregation. Years later, after Narayana had grown up and married, cholera broke out in the village, and he was pressed to join in the worship of the cholera goddess. He refused to do so, and that night he had a dream in which he was wrestling with Satan, who tried to strangle him because he would not worship the goddess. Then, he reported, Jesus appeared in white robes and rescued him by killing Satan. For three years, Narayana took no outward steps toward worshiping Jesus, but when his wife became very ill before giving birth, he took her to the Christian hospital in Medak, where she had a safe delivery. In gratitude they named their son Swamidas, "Servant of the Lord (Jesus)." Two months later, after she had developed a severe abdominal pain, she dreamed that she saw Jesus and felt him touching her abdomen and putting three pills in her mouth. The following morning the pain was gone. After this second dream of Lord Jesus, Narayana and Satyamma decided to become Christians, even though that meant joining a congregation then consisting only of Dalits. Narayana was given the baptismal name of Paul; he soon became a leader in the congregation.[3]

The longer story about a dramatic healing told in *Village Christians* is about a lay Christian leader who came to be known as Sadhu Joseph.[4] During the

---

2. See chapter 7.
3. Luke and Carman, *Village Christians*, 154-55.
4. Luke and Carman, *Village Christians*, 148-54.

Lukes' stay in Kondapur, they noticed several Hindus from three traditionally labeled "upper castes" attending night prayers at the church. They all said that they had been healed of various diseases after being blessed by the sadhu at one of his healing services a few weeks before, held in a village near Medak, ten miles away. Only one was baptized and joined the congregation. The others withdrew after the threat of ostracism by their caste leaders. The one man who became a Christian was convinced that he had been healed of leprosy by the power of Jesus Christ.

Botumanchi Joseph was born into a Christian family in the part of the Hyderabad Methodist District that is now part of the neighboring CSI Karimnagar Diocese. He said that he never attended school as a child and was thus illiterate. In his teens, he left his village for a year or two to work as a coolie in an Indian army encampment further north. The money he saved while away helped him to arrange a marriage with a Christian girl from another village. The couple had two sons, one of whom died. Five years after his marriage, Joseph contracted leprosy, as a result of which his parents and friends shunned him, and his wife went back to live with her parents, taking their son with her.

Joseph was so depressed by his illness and by the rejection by his family that he decided to commit suicide. He said that he tried twice. Once he jumped into a deep pit full of mud but found himself on the bank, as if someone had pulled him out. Then he tried to hang himself in his room, but he fell down to the ground and found that the rope that he had tied to a beam had been sliced through, as if with a knife. He could not understand what this meant and lay weeping in despair. He said that about midnight the room was flooded with light, and he heard a voice saying, "Oh, Joseph, why are you weeping? Are you worried about your loathsome disease? Get up! I have healed your dreadful disease of leprosy. Now go in peace out into the world, take the Bible and heal all manner of sickness and disease in my name!"[5]

The following morning he found that all signs of leprosy had disappeared. Leaving home with a Bible from one of his friends, he went out into the jungle to live as a sadhu (a Hindu ascetic), spending his time in prayer and meditation. Now miraculously, he said, for the first time in his life he could read the Bible and pray to Jesus. This happened in 1954, when he was twenty-five. By the time of the previous study he had already spent five years going from place to place, camping in a tent given him by an American missionary, and healing diseases in the name of Jesus Christ. His wife rejoined him, but since he was now an ascetic, she lived as a "sister" in a separate tent. At the time he ate no

---

5. Luke and Carman, *Village Christians*, 150.

solid food, but subsisted on milk and orange juice. He grew his hair long and wore a cassock with a silver cross on a string around his neck.

Sadhu Joseph held healing services three times a week, which began with his wife leading the crowd in Christian songs, singing each line before everyone repeated it. Then he would preach for two hours, expounding some passage from the Gospels that contained several miracles. In the healing part of the service that followed, he would bless the castor oil in a bottle and sugar and honey wrapped in a leaf, which people had brought with them. Barren women seeking a child would bring a piece of fruit. People would come to him one by one, or he would go down a row of people sitting or kneeling. He would place his Bible on each person's head and on the food they had brought and bless one after another in rapid succession. With a large crowd, this could take several hours. Many lepers came to receive the blessing, believing that Jesus who healed the sadhu would likewise heal them. He would camp in one place for three to six months, and many thousands would come to his healing services. Many went home saying that they had been healed, having experienced the power of Christ.

Sometimes there was strong opposition from members of the Arya Samaj and some Hindus in political parties. On Palm Sunday in 1959, just a few weeks before the Lukes came to Jangarai, a group of men came after the service near Medak when the crowd had left; they burned down the sadhu's tent and destroyed his possessions. It was later determined that men from both the Congress Party and the Communist Party were involved. Some weeks later a service in Hyderabad was disrupted when men threw stones at the sadhu and his audience. The police commissioner then stopped the service on the grounds that the sadhu was disturbing the peace. Protestant and Roman Catholic spokesmen, working together, were able to convince the government that it was autorickshaw drivers hired by the Arya Samajists who had caused the trouble.

Sadhu Joseph continued his ministry for many years, going to many places in Andhra Pradesh. He is now living in retirement. In some respects his ministry resembles that of more recent independent pastors; in other respects it differs. Luke reported that Sadhu Joseph emphasized both the physical and the spiritual healing wrought by Christ, but said little about the Holy Spirit. The sadhu spoke about repentance but did not make it a condition for healing. He did not stress any moral requirements but urged his listeners to worship Jesus and to make an offering to Jesus when they returned to their own village. He left it to his listeners to decide whether they should seek baptism. He did not claim any supernatural power for himself, but said that it is Jesus alone who heals. He insisted that everyone should listen to the word of God, which itself creates faith in them and aids in healing.

Sadhu Joseph differed from the independent pastors in making no effort to establish his own church. He worked together with the church leaders in the area where his meetings were being held. In consultation with the local pastors, he baptized those who wanted no one but the sadhu to do this. In 1958 the entire Madiga community in one village in the CSI Bodhan pastorate asked Sadhu Joseph to baptize them. With the presbyter's concurrence, he held a service of preparation on the day before the baptisms. The following day, after making the sign of the cross with oil on the forehead of each candidate, he baptized them all by immersion in a nearby canal. The new converts then built a prayer hall and helped construct a house for the evangelist appointed for their new congregation.

While relatively few of the many thousands he helped from "upper castes" were willing to join the all-Dalit congregations in their home villages, their faith in Christ may have helped to change the attitude of Hindus of other castes toward the Christian message and those who proclaimed it. Both CSI and independent pastors have generally agreed with Sadhu Joseph that Christ's power to heal precedes human responses, but the pastors are more concerned to spell out and emphasize the expected moral changes in new Christian believers.

Ministry of Some Independent Pastors

Why has there been such a dramatic increase in the number of Christians belonging to independent churches, all of them starting within the past thirty years? We get some clues from what the independent pastors have told us about their own ministry.

Only a few of the independent pastors we interviewed broke with a Hindu family to join a Christian fellowship. Instead, they are what might be called "vocational converts." Some of them were brought up in Christian homes in villages or cities, either in the Medak Diocese or in other Protestant churches. They felt called to a ministry beyond their family expectations of what it means to be a Christian. Through some preaching they heard, some miraculous healing they witnessed, or their own encounter with Jesus in a dream or a healing — or all three combined — they came to believe that Jesus has real power today and that they were obligated to share that good news. Most of them had limited schooling, with less than a full college education. Then they had a brief course of ministerial training, in which the Bible was interpreted from the vantage point of Jesus' present power. They were taught how to persuade village people to try this gospel message out themselves, often by accompanying experienced and enthusiastic pastors on their preaching tours.

One of the pastors, Nathaniel, was brought up in a Hindu family in the

Mudhiraj caste, none of whom in his village was Christian. He started going to services in the Medak cathedral, where many Hindus attend, especially at the time of Christian festivals. He also went to the healing services of Tharamma nearby, where prayers were offered for the sick. He said it was there that he came to know Christ and "grow strong in the Lord." After his baptism he used to go into the forest and spend time alone with God. In 1985 he felt called to become a minister. He had only a grade school education and no formal theological training, but he began to preach and also to pray for people who were in need of healing. Some people responded to his ministry, and for them he constructed a church in his home village. He also visited a neighboring village, but he got no response until he was called to come and exorcize the evil spirits tormenting a woman there. He conducted a series of prayer meetings in the woman's home, week after week. After a few weeks, the woman was freed from her spirit possession and was baptized.

Seeing the success of this Christian prayer, a young relative of this same Mudhiraj caste was convinced of the power of Christ. He and his wife were baptized, and he (Joseph) became the lay leader of the small congregation that the outside pastor, Nathaniel, continued to visit. This congregation grew over the next five years to five Mudhiraj families and five Dalit families. For some time, Nathaniel was supported by Christu Sangam, a mission in Hyderabad. Later, Nathaniel was connected with another Christian organization, Little Flock India, which temporarily provided financial support for Joseph.

Another independent pastor, Sanjeevi of Chegunta, grew up in a Christian Dalit family in a CSI church. He completed two years in college, in a bachelor of science program, before trying in vain to get a government job. Then he decided to prepare himself for full-time ministry. When he was unsuccessful in applying for training as an evangelist in the Church of South India, he turned to a Pentecostal organization in Hyderabad and received two years of theological training there. At its conclusion, he was offered a pastor's position, provided that within forty days he could "bring thirty people to Christ." Although he did not quite make the goal (he reached twenty-six), he was given the position and was supported for six months by the Pentecostal Mission.

Sanjeevi told us how he would go from house to house inquiring about people's welfare. When they related their problems, he would read an appropriate scriptural passage and pray for them. If people were sick, he would read a Gospel passage about Jesus healing the sick and tell them that if they believed in Jesus, he would heal them. On subsequent visits, the pastor learned that many had resolved their problems, and some had been healed. Out of the experience of God's grace in their lives, those people committed themselves to Christ and kept coming to the pastor's worship services.

Later Sanjeevi was visited by evangelistic teams from New Zealand and Australia, who gave him a motorcycle. A church in New Zealand and the "mother church" in Hyderabad made a contribution toward constructing a church building. Because of the opposition of militant Hindus, he had to stop inviting people from the surrounding villages to come to his church. Instead, he arranged a schedule of visits to those villages, six of which he visited every week. On these visits, he preached and prayed for the healing of the sick. On his first visit to a village, he went alone to introduce himself. If some people were interested, he returned with a team of assistants, some of them coming out from Hyderabad during their ministerial training.

A third independent pastor, Hanoch, also raised in a CSI church, came to his ministry in a different way. His wife, the granddaughter of a CSI evangelist,[6] got a government job in Jangarai running the nursery school. In order to accompany her, he left his job as an agricultural laborer. They were able to rent a house from a Mudhiraj family in the main part of the village. He says that he was then just a nominal Christian, but he and his wife held evening prayers in their home. Their neighbors grew inquisitive, and eventually some young people joined them. He also tutored school children in the evening, and the neighborhood grew more and more friendly.

In 1993, while asleep at night, he heard a voice telling him to read Luke 18:1-8, which tells of a widow pleading for justice from a judge. Thereupon he surrendered his life to God and resolved to dedicate his life to a full-time ministry, leading Sunday worship. By this time he was also visiting two independent pastors in other villages. Both of them encouraged him. He then went to the town of Toopran (on the road to Hyderabad) for a six-month training course run by the independent Baptist church, which also gave him the money to construct a small church building. In addition to shepherding a small congregation, he makes evangelistic visits to two other villages.

One other pastor, Satyanandam, came from a Dalit family but was not himself a Christian. He got married in 1979, but unfortunately, the following year, his wife began to suffer from the effects of black magic. He took her to the Pentecostal pastor in Narsinghi, who prayed for her and asked him also to pray to Jesus. Gradually his wife recovered, and with the encouragement of the pastor and his wife's brother, he accepted Christ and was baptized in 1982. He was also encouraged to enter the ministry, and he went for six months to the Pentecostal training center in Hyderabad. On his return, he started a church in his home village of Chitrojpally.

---

6. Her grandfather, Noone Bhooshanam, served in Ramayampet pastorate and settled down in Nandigam village, where he constructed a church.

The Independent Churches

Several years later, when Satyanandam could turn over that congregation to his son, he took over the Pentecostal church in Achampet, a village with a neglected CSI congregation of Dalits (all Madigas). When he and his wife were threatened by five young men from the leading landowning caste (Reddy), some members of the CSI congregation defended them, gave land for a church building, and helped with its construction. Although the Madigas no longer attend the church, persons from eight other castes come regularly to worship and say that they have come to know Christ. The pastor reports that healing meetings are held every May, attended by about five hundred.[7]

M. C. Babu is the pastor of the independent church in Wadiaram. When he came to this area in 1989, he was working as a production engineer in the metallurgical industry. While living in Toopran in 1990, he attended the independent church of Pastor Nathaniel and there became acquainted with Nathaniel's friend, Nehemiah, who since 1975 had been the pastor of the church that Pastor Babu now serves in Wadiaram. In 1991 he married Nehemiah's daughter, Suvarna, resigned from his job, and started a full-time ministry. He said that in 1989, looking down from the top of a building, he was "shaken in his heart" on seeing a girl from the Budagajangala tribe begging. He said that he heard a "slow voice from the sky" asking, "Who is going to teach my gospel to this kind of people?" He answered, "I am here to teach your gospel to them."

In the first village where Babu ministered, a woman with cancer came to him for prayer, whereupon the Reddy landowners came and beat him. He went to another village, Kukkunur, where he gradually built up a congregation of 150 families. There he met a disciple whom he trained and to whom he eventually turned over the congregation. While he was living there, he went to Hyderabad to complete a bachelor of theology course at the Harvest Time Bible College. He also started a church of twenty families in Dharmaram village and another multi-caste congregation of the same size in Dharipally. After he moved to Wadiaram to assist his father-in-law, he returned to Kukkunur once a month to conduct Holy Communion.

For twenty years (1975-95), Babu said, his father-in-law, Nehemiah, had maintained a school for orphans. After the school was closed, Babu wanted to provide a place for the orphan children of another pastor who had died. All seven children were attending a government school. He gave them clothes, books, and food, and his wife took care of them, including some who had AIDS.

Pastor Babu's opportunity to minister to the Budagajangala tribe came during a visit to a Christian family from that tribe in a nearby village. This happened to coincide with the visit of a relative and his companions after

---

7. See other references to this church in chapters 1 and 5.

they had performed an all-night drama based on Hindu stories. The pastor took the opportunity to challenge the visiting actors about the stories they were depicting. They should rather believe in Christ, he said. This enraged the actors, who responded that Jesus Christ was the god only of the Malas and Madigas, but it was the goddesses Yellamma and Poshamma who fulfilled all their needs.

Some time later Babu visited the home village of the tribal group and resumed the conversation. He started visiting every week, praying in every home and sharing the gospel. After his repeated visits, he said, several were convinced and willing to be baptized. One of these was a woman related to the Christian family in the other village. Her husband, who was one of the actors involved in the original argument with Babu, was not convinced, but he did not object to her faith in Christ or to her being baptized without him. Six months later the husband began to change his mind, though he continued to argue with the pastor. Two months later, Babu reported, the husband surrendered his life to Christ and was baptized as Daniel, along with two of his fellow actors.

Daniel and his previously baptized wife, Kazia, came regularly to worship, and once a month he and his two fellow actors cycled to Babu's church in Wadiaram to share in the Lord's Supper. Daniel started jotting down Babu's sermons, and a few months later, he began to accompany the pastor on his visits to other villages. After three years of this training, Babu appointed Daniel to be the local pastor of a congregation consisting of twenty-one Budagajangala families and four landholding families of the Mudhiraj caste, whom Babu had also convinced to become Christians. Daniel was briefly supported by Babu's World Evangelism Mission, but now he is supported by his own congregation.

Babu has a supervisory role in Daniel's congregation and in three others, but his major responsibility is serving as pastor of the independent church in Wadiaram, which he inherited from his father-in-law, Nehemiah. This is a congregation of one hundred families, including many from villages nearby. Since he had preached on the importance of tithing, he was asked whether his congregation was able to tithe. "No, they are all from a poor background, begging in the morning and catching birds to sell or to eat in the afternoon. Only three families are able to give a tithe."

Babu is also chairman of the association of 120 independent pastors working in the Medak District. The association meets on the last Saturday of every month. Since many of the pastors have only a loose connection, and sometimes none at all, with the mission agency that originally sent them out to the villages, this association is potentially important, the more so because the independent churches are related to several different denominations.

The Independent Churches

Five Women in an Independent Church

Just a few weeks before his death in May 2011, Pastor Sanjeevi arranged for interviews with five women in his church, the International Outreach Church in Chegunta. These women were at home or otherwise reachable, though one woman had to leave in the middle of the interview.

Jeja Saraswathi was one of the first converts in Chegunta. Her husband used to work for the railways; when he became paralyzed, her Christian neighbors introduced her to Pastor Sanjeevi. After his prayers, her husband's health improved. Later, after further prayers, her younger son was healed. When she herself suffered bleeding for thirteen months, she did not go to the hospital or take any medicine. She says that she was healed by prayer and, after receiving her husband's permission, was baptized. She does not worship Hindu deities or observe the associated rituals, although her children still do. She says that she is the only one in the family to believe in Christ.

After Saraswathi's husband died in 1995, their son, his wife, and their children came to live with her. Her younger son is studying for a college degree. Both sons have recovered from road accidents, and she counts their recovery among the great blessings she has received from God. She attends Christian worship four times a week: Sunday communion service, Saturday fasting prayers, and Wednesday and Thursday cottage prayer meetings. Other blessings she recounted include being able to pay off the debts incurred by her son's marriage and reconciliation with the family's relatives and others in their Mudhiraj caste, who had earlier spoken against her because of her faith. The last blessing she mentioned was that, though illiterate, she learned the Telugu alphabet in an adult literacy class.

Two of the other women are sisters who belong to the same Mudhiraj caste as the first woman. The younger sister has no children. Her husband was adopted into her parents' family because they had no sons, but he quarreled with her and left her. When she was suffering from dysentery, Pastor Sanjeevi came, blessed some water and oil, and gave them to her. She used them daily and was healed. She says that she then believed in the Lord and was baptized. She goes regularly to Sunday worship and finds her greatest joy in praying. "We also have regular family prayers," she says. Previously, when she worshiped other gods, she felt no peace, but she found peace when she prayed to Jesus. Another prayer was answered when she received a two-room house as part of a government project. "Whenever I have problems, I pray, and God answers, 'I am here.'" On Saturday night the pastor and others from the church conduct fasting prayers in her home, and on Sunday she goes to the church for Holy Communion. She does not take part in the worship of local goddesses or follow any Hindu rituals.

After she and her husband were married in a Hindu ceremony, he told her that she was free to believe in any god, but "two months later he told me to stop going to church. He believes in Lord Narasimha [the fierce man-lion avatar of Vishnu]; that is why we quarreled many times, and because he listened to his family, we broke up. The seven words that God spoke on the cross are very touching to my heart, especially the third, 'Woman, here is your son.' Since I do not have a husband, these words are a great comfort to me. Once I did not have food to eat, and God gave me this small shop. When I pray with tears in my eyes, God answers my prayer, saying, 'I am here.'" Six months prior to this interview, two men came into her shop and stole her gold wedding necklace, but she was not harmed. For that she is grateful to God, and she is also grateful that she has no debts.

The other sister, older by three years, is a widow with four children. She supports herself by farming and by making country cigars. She says that she believed in God because of the healing of her husband and children. When her husband had blood pressure problems and was suffering from diabetes, she got the pastor to come and pray for him. Her husband's health improved, and when her sister was healed, she started going to church. Later, after their daughter's marriage, her husband died. He was a Hindu throughout his life and never took part in Christian worship; nor do her children. "I like the Jesus way," she says. She was baptized only a few weeks before this interview. She is the only one in the family who goes to church, which she does every Sunday, carrying her Bible and song book. As an immediate answer to her prayer, she says, God gave her a two-room house. "God helped me by making possible a good marriage for my daughter. When we had economic problems, God gave me a home, and now God has given my daughter a handsome son."

The oldest of the five women, Ramamma, is a seventy-five-year-old widow belonging to the herder caste. She is a vegetable vendor who goes from village to village. She lives in a hamlet at the edge of the town, where she owns a house and two acres of land. After her husband died, she adopted a son to marry both her daughters. One daughter had four children, the other three. Later, their husband in common died. At the time when Ramamma's husband died, both were Hindus. She describes her conversion as follows: "Ten years ago I experienced a severe numbness in my left leg. My relatives told me to believe in God, but I did not do so. Then because of the prayers of Pastor Sanjeevi, I was healed with prayer oil." After her healing she was baptized.

Since then, the son of one daughter and the two daughters of the other daughter have been baptized, and the granddaughters have had Christian marriages. Ramamma would like all her grandchildren to have Christian marriages. Ramamma now has the Christian name of Marthamma. She explains that they

The Independent Churches

are a joint family of seventeen, owning three Bibles and four song books. "Our whole family attends the Sunday worship service. There are only four in the family who do not believe at all. Our joint family includes children, grandchildren, and great-grandchildren. That God can feed this big family is a miracle! We do not celebrate Hindu festivals. All in the family love Jesus, but some have not been baptized. We do not eat food that has been offered to idols. Every day, we have family prayer." The answers to her prayers include the successful construction of her house with the aid of government funds and getting her elder daughter's children married. (Pastor Sanjeevi added that she always contributes a tithe.)

The fifth woman, Pendula Padma, is much younger (twenty-five) and lives with her thirty-year-old husband and their son. They belong to the Dasari caste, whose members are peddlers, going from village to village, selling small items. They also used to put on dramatic performances, but now, she says, there are "many good movies on television; no one would want to watch our dramas." When her husband accumulated many debts, he was so depressed that he poured kerosene over himself, tried to set himself on fire, and was partially burned. They went to Pastor Sanjeevi, who prayed over some water that all of their troubles would be resolved. Her husband's burns healed. She says that they "used to suffer from the evil eye." This, too, was reduced through prayer. They attend worship regularly and at the time of the interview were preparing to be baptized a month later. When asked about blessings in her life, she replied, "Blessings are from all sides. Previously we used to have troubles. Now we get answers to our prayers immediately."

At this point in the interview, Padma excused herself to go out to sell vegetables. Her father took over and said that he would finish the interview for her. He said that he would like to go to church as his two daughters and his wife do, for "when I pray, all my troubles are gone." Since he worships the two village goddesses and eats and drinks at their festivals, however, "it is a bit difficult to come to church, but I go to the pastor for prayers." He said that when his daughter had no children, he made a vow to the snake goddess that if she gave the daughter a child, he would name the child after that goddess and hold a festival in her honor. His daughter did have a child, who died soon after birth in the Narsinghi hospital. "Since then," he said, "I do not like any village deity." He continued, "I believe in Jesus. He has given my daughter a wonderful son. We went to church; the pastor prayed over water and oil, and then he named my grandson. The child is now a year and a half; this was an unforgettable event in my life." This Hindu father, who makes no secret of taking part in goddess worship and following Hindu rituals, nevertheless also said, "We like Jesus; he will give us all our desires. If we want ten rupees, we will get it. If we need to pay off our debts, he helps us to do so."

Those who were interviewed in this very small sampling were chosen at least in part because they were available. They range from three who had been Christians for several years to one who, with her husband, was preparing for baptism. All the women interviewed were first-generation Christians or about to become so. In contrast, most of those interviewed in two CSI congregations[8] grew up in a Christian family. Here, in this independent church, only the pastor and his family, along with a few families moving to Chegunta from other places, were brought up as Christians.

All of the women who were baptized were given Christian names at that time. They also had the Hindu names they had received as babies in the traditional naming ceremony, names that they used most of the time. In the older CSI congregations, too, most members have Hindu names that are used more often than their Christian names.[9] These new members of an independent church say that they use their Christian names only in church or when the pastor visits their homes. The length of time since the women's baptisms varies considerably. Each one links her decision to be baptized to her own healing or the healing of her husband or other family members. All of them attribute their healing to the power of Jesus. The water or oil blessed by the pastor became the immediate agent of the healing.

In answer to the question about caste relationships, one woman mentioned verbal abuse from fellow caste neighbors that has now come to an end. Another interpreted the question to refer also to inter-caste relations and affirms, "We are in unity with the caste and the village and the church." Another added, "People of all castes eat together at all church gatherings." The great-grandmother heading her joint family said, "We are in unity with people in our own caste and with our neighbors, and we are at peace with all members of the congregation." To that she added that her grandson, John, brought the young people together to decorate the church at Christmas. The question about the unity of the Christian community clearly evoked a different response in this multi-caste Christian community than it would in a congregation where everyone belongs to the same Dalit caste or in an all-Dalit church with a long history of rivalry between the Madigas and the Malas. All those interviewed in this independent church emphasized the unity among church members coming from different castes.

The lack of a more defined theology is due in part to the questions that were asked. These Christians believe that Jesus is God and that he responds positively to specific prayer requests. This was also the belief of the Hindu father substituting for his newly Christian daughter. Christians in this church, it appears,

---

8. See chapter 9.
9. Luke and Carman, *Village Christians*, 190-92, 233.

The Independent Churches

believe in Jesus as the God who does what Hindu deities had failed to do for them: answer prayers for healing and for material blessings. For some, God's answer begins with the assurance, "I am here."

Worship in an Independent Style

All seven of the independent churches in which we attended a worship service have free-standing church buildings, instead of using the veranda and courtyard in front of the pastor's or evangelist's house, which was the practice in the older village congregations of the Wesleyan Methodist Mission and the CSI Medak Diocese. All seven churches have names: Bethesda Prayer Temple, Bethel Prayer Temple, The King's Prayer House, Hermon Church, Independent Baptist Church, Gospel Church, and Pentecost Mission. All these churches have members from different castes, with Dalits often in the minority, and, as in the CSI congregations, the majority of worshipers are women.

Laypeople, both men and women, helped to lead all these services, sometimes with prayer or short testimonies, and always with scripture reading. All the worshipers participated actively in the singing and prayer responses, and all would shout "Hallelujah" or *Stotram* ("Praise") during the prayers or the sermon. The songs or praise-hymns came from booklets or, in one case, audiocassettes, and generally used simpler Telugu words and more repetition of the same words than in the hymns in the Andhra Christian Hymnal used in CSI churches. The lyrics in these independent churches are closer to the style of the Hindu *bhajan;* one worshiper called the whole service a *bhajan.*[10] Some of the first lines in one service were: "Jesus is worthy of praise," "What a good God is Jesus," "Jesus' blood, blood, blood!" "God who consoles the disturbed in heart," and "You are my mountain and palace; you are my hiding place." In some of the services the singing was accompanied by hand clapping and by a few instruments, including cymbals, drums, and tambourines. The very new church of the Pentecost Mission had the most repetition of "Hallelujah, *Stotram.*" Some of the hymn titles were "Praise Jehovah," "My Savior Jesus Is Alive," "The Victorious Ones Will Inherit the Throne with Jesus," and "Holy Spirit, Give Us Power."

In most of the services, the final hymn before the benediction followed the offering, which took several forms. In two services the offering was collected in bags, as is often done in CSI churches. In two other services, worshipers came forward to place their offerings in a box by the altar. In two other churches, the

---

10. A *bhajan* is a short devotional song that all the worshipers sing together.

money offered was placed in an open Bible, which was passed around. In one church, there was also a special thank offering by a few, which was brought forward in envelopes. In another service there was no general offertory, but five people brought forward their thank offerings. Only in one service were various vegetables brought forward, as well as gifts in cash.

Many of the lay prayers consisted of a few words of thanks or a brief confession of sins, the latter accompanied with sobs or tears. The lay leader in one service began with, "Rabbi, Rabbi, have compassion on us. *Stotram.*" He also said in English, "Praise the Lord!" He then continued with the following prayer:

> Pour out your Spirit on us, O just God. The Spirit that you poured out on Joel, now pour on us. Safeguard the word in our hearts that will be delivered by your servant. In order to take the word to the ruthless people of the world, have mercy on us. In Jesus' name we pray.

An eight-year-old girl gave a brief prayer: "God, thank you for giving me good health, and while Pastor is preaching to us, be in our midst, Amen." In another service, a layman led a prayer of thanksgiving:

> *Stotram, Stotram, Stotram,* Hallelujah, Hallelujah! Lord, we are humble people of no worth. Your works are very great in the lives of sinners like us. You have given us healing, health, and blessings, and for this we praise your name, O Lord. You suffered because of our sin, and for us you have sacrificed your life. Our King, we thank you. Bless our pastor and his family and our congregation, and help us to grow in faith. We ask this in Jesus' name, Amen

The same layman also offered a more personal prayer: "O God, when I was sick and prayed to you, you gave me healing. I pray that you would keep your Holy Spirit with us. Amen."

Later in the same service, a laywoman and another layman offered intercessory prayers, both kneeling as they prayed. The woman lifted up her hands to God and began by chanting, *"Stotram, Stotram."* Then she prayed:

> O God, bless Pastor and Mrs. Pastor and their children; give them health; make the congregation grow. You said, "Ask and it shall be given unto you; seek and you shall find." While we are constructing the church, there is need for a lot of money; give us money to finish the construction; bless all those who have helped. Bless all the persons in our village; give us good crops. Give health to all those who are suffering with sickness in our con-

gregation. Sir, give healing right now. If our lives are still without change, kindly transform us all. Father, we ask in Jesus' name, Amen!

The man said the following prayer:

We look unto the hills; give us help, O Lord. Bless our nation, our state, and our village elders. Help us all to live spiritually. Give us a nice temple for worship, and help us in completing its construction. Jesus, bless us, our works, our land and fields and their produce. Give wisdom and understanding to those who are studying. Bless our pastor and his family, and his service. Bless all those who have come for worship and also those who were not able to come. Be with us in the works we do. Remove the difficulties from those who are suffering. I request you to accept this small prayer of mine, in Jesus' name, Amen!

In half the services observed, though not in this one, a few brief testimonies were offered, usually by laypersons. In one service, the visiting preacher gave his own testimony somewhat before the sermon. Before that, a forty-five-year-old layman testified that he had suffered from kidney problems causing such pain that he could not sleep. He went to many hospitals, but was not healed. Then, some Christians told him to accept God. After he read some books, he felt he came to know God. One day in 1991, while he was sleeping, he said, the Lord spoke to him and said that he was Jesus. In his dream, the man's body was filled with blood, with which, he said, God was washing him clean. After the dream, he was totally healed. He said that he wanted to serve the God who had healed him and to preach the gospel to people. For this, he solicited the prayers of the congregation.

In another service, there were three testimonies from members of the congregation. One woman said that when her family was without rice, they prayed to God for help. Although they did not ask any of their neighbors for help, one came to their house and gave them a temporary loan of five hundred rupees. Another woman said that two snakes had come onto their premises. "We prayed to God, and the snakes passed by our house. Later our neighbor spotted the snakes near his house and killed them. Hallelujah!" The third testimony was from a man who had just gotten married. The marriage ceremony went well, he said, "since we prayed to God." Many things could happen to disturb a wedding, such as storms or quarrels. "But God blessed us, and the wedding took place without any disturbances. Hallelujah!" To all these testimonies, the congregation responded with "Hallelujah!"

In a different church, one woman had a similar testimony about God saving her from a snake, while another said that her two-year-old son had developed typhoid fever. "I fasted, cried, and prayed, and the sickness left my son. For this, *Stotram* to God!"

In many of the independent churches, there is a deliberate effort to foster fellowship in their multi-caste congregations by joining in a time together after the Sunday worship service. This took place after only two of the services we attended, in one case with the serving of cool drinks, in the other case with a special meal. The meal was sponsored by a family who celebrated a traditional lifecycle ceremony, the baby's first haircut, in a Christian setting. After the sermon, the pastor cut baby Esther's hair three times, "in the name of the Father, Son, and Holy Spirit," while the congregation clapped. As it happened, this ceremony took place on the parents' wedding anniversary, and the baby's father had been the pastor's assistant for some time. After the service, the whole congregation was invited to a special lunch.

This congregation tries to have a lunch every Sunday, sponsored by someone in the congregation. Since many come from villages several miles away, this is particularly welcome. Eating together across caste lines is a symbolic as well as a practical expression of inter-caste harmony.[11] When it comes to marriage alliances, these newer Christians, like the members of the older congregations, seek a family in their own caste, but they try to find other ways to represent and to realize their unity in Christ. One of these other ways is to give Christian significance to those special events that, in the eyes of all villagers, mark the stages in every person's life.

Preaching of Independent Pastors

The independent pastors are "independent" not only because their churches are not part of the hierarchical network of the Church of South India, but also because they themselves are less, and sometimes not at all, dependent on a

---

11. These common meals in which people belonging to different castes take part are a distinctive witness to Christian unity in a village society in which the superiority of one's own caste to some other castes is shown by refusing to eat the food prepared by members of those other castes. Many Hindu sects or devotional communities share food at their temples, disregarding caste differences, but this is often regarded as an exceptional act appropriate only in the sacred space of a deity who is above caste distinctions, but not part of day-to-day living. The question for Christian congregations is whether eating together at church on Sunday also represents a rejection of feelings of caste superiority during the rest of the week. Many Christians believe that it does, but they consider this a separate issue from maintaining the strong Indian tradition, among Christians as well as others, of marrying only within the same caste.

superior church authority in Hyderabad or Medak. While most of them were supported financially by a mission organization at the beginning of their ministry, that support was usually temporary, and some have broken their ties with that organization. These pastors depend on their congregations for financial support, expecting wealthier church members to tithe. They have only a loose fellowship with other independent pastors.

The pastors expect to preach almost every Sunday in their home church, with only occasional visiting preachers, and some of them lead a second Sunday service in another village. During the week, they have the pastoral care of their home congregation and often a program of evangelistic visits to other villages as well. They seem to have greater authority in their congregation than many CSI pastors. They expect their church members to live up to the moral standards they have set and to share their theological position. Many members do meet their expectations, but there are also many new Christians and Hindu inquirers who "float" among several churches.

The worship services visited showed that there are many differences among independent pastors, both in personal style and in church tradition, and, of course, there are also differences from week to week. One common feature of these services was a high degree of lay participation. Individuals led prayers, read scripture lessons, and offered personal testimony, and the whole congregation sang hymns and took part in the prayer responses. Both laypeople and pastors frequently interjected with "Hallelujah, *Stotram!*" There is thus a certain common Pentecostal style, regardless of denominational affiliation, but only in one service was there any "speaking in tongues." As we have seen previously, most of the new members of these independent churches have experienced healing through prayer, and independent pastors themselves expect to engage in prayers for healing. They urge the members of their church to do the same, both during the Sunday service and in many family prayers during the week.

Unlike many of the CSI sermons from fifty years ago, summarized in *Village Christians,* there were no texts relating to Jesus' death and resurrection, or to the Last Supper. This may be partially explained by the fact that none of these services included Holy Communion, whereas the CSI Sunday service conducted by an ordained presbyter is expected to include communion twice a month. The greater frequency of celebration may point to the greater importance of communion in the CSI congregations. Some lay Christians in the CSI congregations link the blood Jesus shed on the cross to the communion "grape wine."

The emphasis on divine protection is clear from the texts from the Psalms. "And those who know your name put their trust in you, for you, O Lord, have not forsaken those who seek you" (Ps. 9:10, NRSV). This text was interpreted to mean: "We cannot be safe without the grace of God . . . If you believe in God, he will be your refuge." The whole of Psalm 91 is understood as a call to turn to God for protection: "We must hide behind God. He is our place of refuge. He protects us from falling prey to the hunter, who is Satan."

One sermon gave several illustrations from village experience to bring out the meaning of Psalm 123:2: "As the eyes of the servant look to the hand of his master, as the eyes of a maid to the hand of her mistress, so our eyes look to the Lord our God, until he has mercy upon us." The illustrations all relate to general village experience: the way villagers look at the image of the elephant-headed Ganesh during a Hindu festival, or the wonderment when the image of Shiva appears to arise miraculously out of the ground because the wet grain under the image expanded. One line of the verse is paraphrased: "A servant looks toward his master, expecting something from him." Again, there are two illustrative comparisons. The first is when an order given to a waiter in a restaurant is shouted on to the cook: "In this way you come to church and tell me your troubles. Like the waiter, I will shout to God what you need." The last comparison emphasizes the worshiper's eagerness to be fed: "As the dog looks to his master, so we look to God."

The rest of this sermon put the emphasis on the divine requirements that must be met if we are to enjoy God's protection. It started with the angel's rebuke of Hagar for her pride (Gen. 16:8-9) and then became a sharp critique of a member of the congregation for whom the pastor had prayed earlier in the service. The man was severely injured in a road accident and taken to a hospital, where the pastor had visited him. The man "who suffered the accident never gave his tithe to God. When he did not give his tithe, God took that money in a different form . . . God gave him profits in his shop, but he did not give a tithe; he became proud, but God is now extracting his due from the man through his accident." The end of the sermon returned to a positive note, that we must experience God's healing presence: "God is a God who heals . . . He hears prayers. God healed me when I met with an accident. I have experienced it . . . Our eyes must look to God."

Another sermon focused on three verses in Psalm 111. "In verse 1, the Bible tells us that we should worship God. The Israelites worshiped God because he delivered them from Egyptian slavery and did many great deeds for them. We forget to worship God, though he is doing many great things in the lives of our families. When we are sick and pray to God, God heals us. Our troubles roll away." Commenting on part of verse 9 ("Holy and terrible is his name," NRSV), the pastor moved immediately to the holiness expected of the congregation: God wants us to be holy, but we do all kinds of unholy things, drinking, taking drugs, and smoking. God will not come into our unholy heart. "Leave those habits and come into God's presence; confess your sins. He will forgive you. He will save everyone. He will be with you in sufferings and sadness."

One other sermon took Psalm 15 as its text, summarized as, "Who lives in the tabernacle of Jehovah? Who can be a guest with God? Only the one who does not lead a fallen life." The pastor went on to specify the righteousness that God requires and urged his listeners to examine themselves, "looking at our lives" as we see them reflected "in the word of God." The end of the formal sermon was followed by the pastor asking the congregation a series of questions, to which they responded, one after the other and many with tears, "Yes, Lord, help us to lead a righteous life."

One pastor preached a second sermon in the same service on a verse from Proverbs (19:8), which he interpreted as, "It is better to gain wisdom than wealth." There was also one sermon on Abraham's near-sacrifice of Isaac (Gen. 22:1-19): "God tests a human being, as children are tested in school." The pastor took both Abraham and Isaac as models for Christians: "We must be like Abraham with devotion and valor, and God will bless us . . . Abraham believed in God; that is why his progeny increased . . . Jesus Christ died on the cross so that we may live a good life. We all, like Isaac, without questioning, must look to Jesus in all things; if we do that, God will bless us."

Only in the second part of one sermon was there a focus on a New Testament passage (John 14:1-6): "I am coming again and I am going to prepare a place for you. Through this message, faith was established in the lives of the disciples. Jesus will certainly come again . . . Your faith will save you. God will bless those who give a tithe."

Tharamma of Medak: The Healed Victim Who Became a Healer

In our description of witchcraft in chapter 4, we commented briefly on the life story of a woman healer named Tharamma. After growing up in a village Christian family, she became a school teacher, working in various places. For many years, she has lived in the town of Medak, where her house is in the Christian colony within the cathedral compound. Like so many others, she first sought release from black magic through counter-magic or "light" magic, but most of the healing from the various serious illnesses that have afflicted her has come through prayer. The first magician she consulted told her that someone had cast a spell on her. He gave her the choice between an amulet, which she refused because she was a Christian, and a ritual "smoke," which made her fall down.

When a fellow teacher who also knew counter-magic came to her house, her heart started to pound, and she was unable to speak. He lit an earthen lamp on the stone floor and asked her to stare at the flame. She saw the flame expand and saw a dark woman within it, after which the flame divided and fell heavily on her chest. This signified that the spirit that had been attacking her from outside was now confronting her directly. The magician-friend then questioned the spirit: How many ills did it intend to bring, and who sent it? When the spirit refused to get into a bottle, the friend made a smoke-fire and covered Tharamma and the smoke with a blanket. When that did not help, he brought in a branch from a tamarind tree and hit Tharamma with it until she was black and blue. She then fell unconscious, slept for a day and a half, and woke up in great fear, imagining herself to be a corpse covered with a white cloth. Her friend said that she should continue the flame ritual for forty nights; only then would the spirit leave.

After twenty-one days, a neighbor came and prayed for Tharamma's healing with "much agony and tears." Tharamma first experienced heart palpitations, but then she heard "heavenly music," and for the first time in that period of trouble, she felt happy. The following day, a well-known Christian healer came to Medak and had an experience of the Holy Spirit. When Tharamma's husband took her to the healer, he told her that her neck and body were "pierced with needles" that could kill her within fifteen days, but that "God would save her." She should come for the evening healing prayers that he was conducting in front of the cathedral. When the healer put a New Testament on Tharamma's head, she fell down, writhing in pain, and said over and over, "I am dying, I am dying." The healer replied, "It is Satan who is dying, not you." Then he hit her with the New Testament and told her to go home, eat, and sleep.

The following morning Tharamma sat alone to pray, repeating the two words "Hallelujah" and *"Stuthi"* (praise) louder and louder until all the neighbors came into the house. While they were watching, she fell unconscious. She says that she saw the whole room full of bright light. When she became conscious, she began to read the second chapter of Acts (about the descent of the Holy Spirit at Pentecost), sharing the meaning of every word as God revealed it to her. The neighbors thought that this extraordinary performance was the moment of insight before her death, but she heard a voice saying, "My daughter, tell them not to cry. I will make you live." When the Christian healer was told what had happened, he said that Tharamma had been anointed with the Holy Spirit.

After that, the whole neighborhood of two to three hundred people gathered at her house. When Tharamma began to preach, one woman fell unconscious. Tharamma heard the Holy Spirit command, "Rebuke in the name of Jesus of Nazareth." She continued her inspired utterance, believing that the Holy Spirit was revealing the secret sins of each person who came for her blessing. For three days, people kept pouring into her house, and the women in the neighborhood were too distracted to cook. The evil spirits that had possessed people began to leave them. One woman shouted, fell down, and seemed to have died, so some neighbors said that Tharamma would face charges from the police. When the woman "came back to life," she testified that "I died, but Jesus took me on his lap" and sent her back to earth to take care of her crying daughter. "Many people present were bewildered, yet some accused Tharamma of pursuing every manner of black magic."

Indeed, many neighbors in the cathedral compound believed that she was possessed by a "big devil," and they avoided her. That night she had a dream of Jesus grasping the outstretched arms of a man kneeling before him. The following morning Tharamma went to the Rev. P. Y. Luke, who was living in retirement nearby, who interpreted the dream: "God gave you a vision in order to break down the powers of the evil one."

For a whole year, Tharamma reports, she struggled with Satan, who sometimes caused her to bleed. Once she had a vision in which three hundred Hindu deities tormented her. Each deity that appeared she rebuked with the words, "In the name of Jesus of Nazareth." Then she was so weak that she prayed, "God, take me," but Jesus came in a vision, she said, put her in a sheet, lifted her up, and lowered her down. Feeling a great shock, she realized that she had regained her strength. After that, she conducted regular prayer meetings at home, but her Christian neighbors accused her of using magical spells *(mantram)*[12] and of starting a different church. Her healing services were held after the morning church services, and attendance kept growing to between three and four hundred. People finally put up a big shed, filling her yard. Sometimes as many as fifteen people affected by witchcraft were running crazily about. One possessed woman is said to have died, but after Tharamma fasted and prayed all day, the woman "came back to life."

In the initial stages of her ministry, people who were healed went to the cathedral to be baptized. Bishop Prasada Rao baptized them by immersion, but later Bishop Premasagar refused to do that. He was willing to baptize them by sprinkling, but not by immersion. The new adult converts, however, very much wanted to be baptized by immersion. Tharamma did not know where to take the new Christians, especially since many church members opposed her ministry. After a few days a Baptist pastor arrived from Warangal, a city 120 miles away,

---

12. A *mantra* is a sacred word or phrase, originally referring to a Vedic chant, but later often referring to the secret word whispered into the initiate's ear at the climax of the initiation ceremony. The term may also designate the word, both sacred and powerful, that a magician utters to make his charms or spells work. From this use comes the word *mantrikam*, which means "magic" in a general sense. These Christian neighbors, however, were using *mantra* in the sense of harmful magic, that is, black magic, witchcraft, or sorcery. The proper Telugu term is *banumathi*, in contrast to good or "light" magic, which is *bhutavaidyam*, the "medicine against the (evil) spirit." See "Christians Possessed by Village Goddesses" in chapter 4.

saying that God had sent him to help someone he did not know (Tharamma) to baptize converts in a town with which he was not acquainted (Medak).

The cathedral committee resolved to ask Tharamma to conduct her prayers in the future somewhere outside the old mission compound. After the municipal chairperson arranged for her to get land on which to build a separate church, the Christians in the neighborhood accused her of occupying the land illegally and brought a court case against her. She borrowed money to start construction, but after her husband had a stroke, the family ran out of money and construction stopped. Local Christians continued to vilify and threaten her, but Tharamma continued in prayer. Neighbors also tried to force her to leave her home in the cathedral compound, but after a boy afflicted with witchcraft was healed in her presence, the Christian young men turned to support her and persuaded the pastorate committee to let her keep her house.

The early 1980s saw the completion of a church building that holds two to three hundred people.[13] Tharamma is now the senior minister of this independent congregation, which is outside the cathedral compound. She has assistant ministers who help her with a ministry that extends to scores of villages in the area, in many of which new independent congregations have sprung up, cared for by independent pastors. Tharamma begins the Sunday morning service with singing led by a women's choir. During the singing, some women also dance with the same step as women possessed by local goddesses. People who are rolling around in pain are cared for by stewards. Tharamma and others "speak in tongues." Some cry; some shake; some shout. There is a Bible reading and a sermon, which she herself sometimes gives. Often there are guest preachers or other visitors giving testimonies of how Jesus has helped them or even miraculously healed them.

Then the healing prayers begin. People come forward with their own coconut oil, which Tharamma first prays over and then smears on their foreheads or on the afflicted part of the body. People sometimes bring water that she prays over before they drink it. For barren women, she blesses five dates as a symbol of the "fruit of the womb," "in the name of the Father, Son, and Holy Spirit." "Three dates are to be eaten by the woman and two by her husband." She explains that Hindus are used to tangible things in their ritual. She will not give amulets because "Jesus is not a magician." "Every word that comes out of the mouth of Jesus heals and opens up the womb." She likens her use of physical means to Jesus' use of "spittle" and "mud" to heal the blind.

13. Vasantha Rao and his brothers performed *burrakatha* at the inauguration of the new church and, before that was completed, at the time of the annual revival and healing meeting that Tharamma held in the cathedral.

The Independent Churches

Tharamma gives many accounts of how her prayers were used by God to bring many people to accept Christ. She says that God said to her, "My daughter, I will build a church through you; I will build a congregation anointed with the Holy Spirit; I will use you as spiritual mother to many in this region." Her path has not been easy. She has suffered from typhoid, kidney failure, and malaria, and she testifies that each time she was miraculously healed. She also escaped an attempt on her life by hired killers. She underwent five major operations in which she says that Satan's attempts on her life were thwarted, so that she is healthy at present, except for knees weakened by so much time spent kneeling in prayer. She did not think that she could preach, but through visions, God convinced her that she could preach God's word to both Christians and non-Christians. Her children and grandchildren complain that she has neglected them, but she says that the people to whom she ministers are also her children, conceived in the Spirit.

This is yet another unfinished and continuing story. It concerns not only Tharamma's own life and ministry but also the many lives that, through her prayers, have often been decisively changed. It also concerns the future relation between the new church that she was almost forced to found and the older community of her suspicious Christian neighbors.

Conclusion

These independent churches may be just at the beginning of their history, both in their internal congregational life and in their effect on the whole religious landscape of this part of South India.

There are earlier movements behind the spread of independent churches to an area where previously the only Christians were in the CSI Medak Diocese. The first Pentecostal churches in India were inspired by earlier revivals in India and by Pentecostal developments in other parts of the world, especially the United States. The independent Baptist churches continue a style of organization and church life that had developed a century earlier in other parts of the Telugu country. While Pentecostal leaders from a Syrian Christian background in Kerala initiated the early spread of their churches into Andhra Pradesh, the leadership is now almost entirely Telugu, with most of the pastors coming from older churches. Within the very small area of our study, some of the independent church members come from Dalit castes, many of whom have grown up in neglected congregations, but the majority are new converts from many other castes in which there were very few Christians. The caste most widely represented is one of the elite landholding and ruling castes; it proudly calls itself Mudhiraj.

There are questions that outsiders may ask about these new multi-caste churches: Can they hold together in a society in which caste differences are so sharply felt? Will Dalit Christians continue to be a part of these newer churches, especially if they are in a minority, and will they be accepted as social equals by Christians who belong to castes that consider themselves higher than Dalits? Members of these churches do not seem to be troubled by these questions. They testify to their unity, and they are confident of the continuing empowerment and guidance of the Holy Spirit. One church lost most of its members to newer churches in other villages belonging to different denominations, but this seems to have been because the laywoman who founded the church no longer visited. All these families were Dalits from a neglected CSI congregation. In Achampet, some Dalit Christians left the new Pentecostal church when their old CSI congregation was revived, but the new church has continued.

As in the CSI churches, the majority of worshipers are women. Some of them are the only Christians in their respective families. Both women and men give brief testimonies during the worship services to the way that Jesus has healed them or other members of their families, or rescued them from financial distress. Both laity and clergy sometimes share their experience of seeing Jesus in a dream or hearing him speak. The pastors' sermon texts from the Psalms often deal with God's protection in perilous circumstances. Some of the healings reported come after fervent prayer. Sometimes the healings occur after water or oil is applied that has been blessed by the pastor or some other Spirit-filled person. Tharamma of Medak explained her use of such aids by referring to the precedent set by Sadhu Joseph, as well as by the use of such material instruments of blessing in much Hindu practice.

The life story of Tharamma is different from all the other accounts. She was a Christian school teacher who demonstrated an unusual gift of healing after she herself was dramatically healed. Her powers frightened some of her Christian neighbors, and her claim of spiritual authority offended some of the clergy at the Medak cathedral. She was helped by some CSI pastors and by independent pastors. While not in the tradition of any of the Pentecostal denominations, she sometimes "speaks in tongues." Her healing ministry has had wide effects in the villages around Medak, in both CSI and independent churches, extending all the way to Wadiaram. While Sadhu Joseph moved about and avoided setting up his own church, Tharamma has worked from a center near her home that has become a new independent church, but her ministry has touched individuals in many other churches.

The following chapter also focuses attention on a remarkable laywoman. Mrs. Raduva Deevenamma Mithra, in her ministry, has moved between the CSI and the independent churches. The effect of her ministry may be to bring a new zeal into the life of many CSI congregations in the Wadiaram pastorate.

CHAPTER 7

New CSI Congregations of Different Kinds

One Small Multi-Caste Congregation at the Pastorate Headquarters

Thus far we have described the decline of many of the older CSI congregations during the past fifty years and the establishment of new independent churches in the past thirty years. There is still another story to tell, describing three different developments that have all led to new CSI congregations.

The first development concerns the small congregation worshiping in the church building at the pastorate headquarters in Wadiaram. This pastorate did not, like many others, begin with a Methodist mission station at its center. Most of the village congregations in the present pastorate had been part of the very large circuit around a mission center in the town of Ramayampet to the north. In 1931 these congregations were separated from that circuit to form a new Wadiaram circuit with a resident pastor, who for several years was supervised by a senior minister in Medak or Hyderabad.[1] The presbyter in charge of the Wadiaram pastorate has lived in a parsonage on the church property, which also includes a school and, more recently, a junior college. There were regular Sunday services attended by Christian teachers and students at the school, as well as by some of those at the New Life Centre, where girls who had dropped out of school came for vocational training. For many years until 1998, there were also some theological students from the ACTC in Hyderabad living at the Village Theological Centre. They attended services at the church and helped to conduct worship. There was no community of Dalit Christians in the town, however, comparable to one of the village congregations.

---

1. Luke and Carman, *Village Christians,* 63-64.

The church building was the meeting place for the monthly and special gatherings of the evangelists and the lay members of the pastorate committee. As it happened, just behind the church on the same property there was a small shrine to the village goddess Mankali, so that fifty years ago the townspeople called this church property "the Mankali compound."[2] More recently, a much larger shrine has been built and a fence put up around it. "This churchyard with two names" is no longer, as in *Village Christians*, just an apt metaphor for the presence side by side of "both Christian and traditional beliefs and practices" within the Christian community.[3] Now the adjacent places of worship and the fence between them also signify a Hindu challenge to the land claims of any minority religious community.

Until thirty years ago, there were only four or five Christian families who came to worship at the headquarters church. In 1989, however, the congregation wrote to the bishop that there were new converts from various castes, including Lambada (Gypsies), Wadla (carpenters), Sakali (washermen), and Bestha (fishermen) because of the evangelism of one lay couple, Mr. B. Vijaya Rao and Mrs. B. Yesumani.

Some of those converts, interviewed in 2008, told how Yesumani helped at least four families who were suffering from the effects of black magic. At different times she took two women from the fisher caste to the lay healer Tharamma in Medak. The first woman, named Laxmi, fell down unconscious when Tharamma started to pray for her and then remained unconscious for a week. When she finally recovered consciousness, after Tharamma's repeated prayers, Laxmi was completely healed. After returning home, she convinced her husband and children to be baptized with her at the Wadiaram church. When their caste community heard that they had become Christians, the men became furious and started out to beat up Laxmi's husband, but they stopped, we were told, when they saw a bright light around her husband's head. Ever since, they have been friendly to this family. Laxmi, baptized as Mariamma, herself became an agent for the healing of her sister's husband and, later, for her husband's brother.

When Yesumani learned that Bhagyamma, another woman from the fisher caste, showed signs of being under a magical spell (she was running around shouting), she took her, too, to Medak, where Tharamma kept her for three months while continuing to offer prayers for her deliverance. When Bhagyamma was completely healed, she returned home and was baptized with her family at the CSI church.

At different times, seven years apart, Yesumani took two brothers from the

---

2. Luke and Carman, *Village Christians*, 165.
3. Luke and Carman, *Village Christians*, 165. See p. 2, above.

washerman caste to the Wadiaram church. There the presbyter successfully prayed for their deliverance from the spell of black magic, and he subsequently baptized them and their wives. The brothers are no longer living, but their wives are faithful members of the congregation.

Vijaya Rao has been active in this congregation in a different way, twice joining in or initiating letters of complaint to the bishop about the presbyters in charge of the pastorate, in one case asking for an immediate transfer. What is remarkable, especially in such a small congregation, is that its members should have been sufficiently organized to make a formal complaint, in one case resulting in a mid-year transfer of the presbyter. In the semi-urban environment of the adjoining towns of Wadiaram and Chegunta, there are now at least six independent churches, most of them much larger than the CSI congregation at the pastorate headquarters. With lay leadership and devoted members, this little congregation seems to be faring well.

Beginnings of Mrs. Deevenamma's Lay Ministry

Much of this chapter concerns the lay ministry of Mrs. Raduva Deevenamma Mithra, who did so much to found the other two new congregations in the Wadiaram pastorate. Until her retirement in 1990, she was the head nurse in the Secunderabad railway hospital. She is a member of the CSI church in Mushirabad, which is part of Hyderabad City. When her husband, Mr. Raduva Mithra, retired from his post as manager of the Charminar Cigaret Company, they resolved to serve God for the rest of their lives.

Deevenamma told us about her unusual childhood. Her birth father was a CSI junior evangelist. His friend, Shadrach, a "superintending evangelist," asked after her birth whether her parents would give the baby to him and his wife to raise since they had only sons. Her birth parents agreed, so at the age of three months she was taken to Shadrach's home. Several years later, after Shadrach had tried to settle a quarrel between two groups of villagers, the losing group caught Shadrach in a forest and murdered him. From then on, Deevenamma was brought up by Shadrach's wife. When she grew up, she married her adoptive brother Mithra, who was five years older and with whom she had played as a child. Deevenamma said that she grew up wanting to serve God as her adoptive father had. Before her retirement, she took a group from her church to visit villages where there were no Christians. Before doing so, she took the precaution of securing the permission of village leaders.

In a later interview, Deevenamma gave us the following account of her call to ministry:

In 1989, one year before my retirement, I had a vision in which God showed me the verse from Hosea (10:12), "I am giving you the land which was never tilled." While this verse was going through my mind, I attended a prayer meeting led by Brother Matthew, who looked at me and said that I should write down my visions. After that I began to pray fervently to God, asking, "Why, O God, when others ask you, you have given them good fields, as shown in Joshua 15:19, but to me you have given barren land?" However, Brother Matthew told me that my vision of Hosea 10:12 means that God has given me an opportunity to tell people the good news of Jesus Christ, especially those who have never heard of him. So the verse is fulfilled in my preaching the gospel to the Gypsies (Lambadas) living in this tribal settlement near Jangaraig

Before that, when I frequently visited the Medak cathedral, I used to give money to beggars. But when I saw them using what I had given them to buy and smoke cigars, I was led to another form of giving. With the help of my brother, Mr. Putra, I would cook food and distribute it to beggars. Once when I saw some Gypsies eating dry chapatis with raw chili paste, I invited them for a cooked meal. When they joined us, I learned that they had brought a family member named Sony to be healed from witchcraft. She had been behaving strangely, sitting in a tree, removing her clothes, or eating human excreta. She broke a coconut on each step going into the cathedral while praying for healing. They invited me to go to their village, but that day I did not go.

Another time when I went to the Medak cathedral for a wedding, I met a Christian Gypsy from some distance away. He took my brother, Putra, and me to the village of the Gypsies we had previously met, and thus began our ministry in the Jangarai Gypsy settlement. The three of us prayed before entering the village. I remembered that I had been cautioned by a CSI presbyter not to lay my hands on Gypsies because they are so frequently possessed by evil spirits. I went against this advice, always praying for them while laying my hands on their heads, and God gave healing. This has led to many baptisms and even to a wedding conducted according to Christian marriage rites.[4]

The woman named Sony who was suffering from the effects of black magic was one of the two wives of Poolsingh and the sister of the first Christian convert in this Gypsy settlement, Banoth Badia. In the following section, we present their own story of their Christian pilgrimage.

4. Interview with Vasantha Rao, 2011.

New CSI Congregations of Different Kinds

Six Christian Families in the Gypsy Settlement

The baptism in 1984 in the Medak cathedral of seventy persons from the Gypsy (Lambada) settlement near Jangarai might have been the most dramatic conversion since the 1959 study, but later events were to follow, so that we now have a very mixed picture. One of the leaders in the group was Banoth Badia (sixty-one years old in 2008), who took an active part in tribal festivals, in arranging marriages, and in settling disputes. He reports that sometime before 1984, a disgruntled group, angry with his exercise of power, arranged for him to be targeted with witchcraft. He suffered and his health deteriorated. His arms and legs lost strength; he became too weak to do anything. He went to many doctors, and he tried to get magicians to employ a stronger counter-magic to lift the spell. He tied amulets all over his body. His Gypsy neighbors and some Hindus suggested that he go to the Medak cathedral, for they had heard of many people who had been healed there. A lay Christian from Ambajipet took him to the Pentecostal church in Toopran, without result. After he had twice visited the Medak cathedral, however, he experienced complete healing, and he became the first Christian in the Gypsy hamlet. Since 1984, people look at him once again as a normal person. Many accepted his leadership and joined him in becoming Christians.

This development might seem similar to the old pattern of group conversions among the Dalits, which ended a generation before, but there was a crucial difference. In many cases, only one or two individuals from a family decided to become Christians, and many families remained solidly entrenched in their old Gypsy traditions. Indeed, the conservatives were able to exert pressure on the new converts to abandon their new faith. So effective was their persuasion that the majority of those who had been baptized returned to their old tribal religion. Only five families have stood firm in their faith in Jesus Christ, recently joined by a sixth.

Four of the six families are closely related. The first is Banoth Badia's own family. All its members were convinced of the saving power of Christ by seeing his suffering when he was under the magicians' spell and observing his new vitality and hope after his healing. He says that their "faith in Jesus Christ has been increasing day by day, and they are coming closer and closer to him in their daily experiencing the presence of Christ with them."

The second family is that of Banoth Badia's brother-in-law, Daravath Poolsingh, who has two wives.[5] Both wives suffered, at different times, from the effects

---

5. Having two wives is no longer common among the Lambadas. It occurs only when the first wife becomes ill or does not conceive. The husband must treat both wives equally. Often they are sisters, as is the case with the wives of Thudum Chandraiah of Chinna Shankarampet, a recent convert belonging to the Mudhiraj caste.

of witchcraft. The second wife was the first to be afflicted, and her husband first took her, without success, both to doctors and to spirit healers. Then, with his brother-in-law's help, he took her to Medak. After staying at the cathedral continuously for a few weeks, she was delivered from the magical spell. Sometime later, Poolsingh's elder wife and his cattle were affected by witchcraft. She became weak and unable to work, and his only ox stopped eating grass and just lay down, night and day. Poolsingh then rushed his wife to the Medak cathedral and asked for prayers in the name of Christ. Eventually, she was healed. The ox, however, died. Poolsingh says that there have been problems in relation to his tribal neighbors since his family follows only Christian traditions of prayer and worship and does not celebrate any tribal festivals. Poolsingh's son's wedding was the first Christian marriage ever celebrated in the Gypsy hamlet. His neighbors asked why he was adopting a new god unknown to the tribe, and his family found it difficult to participate in community celebrations because of the sacrifices to the gods and goddesses. These problems, Poolsingh says, were overcome "by the help of the Lord Jesus Christ.... We cast all our burdens on Jesus Christ and he saves us from all our troubles."

Banoth Badia's two younger brothers have families that have maintained their Christian commitment. The middle brother (Deepla) says that his elder brother's spiritual habit attracted him, especially as he attended the weekly prayer meetings in Badia's house. This brought Deepla the resolution of small problems, peace in his heart, and joy in his life. Encouraged by his elder brother's witness, he and his family accepted Christ as their God and were baptized, after which they stopped observing all the tribal religious customs and started following Christian practices in their personal and family life. The youngest brother, Keemya, and his wife, Tulasi, have one daughter and six sons. He says that he was convinced by his brothers to belong to the same faith that they had adopted and to join in the weekly prayer meetings.

The fifth Christian family in the Gypsy settlement is not closely related to the other four, though Kartroth has the same personal name as the eldest brother (Badia). When his first wife, Mali, had no children, he sought medical help, went to Hindu shrines, and got amulets for his wife from local healers. After many years of living in despair without children, Banoth Badia and Poolsingh told him that he would be blessed with children if he accepted Jesus Christ. Kartroth began to believe, and at every prayer meeting he asked everyone to pray that he might have children. Later, when his wife died of snake bite, his six brothers and their families taunted him, saying that his wife had died because he had sought a new god. He did not lose his faith in God, however, and he did not blame God for his wife's death. He asked the other Christians to pray that God would strengthen him in his time of trial. Now he believes that God has granted him a second wife, Kunni, in place of the first. They were married in a Christian ceremony and now have a son and a daughter. He testifies that God never left him and is grateful for this gift of children through his second wife. He remains a strong Christian.

In 2008 a sixth Gypsy family became Christians. The grandfather's name is Maloth Babu. His thirty-year-old son, Kaliya, is married to Salki; they have two daughters and two sons. He farms his own acre-and-a-half and also works for other farmers. The pastor in Bandaposanipally comes every Sunday morning to conduct worship for the six families, moving week by week to each house in turn. Seven or eight neighbors also attend; they say that they have faith in Christ but are not Christians. Once in four months, and also for festivals, the whole group goes to the Medak cathedral. These families look for Christian marriage partners for their sons and daughters, who must marry other Lambadas but with a different surname, which means, from a different clan on the father's side. Poolsingh's first son found a bride who was already a Christian. His second son's wife became a Christian after their marriage. Lambada Christians continue to relate socially to other Lambadas, but they will not participate in their festivals.

During the past fifty years in Telangana, some Lambadas and members of other tribal groups have become Christians. Sometimes an entire village group converts. This conversion was neither of a whole group nor of single individuals, but of four related families joined by two others. Together they constitute a small but firm Christian minority sure of its Christian distinctiveness. For that reason they have an ongoing problem of whether and how to share with their more distant non-Christian relatives and tribal neighbors in all the festive occasions and solemn events that may be the high points in their village life. Different Christians have resolved this question in different ways; many still struggle with it.

Mrs. Deevenamma's Healing Ministry and the Horeb Prayer Church

Even before her retirement, Mrs. Deevenamma occasionally visited Dr. Paranjyothi in Ambajipet.[6] The two women walked together to the nearby villages that Paranjyothi's father, a CSI evangelist, used to visit. Paranjyothi conducted her homeopathic practice while Deevenamma preached the gospel and prayed for the sick. For some time after she retired, Deevenamma spent five days a week with her friend, returning each weekend to her home in Hyderabad. Later she shifted her attention to the roadside village of Chinna Shankarampet and

---

6. See chapter 5.

other villages close to it. Many of those for whom she prayed were healed from their illnesses and became Christians.

The largest group of new Christians about whom we have family-by-family information consists of the fifteen families in the Dalit section of the village of Rudraram, who were evangelized by Deevenamma, beginning about twenty years ago. One widow, Estheramma, says that through Deevenamma's prayers she was healed from "nervous weakness." She has been a Christian since 1993, but was baptized only in 1998. Several other recent converts said that this widow, in turn, helped them. One man, who survived an auto-rickshaw accident in which his two fellow passengers died, says that Estheramma prayed for him and smeared coconut oil on his injuries. She also told at least five others about her own healing and took them to the new church, where they were healed after Deevenamma's prayers. (Two were healed from twisted limbs, one from the effects of black magic, one from polio, and one from a cough and asthma.)

One man was the target of black magic, which made him shout at other people and behave as if he were deranged. He says that he had heard of Christ as a child, but had not followed him. His maternal aunt, who was a Christian, told him to believe in Jesus Christ, who would heal him. He followed her advice, was healed, and was baptized ten years ago. Another victim of black magic was told by a Hindu neighbor that if he believed in Jesus Christ, he would be healed. When he went to Deevenamma's church, she and the whole congregation prayed for him. Not only did he himself recover; his animals, which had been sick, were healed as well.

One young man had abandoned his widowed mother, to her great distress, so much so that she began to cry out during the prayers in church for the return of her son. When he developed chest and stomach pain, he heard from several people that Jesus could heal him. He came to this same church, where Deevenamma prayed for him, and he slowly healed. He and his wife were baptized, and he and his three daughters now go with his mother to church.

Another widow related the experience of her late husband. A burning sensation in his left palm took him to a government hospital in the city, but no cure could be found, and he was unable to sleep because of the pain. Some of the nurses told him that if he believed in Jesus Christ, he would be healed. After he responded to their advice, they gave him a New Testament. When he held it in his painful hand, he was able to sleep through the night; the following morning the pain was gone. When he returned home, he began attending Deevenamma's church and asked her to pray for him. He and his wife were baptized, and the whole family started coming regularly to church.

In the nearby village of Madur, there have been five instances in which the prayers of Deevenamma and her congregation contributed to decisions to become Christians. She began visiting the few Christians there after an independent pastor and his wife had tried to start a congregation, but were hampered by militant Hindu nationalists (Rashtriya Swayamsevak Sangh, or RSS). After Deevenamma prayed for a woman diagnosed with cancer, the woman was healed. Deevenamma and many others have prayed for a girl paralyzed by snakebite and an anti-venom injection. The girl, now grown, can walk with the aid of a stick; she lives at home and helps her mother sell vegetables. A man wasting away and losing his hair was brought to the church and left there until he was healed. This event persuaded several people in a neighboring village to accept Christ. Then the man who had been healed brought to the church a man who was dying from an unknown disease. This man stayed at the church for three weeks; Deevenamma prayed for him daily until he was healed. After he was baptized, this man had a vision of Jesus beckoning him to take up ministry, so he started holding services at home in his own village. The result was that most of the Christian families there no longer traveled for Sunday worship to Deevenamma's church. This development has sparked a still-unresolved competition for the allegiance of several Christian families.

The fifteen new Christian families in Rudraram are all Dalits. Their Hindu relatives initially put pressure on them to continue their Hindu rituals, especially festival worship of the village goddesses. The refusal of most of the Christian women to carry pots of food on their heads to the goddess's shrine evoked an angry response, but their Hindu relatives have now accepted the Christians' new way of life and no longer try to force them to carry the pots or eat meat sacrificed to the goddesses. In this respect, these new Christians follow the customs of the new members in the independent churches rather than the "we can do both" attitude of the majority of families in the older Christian congregations, not only in 1959, but also at present. These new Christians no longer believe that sick cattle have been attacked by spirits. They now know that the cattle get sick from eating insects along with the fresh grass. Additionally, they believe that smallpox and chickenpox should be treated medically, rather than by sacrificing to the village goddesses. This change of belief reflects the influence of modern education and urban culture.

After Deevenamma had repeatedly visited many villages, she first thought God was telling her to build a church in Jangarai. She selected a plot, but the owner would not sell her the land. Then her friends in Ambajipet advised her to build the church in Chinna Shankarampet. After many visits, she bought a plot there opposite the mandal office and the police station. Despite much opposition from local Hindus and Muslims, she eventually arranged to build a church, aided by the cooperation of the mandal revenue officer, who was a Muslim, and the chairman of the village council, who was a Hindu. Not only did she get the use of a tractor to transport building materials; she also had two powerful voices to counter the opposition, especially that from the Hindu Nationalist Party (BJP). While the church was being constructed, she built a small house nearby and lived there. She was helped in the construction by Manikyam, a teacher in a government school, and by her brother, Putra. Every Sunday she led worship in her one-room house. Construction of the church building and a separate parsonage for the Horeb Prayer Church was completed in 1998.

Slowly the congregation grew. In the meantime, Deevenamma's visits to other villages continued. She says that she led thirty members of the Gypsy community in the Jangarai Thanda to Christ and took them to the Medak cathedral for baptism. When the presbyter would not allow baptism by immersion, which they wanted, she called the bishop, who instructed the presbyter to perform the service. Elsewhere, after some families belonging to the fisher caste became the first Christians in their village, she arranged for a presbyter to come from Medak to conduct the funeral of one of them.

In four or five other villages, Deevenamma also built churches, but, to her great distress, each church was taken over by the independent pastor to whom she had entrusted it. When she became too old to minister to the church that she had founded, she appointed Mr. Anandam, from the Telugu Pentecost Mission in Toopran, to be the first pastor. He proved to be gifted in both preaching and pastoral care, but his attempt to sell the church to another independent pastor led to his dismissal in 2006. After that, he established a large Pentecostal church in the nearby village of Ambajipet.

For the following two years, Deevenamma came from Hyderabad on some Sundays to conduct worship. When she could not come, young people led the service. She then decided to donate the church building and land to the CSI Medak Diocese. The diocese reimbursed her for the cost of building the parsonage. Her gift came with the understanding that an evangelist or pastor would be appointed as a resident minister. She has continued her financial support for this ministry as well as for various special programs. She and her husband have frequently come from Hyderabad (a two-hour ride) for the Sunday service and for special events, at which she has given her testimony and prayed for healing.

Deevenamma now lives in Hyderabad with her husband, Mithra, who, after a thirteen-year illness, has now recovered. (In 2010 he was eighty-three and she was seventy-eight.) They have three daughters, two married, and one son, who moved with his family to New Zealand. Deevenamma and her husband attend the Mushirabad CSI church in Hyderabad and now only drive to Chinna Shankarampet for festivals. She says that if the church needs repairs, she will continue to pay for them. When we met her at a festival service in 2008, we noticed that many people in the congregation came to her at the end of the service for her blessing and prayers for healing.

New CSI Congregations of Different Kinds

The worship of the church combines the CSI liturgy with the free style inherited from Mrs. Deevenamma and the independent preachers. There are many shouts of "Hallelujah" during the service. In other respects, too, the church attempts to merge two Christian traditions. There are members from many castes, but unlike the majority of independent churches, Dalits are in the majority. Because of Mrs. Deevenamma's generosity, the church is not at all self-supporting, as are many independent churches. In this respect, it is like the other CSI village churches rather than like the CSI urban churches, which both support themselves and contribute to a wider ministry.

In this church, as in both CSI and independent churches, members pray to God in Christ, giving thanks for all good fortune and healing, whether following their prayers or modern medical treatment. Deevenamma's concern for villagers includes their physical and spiritual needs, and the gratitude and respect she receives acknowledges both her spiritual power and her distinctive place as an educated urban benefactor.[7]

---

7. Another active laywoman, Mrs. Nelapati Sampoornamma, belongs, as do Mrs. Deevenamma and Vasantha Rao, to the CSI Wesley Church in Musheerabad, which is part of Hyderabad City. The following paragraphs summarize a longer tribute sent to Vasantha Rao by Mrs. Sampoornamma's daughter, Theresa Vinola, and her son, Ephraim Nelapati.

After Mrs. Sampoornamma's husband retired in 1986, he had a new residence built as a prayer hall on the ground floor, with their home upstairs. They led all-night prayers there on the first Saturday of every month, prayers that she continued after her husband's death in 2000, up through the twenty-fifth anniversary in 2011. From twenty-five to three hundred people have participated in those prayers. On the anniversaries she distributed gifts to widows. Sunday morning services have also been conducted there by Baptist and independent pastors and evangelists.

On Sunday mornings, Mrs. Sampoornamma would often go to villages outside the city to conduct services in the streets and to preach in people's homes. She helped to raise money to build a church in one village, and she also took her children along on visits to more than five other villages, where she showed religious films and organized healing and revival meetings, some of which led people to make a decision for baptism. She has frequently visited patients in various hospitals, giving them snacks and praying for them.

Every Friday Mrs. Sampoornamma has led a group of women in a "Fasting Prayer Meeting." She expects miracles, and the women with whom she prays testify that miracles are happening in their own lives and in their families. She also spends much time at home in prayer and meditation. She feels such a burden for "reaching the unreached" that she keeps supporting many independent pastors and churches, as well as donating to support gospel magazines and gospel meetings. She was also instrumental in compiling and publishing a book of gospel songs.

While the details of their life stories are different, it is clear that both Mrs. Sampoornama and Mrs. Deevenamma have unusual evangelistic zeal, confidence in the healing power of prayer, and willingness to use their financial resources in their evangelistic mission. Though both belong to the Church of South India, they have worked with and supported pastors and evangelists in other denominations.

Merging Traditions in Worship and Pastoral Care

Will the Horeb Prayer Church play a mediating role between the older CSI congregations and the newer independent churches? Much depends on the pastors whom the CSI appoints for this congregation, on whether they can continue to hold together the older traditions of the Church of South India, both Methodist and Anglican, and the evangelical zeal of the independent churches, with their confidence in the power of the Holy Spirit made evident in the healings by Lord Jesus. The Horeb Prayer Church may also respond to the challenge of forging unity in multi-caste congregations. As in the independent churches discussed in chapter 6, communal meals, as well as sharing in the Lord's Supper, may demonstrate the congregation's unity in the Holy Spirit.

When this congregation was established as an independent church, Pastor Anandam provided energetic leadership and conducted worship in a Pentecostal style.[8] After Mrs. Deevenamma transferred the congregation to the CSI Medak Diocese, a young presbyter, the Rev. Prasanna Kumar, was put in charge of the congregation. He says that when he arrived, only five families from the village of Chinna Shankarampet came to worship, in addition to some families from nearby villages. There were also eighteen young men from the Pentecostal Mission who came because they did not have a church building of their own. "Why should we celebrate Christmas?" they asked. "It is worshiping idols — both the tree and the star." They wanted to take the members in the new CSI church who agreed with them to the Pentecostal Mission. After the new pastor scolded them for trying to do this, they gradually left the church and started worshiping in a neighboring village. One of them tried to persuade the Christians in his home village to stop going to the Horeb Prayer Church. The pastor then went to that village and persuaded the small group of Christians there to continue to come to his church, even paying for an auto-rickshaw to bring them on Sunday. On Mondays he would go to visit those who had not come to church the day before.

Like Mr. Nithin,[9] Prasanna Kumar visited different villages on a regular schedule and conducted family prayers in the homes that he visited. He also arranged for a three-day annual prayer meeting at the church, for which he invited a speaker from Hyderabad and provided lunch and dinner for three days for all who participated. This led to the baptism of fifty people.

In 2008 and 2009, he told us, miracles began to happen. Prasanna Kumar

---

8. See the summary of the sermon he preached in his present church in Ambajipet in the appendix.

9. See chapter 5.

promised barren women that they would have children, and after he prayed for them, they conceived. One man from a nearby village was afflicted by witchcraft, but after two months of living in the Horeb Prayer Church, he was healed. A man from another village, who was similarly afflicted, was healed after the pastor prayed for him and is now in good health. Since witchcraft was so widespread in the surrounding villages, many who were not Christians started coming to church. After the pastor's prayers, people recovered. If a woman was suffering from evil spirits or devils, the pastor would seize her by the hair and say to the demon, "In Jesus' name, I command you to leave this woman. Go away from this house and from this woman!" Unlike other pastors, he says, he is not afraid to remove evil spirits.

After Prasanna Kumar was assigned to a different pastorate, the Rev. Prabhaker was appointed pastor of the Horeb Prayer Church. He has been trying to persuade his congregation to accept the more formal CSI liturgy. He told them that their joining the Medak Diocese was like a woman getting married and moving to her husband's village: just as the wife should adjust to her new family's customs, so should the congregation accept the standard form of worship in the Church of South India. In the sermon summarized in the appendix, however, the pastor was more informal than some independent churches, interrupting his sermon several times to sing hymns, to some of which the congregation responded by clapping or singing. This informal style is also an older Methodist style of village preaching, which is still followed by many CSI pastors in village congregations. It remains to be seen how worship in this newest CSI congregation will evolve and whether it will continue to live up to its name: a house of prayer on the mountain of the Lord.

Conclusion

In an area where there are so many new independent churches, there are in fact three new congregations in the CSI Wadiaram pastorate. Each of them is of a different type. The congregation at the pastorate headquarters is not entirely new since worship has been conducted there for many years, but this church building is now the home of a small congregation with lay leadership. In the midst of a pastorate composed mostly of Dalit Christians, four of the eight families in this congregation belong to non-Dalit castes.

The six Christian families worshiping together in the Gypsy settlement have no congregational structure except for their family connection, but they do have a common determination to remain faithful Christians while continuing to belong to their tribal community. Since so few Gypsies in this area have become

Christians, it may be difficult for these families to find Christian marriage partners for their sons and daughters, but some of them are trying to do this.[10] That in itself distinguishes them from the practice of many families in the older CSI congregations. Of all the congregations in the pastorate, this one has the closest connection with the Medak cathedral, which is where some of the members were healed from the effects of black magic and where all of them were baptized.

The Horeb Prayer Church began as an independent church and might still be one if Pastor Anandam had been a more trustworthy steward. This church still retains some "independent" features, one of which is the presence of members from several castes.

What all three of these congregations have in common is that they consist largely of first-generation Christians, who have made individual or family decisions to be baptized. In most cases, their conversion has followed their being healed from illness or black magic. In this respect, they are like members of the independent churches. The lay leaders of these new CSI congregations have been very important in their development, and the contribution of the retired nurse from Hyderabad, Mrs. Deevenamma, has been decisive. Where these CSI congregations differ from the independent churches is in their close connection with a larger denominational structure beyond their own village that takes the primary responsibility for their pastoral care. This connection has many advantages, but thus far it also has meant that these congregations have not had to raise the funds to pay for that care. Without contributing much more to their own support, these new congregations, like the older CSI congregations, will have to share a pastor with other congregations, who would give them less pastoral care and pastoral presence than they would like.

For the present, these three groups of Christians constitute the third story of this book: congregations of new Christians that in some respect resemble the independent churches but that are now part of the Church of South India. We do not know how this story will develop in the next generation of the present Christian families, nor can we predict whether they will be joined by more new Christians.

In chapter 10 we discuss the two linked topics that are so important in all the new churches: healing and conversion. First, however, we need to look at two dimensions of the life of village Christians: their adaptation of Hindu rituals and Indian artistic forms for Christian use (chapter 8) and their own distinctive formulation of Christian beliefs (chapter 9). Our data for these topics are largely from the CSI congregations, but these aspects of Christian life are important for members of the independent churches, as well.

10. In some parts of Telangana, quite a few Gypsies have become Christians.

CHAPTER 8

Christian Adaptations of Hindu Practices

Dual Adjustments in Becoming Christians

When people become Christians in any part of the world, they undertake a dual process of change. They adjust their lives to the new beliefs and new moral requirements they have accepted, but they also adjust those Christian beliefs and rules to their prior cultural and social circumstances. Their previous religious practices may continue with a new interpretation or in a modified form. Missionaries coming from another culture have not always recognized this dual process. They have sometimes thought that their own Christian culture could be transplanted into new ground. Indeed, both Christians and non-Christians have sometimes agreed that introducing the Christian religion to a culture where it has not previously been present involves importing the foreign missionary's culture.[1]

Other Christians, both those bringing the gospel and those receiving it, have maintained that the gospel has to find a new embodiment in the culture of those who accept it. Incorporating old religious practices into Christian worship or social custom can for some Christians only be justified if there is some biblical precedent. Many Protestants object to Hindu rituals that remind them of Roman Catholic practices rejected by European Protestants in the Reformation.

The leaders of the Hyderabad Methodist Mission, both Indian and British,

---

1. The Indian word *parangi,* applied to the Portuguese and to Europeans in general, and to missionaries and Christian converts, comes from the Arabic term *farangi,* meaning "Frank." In the Middle Ages "Frank" was used as a synonym for "Western European." The Muslims called the Crusaders "Franks." This word may also lie behind the English word "foreign" (if this is not from the Latin word *forās,* or "outside").

went further than many Protestant churches in India in recognizing the value of adapting some Hindu practices and cultural forms for Christian use. They were willing to do this deliberately and to give official approval to what in some cases was happening spontaneously in the communal life of village Christians. Such adaptation seemed preferable to an alternative that we have already noted: having Christians follow two separate religious tracks, one Christian and one Hindu. This chapter describes both the adaptations that were deliberately introduced by church leaders and those that have been developed by the independent initiatives of laypeople.[2]

Adaptations Noted in 1959

The earlier study revealed the large extent of Christians' participation in village rituals, but it also noted various efforts to adapt some Hindu practices so that they could be integrated into Christian worship or at least into a total pattern of life that was recognizably Christian. Some were adaptations by village Christians themselves.

Christian symbols were used as embodiments of the power of Christ and as effective means to ward off demonic powers. Little crosses were tied around children's necks and crosses were painted on the outside walls or door posts of houses. Pictures of Jesus were put on the inside walls of houses, either a Roman Catholic crucifix or Sacred Heart, or a picture of Jesus on the Church of South India pledge card. The Bible and the cross replaced the earthen pots carried in processions to welcome a bride and in funeral processions.[3]

Christian songs in the village Telugu were set to tunes derived from ballads, wedding songs, and work songs. These songs were not in the *Andhra Christian Hymnbook,* but they were in Sadhu Joseph's lyric book. There were also a number of adaptations introduced by evangelists and presbyters. One was processing through the village with drums and marching three times around the place of worship. This was done especially on Palm Sunday and during

---

2. Much of the information in this chapter is drawn from Vasantha Rao's previous research and long acquaintance with many rural pastorates in the Medak Diocese. With one exception, we do not know about adaptations occurring in the independent churches we were able to study.

3. Two generations ago, Christians in many other places in India would sometimes place a Bible under their pillow as a protection against evil powers. This is occasionally still done by healthy people but more often for those who are sick. The Bible is also used to determine who is guilty of theft. Two people hold up a Bible on their thumbs while someone else calls out the names of the suspects. If the Bible turns and falls down, the person whose name was just then being mentioned is judged to be the thief.

Christian Adaptations of Hindu Practices

Christian festivals; it resembled the circumambulation of pilgrims at Hindu temples and shrines.

A second earlier adaptation was singing *Jayam, Jayam* ("Victory, Victory"). These days, too, after singing in the village, the pastor will sometimes shout, "A hymn for God whose name is Jesus!" Then the congregation replies, "God above all gods!" The pastor raises his hands and shouts, "To our Lord Jesus" and the congregation responds, "be victory!" This is an adaptation of a Hindu way of praising a particular deity, with shouts accompanied by drums and cymbals.

Another adaptation of traditional custom was greeting the presbyter with honors due to a guru: touching his feet or washing them. During a festive outside service, the pastor was garlanded and taken in procession to the place where he was to preach. This was one of many customs sometimes incorporated into the celebration of a Christian pilgrimage *(jathara)*, another of which was distributing light refreshments as the equivalent of Hindu *prasadam*.

There were dramatic performances based on Hindu models, with Christian words and stories, and traditional tunes. There was also a special baptismal service with the lighting of the cross outside the worship hall. This took place in April during the Hindu festival of *ugadi* (Telugu New Year's Day) when Hindu women carry pots containing lighted lamps to the shrine of the goddess Poshamma. We describe current forms of these adaptations later in this chapter.

Fifty years ago, equivalents had not yet been developed to many of the customary lifecycle ceremonies. Now, however, all village Christians observe a Christian naming ceremony for a child on the twenty-first day after birth, and the Christian marriage service includes the giving of a *tali* (a gold chain as a wedding necklace) to the bride, along with an optional Brahmanical "seven steps" ceremony.

The treatment of this topic in *Village Christians* concluded that in 1959 there were relatively few Christian adaptations of village Hindu ceremonies because most Christians were so involved in village religion that they considered Christian rites only an addition to or partial substitute for some of the old rites, not as their replacements or theological "fulfillments." Only the Achampet congregation was beginning to see the Christian way of life as an alternative rather than an addition. For most Christians the appropriate times in the annual calendar or the lifecycle were largely under the control of the traditional divine powers.[4] The half century since the earlier study has seen some further integration of the old and the new, both in village Christian practice and in reflection on the lordship of Christ.

4. Luke and Carman, *Village Christians*, 183-89.

Christians and the *Jathara* Festival

The most striking adaptation in the pastorate as a whole is a pilgrimage officially sponsored by the Medak Diocese. It is unique to this diocese and the adjacent Karimnagar Diocese, both of which were part of the former Wesleyan Methodist Mission. This is the adaptation of a Hindu festival, especially as it takes place at a particular site in the region, in order to express Christians' celebration of Christmas or Easter. Such a *jathara* was held in the Wadiaram pastorate in May 1959, during the previous study, and has been observed almost every year since.

During the 1930s, C. W. Posnett, then heading the Hyderabad Methodist Mission, succeeded in instituting this custom, and it gradually spread, being initiated in some places when a new pastorate headquarters was dedicated. Some of the retired evangelists and presbyters reported that "the Christian *Jathara* was begun with the explicit aim of making the new converts feel at home in their worship and religious patterns."[5] During the 1920s, one evangelist related, he used to go to the "Pilgrimage of the Seven Streams" out of curiosity. During the 1930s, evangelists in training were taken to the same pilgrimage "for evangelism, tract distribution, singing, preaching, selling of gospels, etc." and there they discovered some Christians who were members of their own congregations. Posnett "often used to say that we too must have our own Christian *Jathara* — it was his vision."[6] To observe the Golden Anniversary of the CSI in 1997, a *jathara* was celebrated in thirty-nine rural pastorates in the diocese, including Wadiaram.

In 1987-88 Vasantha Rao took up the topic of *jathara* for his B.D. thesis, stimulated by the reference to it in *Village Christians*. He began with a study of the Hindu pilgrimage of the seven streams, the major model for the Christian festival. He then also researched the observance of this pilgrimage in the pastorate that may have been the first to make this adaptation and still has the grandest celebration.[7] The research not only detailed the events at both the Hindu and Christian pilgrimages, but also in both cases included interviews with a number of pilgrims in order to learn what effect the pilgrimage had on them. A Hindu pilgrimage is called a *tirtha-yatra*, a journey to a sacred place, often a place at which pilgrims can take a sacred bath. The Christian festival tries to incorporate certain specific features of this particular Hindu festival. The study was intended to discover whether Christian pilgrims experienced a sacred journey or perceived the site of the pilgrimage as sacred.

The Hindu festival draws pilgrims to an unusual place where a tributary

---

5. Vasantha Rao, *Jathara*, 88.
6. Vasantha Rao, *Jathara*, 89.
7. April 22-23, 1987; Vasantha Rao, *Jathara*, 69.

Christian Adaptations of Hindu Practices

of the Godavari divides into seven streams that run parallel before merging again.[8] The central shrine here belongs to the goddess Durga, whom everyone is expected to worship before continuing on to perform a variety of other ceremonies. One is to crawl through a narrow passage between rocks where one needs the grace of the goddess not to get stuck. Another is to take a sacred bath in one stream of the wondrously divided river. A third is to stay awake through a night of vigil, and a fourth is to share in an animal sacrifice to the goddess. The journey to the shrine is itself an impressive ceremony, with carts from the surrounding villages approaching in a traditional order that reflects the relative importance of each village and the ranking of castes within the village. The sacred center also draws a more secular penumbra: rows of makeshift shops selling sacred pictures and images, but also little toys and all manner of knick-knacks, as well as sweets and other kinds of food.

This particular Hindu festival takes place on the annual "Great Night of Shiva," which falls in late February or early March, and includes a night of vigil during the dark of the moon. Many lights are lit at the shrine of the goddess Durga, and dramas are performed to help keep people awake. One lifecycle ceremony that takes place at this time is a baby's ceremonial first haircut. Animal sacrifices made, as well as other sacrifices, are done in fulfillment of an earlier vow. Consecrated food *(prasadam)* is distributed at the shrine, to be eaten there or to be taken home and shared with one's family. The relationship with the goddess Durga is more than a ritual exchange. "Seeing" *(darshanam)* the goddess is also a "being seen," which confers great blessing and strengthens the devotion *(bhakti)* of the worshipers. As they put their trust in the goddess, they receive new steadfastness as her devotees.

Twenty of the thirty Hindu pilgrims interviewed thought that the *jathara* erases caste differences, or at least causes them to be ignored, except for the procession of carts, in which the order of carts is determined by Hindu caste rank. This traditional order was defended by the executive officer, who said that otherwise there would be much confusion and commotion. Since 1963, the Dalit castes (Mala and Madiga) have at least been allowed to join the procession and have *darshanam* of the goddess. One Dalit, moreover, is now a member of the committee supervising the shrine, though he happens to belong to the local Christian congregation.

A few pilgrims thought that education and new social awareness, rather than the pilgrimage, were responsible for lowering caste pride. Others said that while the *jathara* itself does not wipe away caste distinctions, it at least provides a time and place for mixing temporarily and for binding people together with

---

8. Every confluence of two or more rivers is considered sacred, with each river bearing the name of a goddess. A confluence of seven streams is even more sacred.

a sense of their being one community.⁹ Some said that worshiping the goddess Durga at her shrine had improved their lives morally. Others reported no change, except for an increasing sense of being helped by the goddess and a greater interest in introducing others to the goddess so that they, too, might experience her power and grace.¹⁰

The Christian pilgrimage at Luxittipet brought together many people from four pastorates within the eighty-acre forest around the large church. They formed a long procession, some with their carts, while they sang lyrics about the resurrection of Christ. The procession included not only Christians, who are Dalits, but also tribals, a mixture of Hindus from various castes, and a few Muslims. The bishop led the circumambulation of the church in two circles, with those on foot on the inside and pilgrims in bullock carts in the outer circle. The bishop's wife read a scripture passage and spoke, and the women lit candles, which they placed on the large cross outside the church. The first worship service of the *jathara* was then conducted in front of the church, followed by a play about the cost of discipleship.

The following morning at 7:00 a.m., the Eucharist service was held in the church. Although only Christians who were communicant members were invited to come forward to receive communion, two Hindus, over the objection of the church elders and presbyters, insisted on taking the bread and "wine," saying that they were devotees *(bhaktas)* of Jesus and shared in his grace, even though they had not formally become Christians. Other non-Christian participants, who did not come forward, were present in large numbers. At the end of the service a teaspoon of *prasadam* (made of spices and sugar) was served to each pilgrim in the church, whether Christian or not, and at the same time baptisms were performed. After that, the first haircut ritual was performed by the presbyters present for families who had brought their babies or young children.

Meanwhile, just outside the church, some pilgrims were fulfilling vows made before starting on the pilgrimage by lighting incense sticks and breaking coconuts while saying, "Victory to Christ!" One half of the coconut was left as an offering; the other half was taken home by the pilgrim. A few said that they had already had their sacred baths in the Godavari, which is only a mile away. Those who had observed a twenty-four-hour fast then had something to eat. After the closing service at 7:00 p.m., a film was shown on the life of Jesus. "The experience of joy, hope, and new strength was expressed by many, faith being made strong in Christ, and a feeling of oneness of the community was reported."¹¹

9. Vasantha Rao, *Jathara*, 65-66.
10. Vasantha Rao, *Jathara*, 67.
11. Vasantha Rao, *Jathara*, 75.

Christian Adaptations of Hindu Practices

The Christian *jathara* substitutes a large cross outside the church building for the goddess-image of the Hindu *jathara,* and pilgrims bring oil to keep the wicks on the cross burning. "Christian pilgrims derive as much satisfaction from *darshanam* (beholding) of the cross as the Hindu pilgrims do from beholding the Devi [goddess]."[12] The bread and wine of Holy Communion would seem to correspond to the Hindu *prasadam* distributed by the priests of the goddess, but the communion elements are not given to Hindus. Instead, Hindu pilgrims at the Christian *jathara* receive the "pilgrimage *prasadam*" just described. In some pastorates, coconut pieces with white sugar and *jaggery* (coarse brown sugar or palm sugar) are distributed as *prasadam.*

Although the Christian vigil on the first night resembles the Hindu vigil *(jagarana),* it is not called by that name, and Christians are not supposed to perform the vigil to gain merit. Even so, some Christian pilgrims, under Hindu influence, do consider the vigil meritorious. Ritual bathing has both similarities to and differences from the Christian theory and practice of baptism. The slaughtering of animals that occurs at a Hindu *jathara* does not take place at the Christian *jathara.* At the time of the Hindu New Year's festival *(ugadi),* however, Christians observe a "Passover Sunday" on which chickens or goats are slaughtered and the meat is divided equally among the contributing families. This is understood officially, not as a sacrifice to God, but as a commemoration of the Israelite passover in Egypt.

Central to the *jathara* is the idea of the sacred place, and here the Hindu idea of the "place of merit" seems to diverge considerably from a Protestant Christian view of the church building and grounds. Some churches in the diocese are considered "holy ground," however, and this is particularly true of the Medak cathedral. In these sacred places miraculous healings are more likely to occur. There has also been an interesting new development in some pastorates. A large cross has been erected on a hill or in a forest some distance away from the church building at the pastorate headquarters. These crosses have now become focal points of Christian pilgrimage.

Adapting Traditional Forms of Music and Drama

One way in which Christians have adapted Hindu cultural forms is the use of the folk versions of Hindu music and drama to act out and sing biblical stories and Christian interpretations of salvation history from Adam to Christ. These performances have become a regular feature of *jatharas* and other special

---

12. Vasantha Rao, *Jathara,* 93.

events. Sometimes they are planned by the ministerial leadership, who bring a singer or a drama troupe from elsewhere. Sometimes they are more spontaneous adaptations by lay villagers. This was the case with the drama group in Ambajipet fifty years ago.[13] That was an unusual occurrence because most of the young men and their leader were not Christians; they belonged to other castes than those in the previously all-Dalit congregation.[14]

The performance known as *burrakatha* is a story told and sung to the accompaniment of a single-stringed instrument attached to a shell.[15] Originally the performers were wandering minstrels called *jangama*, a name for Lingayat priests, who wandered from village to village with tiny images of Lord Shiva around their necks, instead of serving the great *lingam* in the temple of Shiva.[16] Although the Lingayats originally rejected caste distinctions, these minstrels were not considered to be regular priests of Shiva, but a wandering group outside (and below) the village caste hierarchy. In this type of performance, the storyteller was often accompanied by his wife. In the current form of *burrakatha* adapted by Christians, the main storyteller sings and dances while playing a tambourine, and two others play the *burra* and interject their comments. The players may be either men or women.[17]

A pastor popularized a Christian adaptation of this art form all over the Telugu-speaking area (now Andhra Pradesh). Several other Christian performers have become well known, and a more secular form has also developed. Before Indian independence, this form was banned by both the British government in Madras Presidency and the Nizam's government in Hyderabad State because it was used to spread political messages favoring independence.[18]

The main performer of *burrakatha* wears a ring on his right thumb to clank against a ring on his left hand, while two co-performers play earthenware drums. All three wear anklets, which add even more noise when they dance. The assisting performer on the right side is called the "joker," while the one on the left side is called the "politician" because of the nature of the comments they

---

13. Luke and Carman, *Village Christians*, 156-57.

14. In "Black Magic" in chapter 4, we have described a more recent dramatic performance and the difficulties it encountered.

15. *Burra* means "skull" in Telugu, so the shell is meant to represent a human skull. This "shell" may also be made of clay and pumpkin, or of brass and copper. The name may also refer to the *tambura*, an instrument with a hollow shell and attached strings, resembling the *veena*, which is played by pulling or pressing the strings. The word *katha* means "story."

16. See chapter 4, note 16.

17. From the time that he was in his teens, Vasantha Rao has performed this with two of his brothers many times.

18. See chapter 2.

Christian Adaptations of Hindu Practices

throw in from time to time. The main performer sings the story to specific tunes used for the *burrakatha*. Various Christian performers have concentrated on specific themes or stories. One performer has played the life of Jesus Christ, and another has sung the story of St. Thomas founding the church in India. Other groups have specialized in acting out the story of Moses.[19]

Harikatha, which means literally "the story of Lord Vishnu," is a form of storytelling with singing between the narrations. It is also called *kathakalakshepam*, "whiling away the time by telling stories." It is done by a single performer. The storyteller is supposed to be a learned person who is able to interpret religious texts according to the listeners' context. The original stories were from the Hindu scriptures, interspersed with musical compositions. This art form has been adapted to tell biblical stories. The Rev. Gorre Prabhudas, who served in the Luxittipet pastorate (where the *jathara* described above was held), was proficient in this kind of performance, assisted by a group that repeated his songs after him. The singer is dressed in traditional Indian attire, wearing a *dhoti*.[20] He uses catchy tunes, whatever their source, and likes to give his stories a unique twist. To make his singing more entertaining, he moves his body around swiftly while he sings.

Kolattam is a dance form played with sticks. It may be derived from the ancient practice of playing the drums while an offering is made to the deity in a temple. It has now become a form of folk art. An even-numbered group of performers, ranging from forty down to a minimum of eight, are directed by their leader to form a big circle. Later they divide into two circles, one inside the other. The musician-leader stands in the middle of the inner circle and tells the performers to hold up their sticks, one in each hand, to the end of which are fastened colored strings or balls. The "drum beat" is made by striking one stick on the other. The musicians accompanying the dance group play the *mrudangam* (a double-sided drum), flute, harmonium, and cymbals. All folk songs, as well as the lyrics sung in village Christian worship, can be adapted to *kolattam*.

The *kummi* dance, performed by women clapping their hands together, is thought to have originated long ago when there were no musical instruments. One woman leads the singing and all join in the refrain, after which each of the performers adds a line to the song. The singing and dancing go on until the group becomes too tired to continue.

Stories from the Bhagavata Purana and the Ramayana have long been acted out in the villages by troupes of men who accompany their singing and dancing with hollow sticks and brass wheels. One stick is held by the thumb, the second

---

19. Vasantha Rao has often sung and played the life of Samson or the story of Nehemiah.
20. The long loin cloth (Telugu: *pancha*) wrapped around a man's waist and legs.

stick with the other four fingers, and the two are struck together. The leader of the troupe arranges the event, composes the text, and selects the performers of the various parts. As noted above, this kind of drama has often been adapted to portraying biblical stories, which usually include a character representing God. In many instances Hindu dramatists have written Christian plays and taught them to the actors. These performances have often been done in the Ramayampet pastorate, which is just north of Wadiaram. There, the characters wear costumes and facial makeup. They are normally all men; some play the female roles.[21]

Bathukamma is a traditional dance in an autumn festival ending two days before *Dasara*. It was customarily performed by women belonging to what was considered a low caste in the Hindu hierarchy. The women danced around a cone of flowers composed of seven concentric layers as their way of worshiping the goddess Gauri, while they sang lively folk songs. In the Christian adaptation of this dance, women form two concentric circles in which they dance and clap, while singing folk tunes with Christian words. They do not have a cone of flowers; they all move in the same rhythm; and their leader sings while the others join in the refrain.

Other Current Adaptations

Sometimes there is only a slight distinction between Christians continuing a customary village practice and Christians adapting a village Hindu practice to Christian use. We consider the funerals described in chapter 4 to be an example of the former since even though the pastor accompanied the funeral procession, he was unable to persuade the members of his congregation to change the traditional form. On the other hand, we understand the examples given in this chapter to be adaptations, in which Christians either change what they do in the ritual from Hindu practice or change the interpretation of the ritual, or sometimes both. The example below in "Christian and Hindu Involvement in Adaptation" shows a merging of Hindu and Christian practices of remembering the ancestors in an unusual fashion: a Hindu joint family honoring their Christian mother and grandmother with a Hindu feast and Christian prayers.

Some Christians simply continue the ceremonial first haircut, but others adapt it to Christian use. At the end of a Sunday morning service in the large independent church in Ambajipet, Pastor Anandam took the barber's role, and

---

21. In December 2011 there was a performance on the first night of the *jathara* in Sangareddy pastorate, at which Vasantha Rao was asked to preach.

the church took the place of the family home. The "household" in which this ritual occurred was the whole congregation. In this case, the baby's father was the pastor's lay assistant, and he and the pastor provided the lunch for all who stayed after the service. The simple act of cutting a few locks of the baby's hair remained the same as in the traditional ritual, and the ritual continued to have the significance of marking a new stage in the young child's life, but the community to which this child would henceforth belong was redefined. This is all the more important in a new congregation including those from many different castes. Members of these castes do not often cross one another's thresholds, and normally they do not eat together. The haircut in the sanctuary, like the common meal, signifies that all present, including the baby, now belong to a larger Christian family.

One Christian adaptation of a Hindu calendar festival is the *paska* festival, celebrated in these villages about the end of July, more than a month into the rainy season and after the millet, corn, and other dry crops have been harvested. The name is a local mispronunciation of *pachika,* which means "tender green grass." When domestic animals feed on this new grass, they also eat insects in the grass and sometimes get sick. Human beings also suffer from various diseases during the monsoon rains because they drink contaminated water and walk through mud. These illnesses include cholera, stomach upset, and diarrhea. Since villagers believe that the goddess Katta-Maisamma causes these diseases, they make animal sacrifices to appease her. They perform the sacrifices near the dike around the village reservoir, praying that the goddess will store enough water in the reservoir for the next crop after the rains and thereby bless the village.

The Christian adaptation of this festival is held at about the same time and is also celebrated in the fields or nearby forest, or at the village reservoir. Each family may slaughter a chicken, or the whole congregation may buy and slaughter a goat, dividing the meat among the contributing families, with a free share for the pastor. Each family cooks its meat separately; this is not a communal meal.

The adaptation depends on the fact that *paska* is also the word that Telugu Christians use for the Israelite passover. Although the ritual is similar to that performed by Hindu families and is done at about the same time, pastors give the festival a different meaning, saying that it is to remember the passover in Egypt where a similar animal sacrifice was performed. Pastors emphasize the link between the liberation of the Hebrews from Egyptian rule and the liberation of Dalits from oppression, as well as the transformation in Christian lives, all because of the strong hand of the Lord. There is another parallel that could be drawn. In the history of Israel, Canaanite agricultural festivals were linked to decisive historical events. Here, Christians are drawing a connection between a village calendar festival and their own liberation, which is an ongoing historical event, evoking both commemoration of their past liberation and their hope for liberation and transformation yet to come.

All over India and beyond, Hindus celebrate the festival of lights (*Dipavali* or *Diwali*) at the end of October or in early November. Local customs vary from place to place, but the decoration of houses with oil lamps is a common feature. Often it is a time for twirling sparklers, setting off fire crackers, and exchanging sweets. This is a festival in which it is easy to include one's neighbors, since sweets can be shared across the boundaries of caste and religion.

A Christian adaptation of this festival was introduced in the Wadiaram pastorate in 2004 by the Rev. S. Devavaram, after his arrival in the pastorate. He wanted this festival to be celebrated between October 1 and November 15 in as many villages as possible, on different dates, so that all the pastors and their wives could take part in all the celebrations. The English name is the Christian home festival, but the Telugu title is more revealing. It means "festival of light for the home through worship with lamps."[22]

All the pastors meet at the pastorate headquarters and select villages for the celebration. The women's fellowship secretary of the District Church Council is invited to participate in a few of the villages. This celebration must be held in the evening since the women light the cross after dark. Women in the congregation organize a dinner for the whole congregation. When that is not possible, dinner is cooked at least for the pastors and pastors' wives and the guest speaker, and some snacks are provided for the congregation members who attend the service. The celebration starts with everyone gathering in the center of the village. The pastors, young people, and children begin to sing. While the singing is going on, Christian women come out of their houses to join the group, carrying platters of rice, coconut pieces, coins, and earthen lamps. Other villagers also come out of their houses to watch the procession.

The procession is considered a witness to the village about Jesus. Some members of the congregation prepare garlands for the pastors and their wives to honor their ministry and show their own happiness. The group moves from the village center and walks toward the church, singing, playing instruments (drums, trumpets, cymbals, and *kanjar*), and clapping. As the procession moves toward the church, more Christian women come out of their houses with their children and join in. When the procession comes to the cross erected in front of the church, all electric lights are turned off. Even the earthen lamps brought by the women are blown out.

Worship begins with a pastor's wife reading a scripture passage relating to light. A prayer is offered by another pastor's wife. A brief exhortation is given by

22. Telugu: *Gruha Velugu Diparadhanala Pandugalu*.

the special invitee, who is another pastor's wife or the District Church Council women's secretary. After this, one candle on the cross is lit by still another pastor's wife or the special invitee. From this one candle, all the pastors' wives light one another's candles and then the earthen lamps or candles of all the women. After forming a circle around the cross, the women walk around the cross three times, singing hymns. Then they place their candles on the cross and enter the church. The worship emphasizes that Jesus Christ is the light of the world and also the light of the church community, the family, and all individuals. In some villages the Lord's Supper is celebrated at the end of the service.[23]

Christian and Hindu Involvement in Adaptation

Both the spontaneous and the deliberate adaptations reported in the 1959 study have continued. Many village Christians like to continue traditional ceremonies that they find missing in Protestant practice, including those marking steps in the lifecycle and yearly events in the agricultural calendar. Unless they move to a secular view of the world in which no time is different from any other, they need to recognize the special times in their individual and communal lives. Moreover, most of them have Hindu relatives with whom they like to celebrate family occasions, as well as the festivals involving their caste community or the whole village. Some occasions, like the festival of lights, are celebrated in different ways all over India. Christians can more easily join with Hindus and Muslims in some of these festivals than in others. Those that involve eating meat that has been sacrificed to village goddesses pose the greatest difficulty. An alternative to joining in an existing ceremony is the creation of a substitute; many of the adaptations sponsored by the diocese are of this kind.

A final example of adaptation is quite different. In 2008 an unusual celebration of All Souls Day (November 2) took place at the pastorate headquarters in Wadiaram. It commemorated a woman remembered as the first Christian from the fisher caste in this small congregation. Her Hindu name was Ganta Laxmi; she was given the name Yesumani at her baptism. Each year, her four sons and four daughters with their spouses and children (twenty-seven in all) come from Hyderabad to visit their mother's grave since she was given a Christian burial. The eldest son and his family said that they attend a Christian church

---

23. This festival has been celebrated for several generations in the neighboring Dornakal Diocese. It was introduced by the late Bishop Azariah and was possibly inspired by Greek Orthodox ritual. Harper, "The Dornakal Church"; Brown and Frykenberg, eds., *Cultural Interaction*, 196.

in Hyderabad, though they are not baptized. All the rest consider themselves Hindus; the women wear an auspicious mark on their foreheads.

That year, all twenty-seven members of the family came to the Christian burial ground in Wadiaram and held a prayer meeting at Yesumani's grave. Later they had a grand display of fireworks, and cooked and ate a meal in her memory. The ritual in the cemetery somewhat resembled the memorial meals at the dark of the moon festival for the ancestors *(Peddala Amavasya)* two weeks before the *Dasara* festival in October. In addition to their graveside gathering, the entire family attended the All Souls Day service in the Wadiaram church, honoring their mother and grandmother. At the end of the day, the family returned to Hyderabad, saying that they would come back the following year. In fact, they came much sooner, to the Christmas service in Wadiaram on December 25, where they joined the congregation in remembering the birth of Christ.

Church historians might regard All Souls Day as an adaptation of the important pre-Christian Celtic festival at the beginning of November. Perhaps this family's memorial service should be considered, not as an Indian Christian adaptation, but as a Hindu effort to adapt their Hindu memorial service to the calendar of the Christian community that their mother and grandmother had joined. In any case, there is a mixing of memorial rituals, even this temporary fusion, by all the descendants. We know of this occasion because it took place in a Christian setting. What encounters of Christian and Hindu traditions are occurring in many other Hindu homes, both in Hyderabad and in these villages, we simply do not know.

Hindus often have less difficulty than Christians in adopting and adapting a religious practice outside their traditional custom. The family just described adapted their Hindu memorial ritual to the Christian calendar, but by attending the All Souls Day service, they also changed the Hindu ritual and put it in a Christian context. Whether the Hindu or the Christian part of this mixed ritual was more prominent depends on one's vantage point. The family apparently liked the Christian service, for they returned seven weeks later for the celebration of Christmas. Many who are not Christians like to come to Christmas services, especially those at the Medak cathedral. In whatever way this Hindu family celebrates Christmas or remembers their mother and grandmother on All Souls Day, they contribute to a gradual adaptation of initially foreign Christian festivals to an Indian cultural and religious context.[24]

It is part of the nature of public festivals, both Christian and Hindu, that

---

24. The adaptations to Hindu culture by Thomas Christians and later by Roman Catholics started centuries earlier and proceeded differently than the meeting of British Methodist traditions with Dalits in a Hindu society long ruled by Muslims.

Christian Adaptations of Hindu Practices

participants may celebrate them in different ways and interpret them differently. It is too early to tell how these Christian festivals will evolve in India or how they may be reformed in the future. Adaptation includes both altering earlier Christian rituals and changing Hindu ritual forms so that they fit into a larger Christian context. Such a process is inevitable in a vital Christian community, but the distinctive Christian meaning in an older ritual might be diluted or lost. It is also possible for a Hindu ritual incorporated into Christian worship still to convey a Hindu meaning that does not fit the Christian context. The Medak Diocese has gone further than many Protestant churches in India in recognizing the necessity of adaptation and in deliberately trying to plan it. Christian congregations will eventually decide how well the old and the new fit together.

CHAPTER 9

Distinctive Beliefs of CSI Christians

Understanding the Christian Message in One's Own Language

Like the chapter on Christian adaptation, this chapter is concerned with a Christian faith that is expressed in terms of the new Christian community's own culture. Whereas we discussed adaptation in terms of ritual practice and artistic expression, this chapter deals with verbal expressions of faith. These come largely from the CSI congregations that are part of this study and of the earlier one made in 1959. The emotional dimension of faith, which may include joy and sorrow, excitement and fear, affects both practice and belief. Certainly the music of hymns often determines how the words are experienced.[1]

Beliefs that express Christian faith are formulated in words. Through the centuries, Christians have differed as to whether the scriptures should be translated into people's own mother tongue and whether the most important prayers and creeds should be recited in a special, sacred language. Muslims and Christians differ even more sharply as to whether ever to translate a sacred language. Differences between Roman Catholics and Protestants about translation are now much less pronounced. Some Protestants, too, have wanted to keep a more sacred language in their liturgy, even if that is only an older version of the language spoken today. Theology is also often considered to be better expressed in

---

1. In these largely Dalit congregations, the Madigas are the traditional drumbeaters in important rituals for the entire village, as well as for their own caste community. In one village reported in chapter 4, some Malas, too, played instruments in a funeral procession. See Clarke's treatment of the drum, *Dalits and Christianity*, 109-22.

Distinctive Beliefs of CSI Christians

a more learned language than that of everyday speech, and perhaps even better in the original language of that tradition's great theologies.

Christians who affirm the translatability of the scriptures may assume that beliefs central to Christian faith can be expressed in any language. That assumption may underestimate the difficulty of meaningful translation. Many words in literary Telugu come from Sanskrit, just as many words in theological English are originally from Latin or Greek. Such words may seem more sacred or more scholarly to Christian preachers, but they may convey little or no meaning in village Telugu, especially for illiterate people.[2] The much greater literacy of the new generation may reduce the initial problem of understanding words, but beliefs often express affirmations that are difficult to comprehend, so that other words, metaphors from various spheres of life, are necessary to understand the standard words. This is especially the case if the layperson's problem is grasping why certain words seem so important to Christian preachers and teachers.

Beliefs Reported in the 1959 Study

We should begin by recognizing how difficult it is to present "beliefs" in translation. The earlier study noted that these Christians "do not readily articulate their fundamental conceptions and attitudes.[3] Many of the statements of belief obtained are repetitions of the phrases of the evangelist or presbyter, which as such furnish little clue as to whether those Christian teachings have been inwardly appropriated."[4]

Any ethnography recognizes that answers are often affected by the questions asked and by the way they are asked. "Mr. and Mrs. Luke did not conduct any interviews with questionnaire in hand, but tried to keep in mind the questions in the preparatory document drawn up for this series of studies. These questions were an aid in trying to learn from their conversations . . . and from their participation in the collective life of the congregation."[5]

For the purpose of that study, every verbal expression of belief had to be translated from Telugu into English. This involved recognizing the differences between the Brahmanical *(margi)* Telugu of Indian Christian Bible translations, sermons, hymns, and prayers, and the village *(deshi)* Telugu in which those Dalit

---

2. For the importance of translation, see Sanneh, *Translating the Message*.
3. Much of the material in this section is adapted from chapter 7B, "Village Christian Understanding of Christian Doctrines," in Luke and Carman, *Village Christians*, 169-79.
4. Luke and Carman, *Village Christians*, 169.
5. Luke and Carman, *Village Christians*, xii.

Christians experienced the world around them.[6] During their ten months in these villages, Mr. and Mrs. Luke probably spoke with several hundred people. The number whose views they summed up was undoubtedly much smaller, and they may have given greater weight to the words of those who expressed their thoughts with a striking metaphor or a personal example. They had the advantage of many years of experience working in other rural pastorates in the diocese, but in the end, their conversations and their notes had to be translated and "boiled down" into a few pages. In the process of editing, the authors tried to clarify villagers' statements with brief explanations of important ideas in their village culture.

The earlier study summarized village Christians' knowledge of the Bible:

> Most of the Christians . . . know a few of the miracles of Jesus, a little about Christ's birth, and the fact that He was put to death on a cross. Many know nothing about the Resurrection, Ascension, or Pentecost, or the promise of Christ's return . . . Many know of the Virgin Birth . . . [Some] know some stories from the Acts of the Apostles . . . they are especially fond of the story of Stephen and the conversion of St. Paul.[7]

Both Christians and non-Christians were moved by the story of Christ's passion. Any story of persecution and suffering aroused their sympathy, including Muslims' recounting at *Muharram* the martyrdom of Hassan and Hussain. The majority of Christians did not understand the sacrificial significance of Jesus' death. While some of the young men and women had learned the formula, "He died for our sins and rose again," they were not clear as to what those words meant.

The young people were familiar with two Hindu ideas of sacrifice. One is *tyaga,* ascetic renunciation or a less sweeping self-denial for non-ascetics. The other is *bali,* animal sacrifice to a village goddess to avert harm. Neither term had been linked in their thinking to Jesus' death. Young people who had gone to Christian night school or had taken special courses outside the village knew the statement, "The blood of Jesus cleanses us from sin," and they sensed a connection with the purification of a sacred bath *(tirtham):* there is cleansing power in Jesus' blood. They believed that the goddesses liked the blood of the animal sacrificed; and, along with other villagers, they sometimes shared the meat, but they did not identify themselves with the sacrifice or with the

---

6. Classical *(margi)* Telugu can be distinguished from the many regional *(deshi)* varieties. See Schmitthenner, *Telugu Resurgence,* 324.

7. Luke and Carman, *Village Christians,* 169-70.

deity to whom it was offered. Animal sacrifices were not offered to the Hindu high gods or their incarnations. (The *avataras* do not sacrifice themselves.) Since they considered Jesus to be like an *avatara* of the supreme God, his self-sacrifice made little sense. Some of the least educated thought that the shedding of Jesus' blood was to placate Shaitan. (They used the Muslim term for Satan.) The sacrifice or self-offering expected of the Christian was equally difficult to understand, especially since the evangelists talked about it as *samarpana* ("complete offering"), a Sanskrit term from ancient Vedic ritual that had no meaning for most villagers.

Only those who had gone to night school had some idea of what Jesus' resurrection means. Even though they used the word *jayam* ("victory") in their hymns, it was not Christ's victory over sin and death that impressed them but his uniqueness: "No other god but Christ ever rose from the dead!" The lack of meaning in the resurrection might be because village Christians were uncertain whether Jesus was really a human being. The Hindu concept of *avatara* implies the appearance of humanity, but not an ordinary humanity — either an illusory bodily form or a body consisting of a special "pure matter" present only in God's descent to earth in material forms. Christ's return or "second coming" was even less known than his resurrection; it did not seem to have been part of Christian teaching.

The usual name for Jesus was Yesuswami. *Swami* means "Lord" and can signify either God in the form of a human being or a human being with the power of God. Village Christians believed that if they worshiped Lord Jesus, he would heal the sick, keep the family from misfortune, bless their crops and livestock, and give them success in all their undertakings. All such "blessing" is *barakat*, the term used by Muslims and derived from the Arabic (and Hebrew) word for blessing. Jesus was mainly regarded as a worker of miracles and a bestower of blessings. There were a few Christians who believed that Jesus suffered on the cross to save them from sin. They said, "Demons need not be feared, for Lord Jesus is stronger than demons." There was little understanding of Jesus' forgiveness of sin or their need to forgive others.

The Telugu Protestant translation for "Holy Spirit" was used in prayers but little understood, perhaps because it is a combination of two words in Sanskritic Telugu: *parishuddha* ("holy"; but also "extremely clean") and *atma* ("soul" or "spirit," but in Hindu philosophy primarily the nonmaterial self within the material body and the Divine Self animating and supporting the material universe). Christians used the term *shakti* for the "power" of God. This is likewise a Sanskritic term, but it was well known in these villages, for it is the generic name for the local divine "powers," the village goddesses. *Shakti* can also signify the magician's "power." When Hindus heard Christians using the word in Christian prayers to express God's "possessing all power" or "omnipotence" *(sarva-shakti-gala)*, they sometimes feared that the Christians were pronouncing some magical incantation!

Least recognized of all theological terms of educated Christians was *tritvam*: "threeness" in Sanskrit, which is the word used for "Trinity." When Hindu representatives of the Arya Samaj criticized Christians for worshiping three Gods while denying the Hindu "trinity" *(trimurti)*, the three divine forms of Creator (Brahma), Maintainer (Vishnu), and Destroyer (Shiva), these village Christians were simply baffled.

The general term for God used by Telugu Protestants is Devudu (*deva* in Sanskrit, originally a cognate of *deus* in Latin). In some parts of India, Christians use other words for "God" because this generic term for deity signifies the ancient Vedic deities long since considered of much lower rank than the Hindu "High Gods" or "Universal Lords." Here, however, the generic term *devudu* has been elevated to a higher status as the personal name for God (as in English and other European languages), as opposed to the plural *devatalu* ("deities" or "divinities"). Hindus in these villages continue to use *devudu* for any male deity, including the one worshiped by Christians, but not as a general name for a village goddess, who is called a *shakti* or a *devata*. In each case, however, the Hindu deity has another personal name. The High God Vishnu is addressed in worship as Bhagavantudu or Narayana, while the High God Shiva is called Parameshvara. Any of these names can also be used as a general or nonspecific term for the Supreme Deity.

At the time of the study in 1959, village Christians understood Lord Jesus to be the *avatara* of Devudu, that is, the form of the Supreme Creator that is present and active within this world. Devudu was used in more general expressions, such as "God is spirit and omnipresent" and "God is love." There are certain material forms in which God's power is especially present, such as the cross, the Bible, and pictures of Jesus, but they believed that the Christian God does not, like Hindu deities, become incarnate in a material (but "inanimate") image.

Because only the Baptist and Mennonite missionaries wanted a literal translation of baptism as immersion ("dipping" or "dunking"), general Christian usage in India has followed the western European precedent of simply transliterating the Greek word, thus in Telugu, *baptismamu*. By mispronouncing this word, some of these village Christians actually invented a more meaningful term, for they said *baptirthamu*, which picks up the Hindu term *tirtha*, in its meaning of "sacred bath." Baptism also had a connection with the Hindu naming ceremony, a connection understood by many English speakers in the word "christening." "Baptism thus signified the receiving of a distinctive name

Distinctive Beliefs of CSI Christians

associated with the Christian community and the Christian God, and was also considered an act of ritual cleansing."[8]

While baptism was understood as a rite of entry into the church, Holy Communion was understood to be the central part of the more elaborate form of Christian worship. To some extent Christians in these congregations conceived of communion in terms of *prasadam,* which Hindus understand as "divine 'grace' or power concretely present in flowers, fruits or other food which has been offered to a deity and then returned to the worshipper," who takes it home and shares it with other members of the family. When one woman was asked what the communion elements were for, she replied, "Jesus gave them to us so that we may keep them in our pockets to remember Him by."[9]

In all but one of the congregations surveyed by the Lukes, only half the adults had been confirmed and were entitled to share in Holy Communion. These Christians knew that the communion elements were only given to a few people, but they did not understand why others were excluded.[10] While many Christians, along with any Hindu onlookers, simply accepted that Holy Communion was a special *prasadam* given to some instead of to all present (as with Hindu *prasadam*), "some Christians consider Communion as a very distinct rite connected with the crucifixion of Christ, and with His body and blood."[11]

Giving Christian Meanings to Hindu Terms

The 1959 study was also concerned with the way that Christians understood Hindu terms.[12] Educated Hindus might define the highest goal of human life as *moksha* or *mukti.* Both terms refer to release or liberation from the cycle of one life after another and entry into a state of transcendental knowledge and bliss. Most villagers, however, were more concerned with gaining *shubham,* "good fortune," everything that is auspicious, good, or happy, or contributes

---

8. Luke and Carman, *Village Christians,* 175.
9. Luke and Carman, *Village Christians,* 175.
10. The consequences of low communicant membership are discussed in chapter 10 of Luke and Carman, *Village Christians* and summarized in "Dalit Theology and Village Churches" in chapter 11 of that book.
11. Luke and Carman, *Village Christians,* 176.
12. The Swedish Lutheran missionary Bror Tiliander did an extensive study of this subject, focusing on the Tamil terms used in Bible translations and other Tamil Christian literature. (*Christian and Hindu Terminology*). We do not know of any similar study on Telugu Christian terminology, but many of the words Tiliander discusses are similar or identical.

to one's welfare. They would also refer to this with the Muslim term *barakat*, understood as material blessings. *Svarga* ("heaven") is considered philosophically to lie between *moksha* and *shubham* since it is a continuation of worldly happiness after death, but for a limited time. Most villagers, however, did not distinguish between *svarga* and *moksha*, considering this to be a state of eternal personal communion with one's chosen Lord. They hoped to go to *svarga*, which is a pleasant place; bad people would go to the world of Yama, the Lord of the dead. Christians generally shared this language, referring to heaven as *moksha* or *vaikuntha*. While for some Hindus this meant the eternal abode of Lord Vishnu and his devotees, many Christians understood heaven as the place where they would be united eternally with Lord Jesus.

For most Christians fifty years ago, as for other villagers, it was the this-worldly aspects of salvation that were uppermost in their minds. Christians shared with most Hindus and the few Muslims in the village the idea that divine blessing comes in very tangible or material ways. The word Christian pastors have used for "salvation" is *rakshana*, a term long used by the Hindu devotees of Lord Vishnu that has the same advantage as the English words "save" and "salvation." It can mean both divine protection from the dangers in this earthly life and rescue from bondage to evil powers or from earthly life itself. *Rakshana*, however, is another word taken from "high" or Sanskritic Telugu that had little meaning for villagers. Christians may have learned the phrase "Jesus is my Savior" *(Rakshakudu)*, but "Savior" and "salvation" had to be filled with new content from Christian teaching. For many Christians, Luke concluded, salvation was not understood as salvation from sin.[13]

Most of the Protestant Christian theological vocabulary in Indian languages consists of Hindu terms. (Christians in North India and elsewhere where Urdu is widely spoken, like Telangana, also use Muslim terms.) Many of these terms go back to the first Bible translations, catechisms, and liturgies.[14] Many of the official Protestant terms are in Sanskritic Telugu, reflecting both the prestige of Brahmanical learning and the fact that some of the original translators of the Bible into Telugu were Brahmins. These terms often mean little to most villagers, including Dalit Christians. They are like words in a foreign language unless they are translated and brought to life in the language and daily experience of village Christians.

---

13. Luke and Carman, *Village Christians*, 178.
14. The ancient Syrian Christian churches of St. Thomas have a liturgy in Syriac. In the nineteenth century the Bible was translated into the local language of Malayalam. Until Vatican II, the Roman Catholic Bible and liturgy were in Latin, except for some of the Syrian churches affiliated with Rome, which were allowed to continue using Syriac. The Roman Catholic catechisms, on the other hand, were written in the various Indian languages.

Distinctive Beliefs of CSI Christians

There is an opposite problem with words like *devudu, swami,* and *shakti.* They already have Hindu religious meanings familiar to Christians, but those meanings can be either a help or a hindrance in understanding and growing in Christian faith. It was concluded in *Village Christians* that, whatever their dangers, these bridges of meaning "do make it easier for non-Christians to come to some understanding and even acceptance of Christian ideas."[15] The same was and still is true of Christians living in a traditional village environment.

Prominent Beliefs Expressed in Recent Interviews

During the recent study, ten lay Christians in two village congregations, the oldest and the newest in the pastorate, answered a set of questions regarding their Christian beliefs.[16] Their answers were knowledgeable and articulate. All ten belonged to two of the very few CSI congregations that had regularly had a resident evangelist or pastor. While one cannot be sure exactly how representative their answers may be, their words certainly provide a window into the thoughts and beliefs of individual Christians in the Wadiaram pastorate today. Each question is followed by responses.

With what words do you begin your prayers?

The greatest similarity in all answers may lie in the responses to this initial question. "God," "Father," and "Jesus" are named in most of replies. Two include "Holy One," and one adds, "My Holy Spirit God." One includes not only the formal Telugu word for Father *(Thandri)* but also the informal "Daddy" ("Papa") *(Naina).* The verbs are "save us, protect us," and the most specifically Indian expression is "Thanks to your feet."[17]

---

15. Luke and Carman, *Village Christians,* 179.

16. This information was gathered by Mr. Erolla Prabhakar, the theological student who served as our research assistant in 2008-9.

17. This expression reflects the traditional Indian feeling that the feet are the ritually lowest and most impure part of the body, but therefore the part that those of lower ritual status should connect with as an act of obeisance or humble request. If the ritual distance is too great for clasping the superior person's feet, the obeisance is shown by kneeling or prostrating at a ritually safe distance. The pronounced deference, whether to a superior person or to a deity superior to all human beings, is shown by saying "to your feet." The word corresponding to "thanks" in Telugu (*vandanalu* or *vandanamulu*) means "praises." Traditionally it would not have been used to thank a servant for doing his or her duty, but only to thank a superior for a gift. Between equals or within the family, verbal expressions of gratitude would seem awkward or embarrassing. In modern Indian culture, the response to "Thank you" is likely to be, "Don't mention it" (see Carman and

What is the most important thing about Jesus Christ? How did he help you? Did Jesus Christ save you? If so, from what and for what?

The statements about Lord Jesus are slightly more varied. He is "God for all ... He died on the cross. He made us his children." "Jesus is Mary's son. For the sake of the world he suffered, died on the cross, and rose again." "Lord Jesus is really God. He caused us to be born; he will take us to heaven." "He is the essence of truth *(satya-svarupa)*."

"He is God the Holy Spirit. There was no sin in his birth; for the sake of our sins he died on the cross. He led me to salvation." "He is a great God, greater than all the Hindu gods that my parents worshiped." A young woman who was not yet baptized, however, said the following: "I do not know much about Jesus. I consider him one among all the gods, but my paternal aunt tells me to have faith only in him."

There was considerable agreement as to what was important about Jesus, though each expressed this conviction in terms of his or her own life experience, perhaps most directly expressed as, "If you believe in him, you can be successful in anything." One man said that his wife had put God to the test: helping her find her lost earrings. "If you are the real God, then I should find what I have lost." After twenty days she did, so "she thanked God (Jesus), resolved to worship only him, and decided that there is no other God." Another woman testified that "when we prayed to him, good water came in the bore well we dug. When my in-laws scoffed that I would never bear children, I prayed to God, and God gave me the fruit of my womb, a son and a daughter." God also, she said, saved her husband from a fatal electric shock. A man said, "He helped me a lot with my fields. He never let me down with any losses." God also saved his wife and himself through successful operations.

Two persons spoke of God's "favors" to their family: "Through the church of Jesus, after four months God restored her sight." "Through the prayers of the pastor and the pastor's wife, with hands on his head, Lord Jesus saved his life from witchcraft." A student declared: "Jesus (God) helped me in many troubles and with my studies." Another student was more specific: "Last year I prayed to the Lord to help me, and I passed my bachelor of education entrance exams with high marks." Moreover, "God alone" had saved his life after he was badly hurt in a motor scooter accident. A woman stated that after a failed first marriage, God had saved her life when she attempted suicide, and God had answered her prayer for a new and loving husband and a happy home.

Streng, eds., *Spoken and Unspoken Thanks,* especially the article by Arjun Appadurai, "Gratitude as a Social Mode in South India," 13-22).

The testimony of a recent convert recalled how, after a nearly fatal road accident, he had prayed: "Jesus, if you will help me with the healing of my broken bones, I will believe in you." After a six-month stay and daily prayers in the home of a Pentecostal pastor, he was healed and sent home to be baptized at the new church in his own village. Finally, a woman who was not yet willing to be baptized answered rather differently: "Up to now, he has not saved me; he is looking after me well." Her only trouble was being accused of causing the illness of her father-in-law and brother-in-law; but "Jesus is taking care of me; and even my in-laws are beginning to believe in God."

What is the relation of Jesus Christ to God?

Most respondents affirmed a father-son relationship between God and Jesus. One said, "They are related as father and son because Jesus was sent to the world in human form by the Father to save human beings." There were some, however, who said something different. One replied, "God and Lord Jesus are only one, but on earth Jesus took the form of a human being." That oneness was sometimes focused on Jesus: "Jesus is the one and only God. There is no other God," and "Indeed, Jesus is the real God." The one unbaptized woman answering posed her own questions: "Which God? People say that Jesus is God. Where is the other God? How can God die?" Another woman began by affirming a father-son relationship, but then she added: "Lord Jesus . . . prayed to the father for his will. This father prayed to that father in heaven." Here the exalted view of Jesus leads to the title of "Father," but still this is a different father from the "Father in heaven."

How did the Holy Spirit of Jesus Christ come into your life?

With the doctrine of the Holy Spirit, there was some uncertainty in the replies. Four of the six respondents from the older congregation did not give any answer to this question. The other two more or less agreed: "God while going off gave his Holy Spirit to us. Now that Holy Spirit is helping us." This is amplified as "While the resurrected Jesus was ascending into heaven, he gave us his Holy Spirit. It is because of the Holy Spirit that we are able to love and to do our work. He sees everything." The student in the newer congregation hoping to become a pastor spoke more personally: "First we should worship him in spirit and in truth and then the Holy Spirit will definitely be showered upon us. The Holy Spirit came into me through prayer. This made a difference in my life. I began to read the Bible more and more."

Two responses to this same question from the newer congregation describe a divine appearance in their sleep. A woman who had been praying for a child heard Lord Jesus reprimand her for laziness and felt him hit her on the cheek, leaving the cheek "burning with pain." "It was in the same month that I conceived," she said, "and now I have a daughter." The man who had been taken to a Pentecostal pastor's house to recover from a road accident was crying in his sleep about noon, "and then he came. When I turned to my side, I suddenly saw him. He asked me why I was crying, told me not to worry, and said that I would be healed, but in a slow process. Just as he told me, I am able to walk today . . . This is not what someone told me, nor is it from any book, but it is directly what God told me. He told me just what would happen, and it happened just as he said."

Why was Jesus killed on the cross and what was special in the shedding of his blood?

In responding to this double question, most referred to drinking the grape juice at the Lord's Supper. One said, "In this way, we are sharing his blood. We are sinners; for our sake he underwent troubles and accepted lashes. Only due to his death we are living and are holy. His blood has the power to cleanse our sins. He shed his blood on the cross; only with that blood we are made holy." Almost all made this same affirmation, but some began their answer with various statements about the historical cause of Jesus' death: "They killed Jesus because they saw that he was becoming famous." "The Romans put him on the cross. The Jews wanted to stop him when he was preaching the gospel, so they complained that he was breaking the law." "They killed him to see whether he was the real God; would he come to life again? To see whether he had magical powers they lashed him. Because he was healing the lame and the blind they caught him and hit him." "King Herod out of jealousy tried to kill him . . . They could not tolerate the good things he was doing and so they killed him." "The Jewish high priests conspired against him because people were saying that he was king of the Jews."

This respondent went on with a theological statement about the divine cause of Jesus' death: "God made him take the sins of the world upon himself and hence caused him to die on the cross. He gives his blood as wine to those who have received baptism and the Holy Spirit, in the Lord's Supper every first Sunday in the month. When we receive this wine, we must remember his commandments . . . and follow them." A statement closer to the Hindu environment went as follows: "Believers in the (Hindu) gods were terrified that he was attracting these people by saying that he was the great God, so they decided to torture and curse him . . . they hung God on the cross." Finally, on this question, too, the unbaptized woman dissented from the rest: "They only hit him, but they did not kill him; he did not die. I don't know myself, but people here say that he washed away sins that are happening right here."

Why is baptism administered?

The most common answer was "in order to become the children of God." Additions included "in order to bring us together to him," "in order not to be committing sins," "to enter the kingdom of God . . . to live lives of complete faith in God. Baptism is a sign of a change of heart," "so that all the sins we have committed should be gone." Some of the longer statements were the following: "If we take baptism, God will be over us. Otherwise he won't be. He will be in our heart. Otherwise we will remain Hindus, with the mark on the forehead." "Believing that being saved, we go to heaven. Jesus said that he who takes baptism and believes will be given eternal life." "One has to have trust in this God, not go here and there to worship other gods. Under no circumstances will I worship them. When there was a big Hindu festival *(jathara)* the other day, every one else went, but I stayed home. I got some rice and *dal* cooked for me and ate at home."

What is special about the death of Jesus Christ? What is the importance of the resurrection?

This double question elicited many thoughtful responses, which were in general agreement, but with different emphases. One man said that by both his death and his resurrection Jesus proved himself to be the true God. "If he had not died on the cross, we would not have got to salvation," said two others. Some put this more generally: "There is no one like Jesus on the whole earth. He endured a lot of suffering for the sake of the poor. He healed the lame and the blind; he died for all the people."

Several referred to the uniqueness of the resurrection, and some linked it to their "firm faith that in future he will also raise us up . . . He will take our spirit and keep it with him." "By rising again, Jesus made it possible for the whole world to know that he is the great God." "Since he lives, he will also raise us from death through the Holy Spirit." The woman who comes to church but is not yet willing to be baptized gave to this question an answer in agreement with her Christian friends: "First, he is God, and then he comes in the form of a human being to protect people from death caused by sin. He came to save us. Because he rose again, all came to know his greatness. He saw that his children were falling into the trap of death, so he came and saved them."

Is Jesus Christ a human being or an *avatara-purushudu*?

This question about Jesus may have been confusing; it certainly needs some explanation. The Telugu term, coming from Sanskrit, could be translated "a human incarnation of God" or "a divine descent in human form." The question seems to presume a contrast between a Christian affirmation of the full humanity of Jesus and a Hindu belief that the *avatara* only appears to be human. Many Hindus, however, believe that the *avatara* has a genuine material body; it is not a magician's illusion *(maya)*, but consists of a special "pure" matter. Many Christians in India, moreover, use the term *avatara* as an equivalent of the English word "incarnation."

The answers we received reflect something of this ambiguity. It is worth noting how these Christians reflect on the mystery of the incarnation. Only one said, "No, he is not a human *avatara*. Lord Jesus came into the world in human form, living among us in the body of a human being, but he is God." In general, the respondents all tried to affirm both Christ's humanity and his divinity, but with different emphases. Here are some of their statements: "Lord Jesus is only God, but he came to this earth in human form and again went back to God." "Lord Jesus came to this earth as a human *avatara*. With our flesh and our bodily form, God came to earth to be with us." "Lord Jesus is Divinity in human form." "Lord Jesus came into the world in the form of an *avatara*. Jesus is God, but he came in human flesh." "Lord Jesus is God, but he came into the world by being born to Mary in a holy way." "He is God who came to the world as a human *avatara*." "Once he was a human being; when he died and rose again, he is God."

What did Jesus Christ teach about what things are good and what things are bad?

All but one respondent had informative answers to the question about Jesus' ethical teaching. Only the not-yet fully convinced "seeker" said that she had no answer: "I do not know. I am new." Not surprisingly, given the emphasis on learning the Ten Commandments, between one and five of the following commandments are mentioned: not to commit adultery, not to steal, not to kill human beings, not to covet others' things, and not to bear false witness. All nine who answered included some teachings of Jesus, especially those from the Sermon on the Mount. Two began with turning the other cheek, and five included loving our enemies, which implied for them not returning a curse with a curse. Some of the statements were quite eloquent: "Even enemies are to be treated as though they were born from the same mother." "Lord Jesus gave legs to the lame and eyes to the blind. He received bad people. He said to visit others and give them food, and to become friends with an enemy." "He told us to love more if the enmity is more." "Don't stop talking with those who cursed you, but love them and talk to them."

Other words of Jesus were quoted or paraphrased in the following statements: "When children were coming into the kingdom of God, the disciples blocked them, but Jesus told them, 'Let the children come to me. Do not stop them.'" "Give clothes to those without clothes; give water to the thirsty; give food to the hungry. Then you will be known as children of my Servant." A few statements reflected more recent Protestant emphases: "God told us to pray, to work hard, and to forgive those who curse." "Lord Jesus told us to walk a good path, not to drink toddy, not to smoke country cigars, and not to roam about sinning." "He taught us to come for prayers at least one day a week." The student hoping to become a pastor said, "When we talk with others, our talk should bring glory to God . . . We should especially know what is written in the Bible about God."

Do you believe that God has forgiven your sins? Did you ever forgive those who sinned against you?

This question was also a double one. Almost all responded to the first question emphatically: "Yes, I firmly believe that he forgave my sins." The second question prompted a variety of answers, based on specific experiences. Here are some of the responses: "When our neighbors in our own caste attacked me unjustly, I decided not to fight back. Believing that God will look after the matter, I did not return their curses. But today they live amicably with me. All have love toward me. In spite of their curses, I forgive them." A college student replied, "When misunderstandings and quarrels arise among our roommates, we relate to each other with a forgiving spirit, which means that we forgive each other and live with love and cordiality." A wife said, "I forgive all the neighbors . . . I forgave my husband when he hit me. I humbled myself and resumed speaking with my husband. Also, I forgave people who had only harsh words for me since I was reminded of the words of my Lord, who told us to forgive others."

A mother-in-law distinguished forgiveness from necessary consequences: "My daughter-in-law sinned against us; she did something that brought dishonor to our family. We forgave her and sent her back to her parents." (We do not know whether this was a temporary punishment or the termination of the marriage.) The student who wants to become a pastor linked forgiveness with continued prayer for the offenders. "I forgave those people who spoke ill of our pastor. I tell them good things about pastors. I pray to God about them. I am surprised and hurt that they talk like that since they are members of my church. Two of my friends tease me a lot and speak bad words. I pray to God about them, asking God to set them straight." The offenses to be forgiven include physical and verbal abuse, and offenses against family honor and against the honor of the pastor. Eight of the ten were quite specific as to what the forgiveness entailed. Four included a happy result from their forgiveness. For example, "I have forgiven them. Now they are friendly toward me and take the initiative to talk to me."

No doubt differently worded questions would have elicited answers that showed other dimensions of these villagers' Christian beliefs. Moreover, the responses may not fairly represent the Christian community as a whole, since those who took the time and trouble to answer our questions are probably among the more articulate members of their congregations. Nevertheless, this is a remarkable collection of responses, especially from Christians whose religious practice seems to differ so much from that of many educated urban Christians.

We did not ask how the respondents reconciled their Christian practice with their continued involvement in village Hindu rituals. It is, of course, possible that most of them are part of the minority who do not engage in any Hindu rituals. If they do, however, still maintain a double religious practice, their answers show that this mixture in practice does not necessarily mean a diminution of their Christian beliefs or ethical principles.

The responses certainly indicate that at least some members of these congregations have gone far beyond simply memorizing phrases from Christian creeds or frequent pastoral exhortations. They are connecting central Christian doctrines to experiences in their own lives. All of them, including the young woman who has not yet decided to be baptized, think for themselves and think about their faith.

A more thorough study of beliefs might show the connection — or lack thereof — between what village Christians hear from their pastors, on the one hand, and their own personal faith and practice, on the other. For this present study, their statements provide a fascinating though incomplete glimpse into what it means for them, in the midst of contemporary village life, to be Christians.

Conclusion

This study was originally intended to compare the present situation of the CSI congregations with their situation fifty years ago. The comparison we have been able to make is only partial, not only because different kinds of information were collected in the two studies, but also because of differences in the way the

Distinctive Beliefs of CSI Christians

information was gathered and edited. As noted above,[18] Mr. and Mrs. Luke spent more time in some villages than we did and conversed with more people. Many conversations were condensed into the summary of distinctive beliefs that Mr. Luke wrote, however. The "we" in the present study includes not only the two authors but also our eight student assistants, one of whom gave us major assistance with the previous section of this chapter. The interviews gathering information for all parts of this book took place in Telugu; the notes were translated into English and sometimes abbreviated. They were then further edited to fit into various sections of this book. We have tried to retain the individual voices, especially in the statements of belief, to a greater degree than was possible in the 1959 study. All these factors give our presentation a different style and a different content than that in *Village Christians*.

What has remained the same and what has changed? As elsewhere in the world, Christians vary considerably in their knowledge of the Bible and their acquaintance with major Christian doctrines. Jesus was and is understood to be both divine and human, with a heavy emphasis on his divine nature. Moreover, Jesus was and is believed to be presently available to protect and help, especially but not exclusively, those who pray to him and believe in his power. Jesus sometimes appears in the dreams of both Christians and non-Christians and demonstrates that he still has the power to heal. God's forgiveness of sins is believed in and more readily understood than salvation from sin; salvation includes God's protection from misfortune and the gift of good fortune.

It is more difficult to say what has changed. We have tried to convey as closely as possible what our informants actually said, but we do not know whether they are a representative sample of their congregations. If they are, Christians in the active congregations are more familiar with central Christian doctrines than Christians in these same villages fifty years ago; they can engage in thoughtful reflection on difficult theological ideas. Our recent informants were ready to answer the questions in terms of their own life experience. Nor do they represent a single theological viewpoint. On the question about forgiveness, for example, there is considerable variety in the responses, even though all affirm the reality of God's forgiveness and the requirement that they, too, should forgive others.

We did not try to explore the relation between theological reflection and behavior. We do not know whether these Christians observe all the commandments they know how to recite, whether they take part regularly in congregational worship, or whether they are generous to neighbors in need. Nor do we know whether these particular informants share in the rituals of their Hindu

---

18. See "Beliefs Reported in the 1959 Study" in this chapter.

relatives and neighbors, or register themselves as Hindus for the census. While a much more thorough study might have provided some answers to these questions, we recognize that Christians are divided in their estimate of themselves and of other Christians. In chapter 12 we ask whether it is possible to measure a church's "life and growth" or even to count the number of Christians.

We could only catch a glimpse of the faith of a few village Christians as we listened to them putting into words and metaphors the meaning and the challenges of their faith. In the following chapter, we turn to what is the growing edge of village Christianity, which is more evident in the newer congregations. This is healing after prayer to Jesus, especially the healing of those who up until that time were outside the Christian community but who, after they were healed, decided to be baptized.

CHAPTER 10

Healing and Conversion

Multiple Meanings of "Conversion"

Christians have long used the term "conversion" to refer both to the transformation of mind and heart *(metanoia)*, which ideally is expected of every Christian, and to the movement of individuals and groups into the Christian community and, by extension, into any religious community. In the latter sense, the term was politicized in India during British colonial rule, especially when Christians were put into a separate category for provincial elections. Conversion to Christianity would enlarge the relatively small Christian community and diminish the size of the Hindu community, which for electoral purposes was treated as a single bloc. With all Muslims being treated as another electoral bloc, it became important for Hindu nationalists to represent the Hindu community as consisting of as large a majority as possible.

When Ambedkar, leader of the Mahar outcaste (later Dalit) community, threatened in 1935 to lead all outcastes out of "Hinduism" into some other religion, Hindu worries increased. If sixty million Dalits had declared that they were no longer Hindus, the whole political landscape of colonial India would have changed, just at the time when many Muslim leaders were demanding that all states in which Muslims were in a majority should become part of a separate Islamic nation-state. Eventually, just before his death, Ambedkar did lead a half million of his followers to become Buddhists, with many more to follow. Other outcaste groups, however, did not follow their example, and when an India without Pakistan became independent, a presidential order and various state laws provided inducements to Dalits to remain Hindus or even to revert to Hindu status. If many millions of those with Scheduled Caste status had declared themselves no longer Hindus, this might have had profound effects on Indian society. In any case, this did not happen. In most parts of India, Christians have focused on conversion as an individual and small-family decision stemming from some personal transformation.[1]

Apart from the political implications, there have been both practical and theoretical reasons for some Hindus to oppose the conversion of other Hindus to Christianity. Under British rule, outcastes who became Christians were sometimes able to escape lifelong serfdom and other indignities, especially if they became literate and/or moved to a different occupation in a city. Higher-caste Hindus, especially wealthy landlords, resisted such a change and challenged the idea that any Hindus could opt out of the social position into which they were born. (By one hundred years ago, Hindu leaders assumed that Dalits were Hindus, in the sense that they were part of a Hindu hierarchy of castes in which their lowly place was determined by the karmic consequences of their deeds in past lives, even though Dalits were not allowed to enter many Hindu temples.) Attempting social climbing through "conversion" was considered contrary to both cosmic and Hindu law, and many Hindu leaders denied that Christian converts had undergone a moral or spiritual transformation, especially if they were part of a group conversion.

Long before Indian independence, the Hindu reform movement, the Arya Samaj, had not only challenged conversion to Christianity on theoretical grounds but had undertaken efforts to reverse conversions that had already occurred through a ceremony of "purification" *(shuddhi)* by which Christians were readmitted to their former Hindu status.[2] To Hindu nationalists, conversion to Christianity was a betrayal of their country, understood to be a Hindu nation, in which non-Hindus were essentially second-class citizens.

---

1. On October 13, 1935, Dr. B. R. Ambedkar, leader of the Mahar outcaste community, made a stirring speech to the Bombay Presidency Depressed Classes Conference that included the words, "I will not die a Hindu." The conference responded with a resolution that they, representing all the Scheduled Castes in India, "would leave the Hindu religion and join any other religion which promised them equal treatment with others" (Webster, *The Dalit Christians*, 107). Webster comments that "the prospect of sixty million people changing their religion was stunning in its impact" (110). Near the end of his life, on the 2500th anniversary of the Buddha's enlightenment, on October 16, 1956, Ambedkar did lead several hundred thousand of his fellow Mahars into a new form of Buddhism, but only a few other Dalits joined them (162-63). Ambedkar helped to draft a constitution for independent India that outlawed "untouchability," but a "President's order" in 1950 excluded non-Hindus from being considered members of the Scheduled Castes and therefore made them ineligible for land and other benefits to Dalits. In 1956 Sikhs from Scheduled Castes were included, and in 1990 Buddhists, too, were added (137-38). Christians and Muslims from Dalit castes are still excluded.

2. Vasantha Rao, *Heads and Tales*, 17-18.

Healing and Conversion

In practice, not all Christians consider an individual conversion experience to be necessary or integral to the life of faith. They hold that a Christian community develops through a process of social and moral transformation extending over many generations, during which time a new and distinctive lifestyle and theology gradually emerge from a blending of local culture and older "foreign" Christian traditions. On the other hand, for those who themselves experience a decisive turn in their lives, sometimes at great personal cost, such a gradual and historical view of conversion leaves out what they feel is most important: that God has come into their life and changed it forever. For some Christians in the villages studied, their conversion has involved a seeing or hearing of Jesus in a dream or vision to which they must respond for the rest of their lives. What conversion means continues to be debated among Christians as well as disputed between Christians and Hindus. For the purpose of this study, we understand conversion both as a formal entry into the church and as an ongoing process of conforming one's life to the call of Christ. In this chapter we see both the individual and corporate aspects of the conversion process, as well as the variety of its forms. Since the word itself is now so controversial in India, we try to describe each change in a person's life in as specific terms as possible.

Previous Conversions in the Jangarai Section

All nine of the original congregations in the Jangarai section, the first in 1912 and the last in 1950, were established as a result of group decisions to become Christians by one or both of the Dalit castes, the Malas and the Madigas. In many cases, one individual or family took the lead in persuading the other families in a particular caste community. In Ambajipet in 1914 a young Mala man became a Christian at his Christian father-in-law's insistence. His family converted with him, and they persuaded all the other Mala families to join them. Their motivation would have included family and caste *(kulam)* solidarity; this was a time when many Malas in the area were becoming Christians. In 1920 the Madiga families in the village also became Christians and joined the congregation. In some villages, evangelists were active in the persuasion, holding out the hope of education for Dalit children and escape from compulsory labor and the tyranny of village officials.

Three other early congregations had almost disappeared by the time of the 1959 study. The congregation in Chettipalli, founded in 1917, consisted of both Malas and Madigas. The congregation in Edulapalli began in 1927, and the one in Mirzapalli was also founded in 1927. The few remaining Christians there in

173

1959 expressed their bitter disappointment that they had been so long neglected by the presbyter and the evangelists.³

The last three congregations established involved the entire Madiga community in each of these villages. They were not joined by any of the Mala families, and they continued to be single-caste congregations. As related in chapter 4, all the Madiga families in Jangarai converted in 1927 after Mr. Posnett visited the village at their request and helped to bring to justice the village police official who had unjustly arrested and beaten a man in their community. Five years later, in 1932, in Achampet, all the Madigas became Christians. They had heard from their relatives in Jangarai about the evangelists' teaching there. In 1950, in Gawallapally, Konka Yesudas returned to the village after being healed from leprosy and persuaded all the Madiga families to join him in seeking baptism.⁴

In contrast, the conversions at the time of the previous study, mostly in 1959 and 1960, were of individuals and small families, many of whom said that Lord Jesus had healed them or members of their family, very often in a miraculous way, or had blessed them with a child after they had prayed to him. Most of them were not Dalits, but they joined otherwise completely Dalit congregations.

Just before the baptismal service for two families in Ambajipet took place, another young man from the potter caste, who had also attended P. Y. Luke's evangelistic services, said that he wanted to be baptized with his friends, who were the men in those two families. After some questioning, the presbyter was convinced of his sincerity, baptized him, and gave him the name John. It was John who took to heart Luke's admonition not to take part in Hindu dramas, and that decision eventually led to the entire drama group (fifteen Hindus and three Christians), using the same music and dramatic style, to present plays on Christian themes.⁵

Recent Conversions after Healing

Our recent study suggests a strong correlation between the experience of healing and personal decision to follow Christ. In 1988-89 a lay Christian woman named Shanthamma came out from the Hebron Church in Hyderabad⁶ to preach the gospel in the village of Mirzapally. Decades before, evangelists had stopped visiting that congregation after they were threatened by a powerful

---

3. Luke and Carman, *Village Christians*, 64-65.
4. Luke and Carman, *Village Christians*, 65-69.
5. Luke and Carman, *Village Christians*, 156-57.
6. Founded by Bakht Singh, a Punjabi convert.

landowner. Without worship services, the congregation had ceased to function. By 1959, it had almost disappeared. Thirty years later it was only a dim memory. The village has the reputation of being the home of powerful magicians practicing witchcraft, and many in the village were suffering from its effects. Shanthamma is reported to have brought seventeen individuals or families to Christ, all from the Dalit castes whose ancestors had become Christians sixty years before. In at least eight families, someone suffering from a magical spell was healed after the lay evangelist's prayers. The new congregation was named the Philadelphia Church.

For some time, Shanthamma continued to visit and conduct worship, but after she stopped coming, attendance at worship dwindled, and the congregation has now divided into three groups. Eight families go to a Pentecostal church some distance away; five families have shifted their allegiance to Mrs. Deevenamma's church, which is also in another village; while the remaining five families continue to consider the Philadelphia Church their home. A layman in the congregation conducts Sunday worship.

In our recent research we have documented about seventy instances of a healing after prayer to Christ. Almost every healing led to a conversion, which we understand as coming to faith in Christ, leading to baptism into the fellowship of the Christian church. Some of the healings also led to the decision of family members or neighbors to be baptized. The number on which we could report would be much larger if we had specific details about those who have joined the larger independent churches.[7]

Of these cases, twenty-nine were reported as healing from the effects of black magic, three as the expulsion of evil spirits, and thirty-seven as healing from a variety of illnesses or successful recovery from serious accidents. The symptoms of black magic include stomach pain, paralyzed legs, "mental torture," lunatic behavior, attacking other people, and showing abnormal physical strength. Some of these symptoms are fairly close to the cases described as illnesses: "nervous weakness," crippling of limbs, cough and asthma, "wasting disease," stomach pain, ear infection, diabetes, leprosy, and cancer, as well as several unspecified "serious illnesses." These are not physicians' diagnoses but reports from the person healed, a family member, or someone else in the congregation. The common factor is that all these people ascribed their healing to prayer and Jesus' power; they therefore chose to be baptized.[8]

---

7. Tharamma of Medak is an exception since she was already a Christian when she was delivered from black magic. Her story is in chapter 6, and the account of the two women whom Yesumani brought to her from Wadiaram is in chapter 7.

8. The distinctions between types of healing are made by people who reported these events. Outside observers might see more overlap or make different distinctions.

We heard of a few cases where a healing after others had prayed did not lead to faith in Christ or where the recognition of Christ's healing power did not lead to the person being baptized and joining the Christian community. There were also about ten people who said that their prayers had been answered, but not by a healing. These prayers included a woman being blessed with a child after years of barrenness, the restoration of family harmony, financial assistance in building a house, relief from pressing debts, or a successful harvest. Such answers to prayer were more frequent after the decision to seek baptism, whereas the healings led up to that decision.

All of the five women interviewed in one independent church said that they had been or would be baptized because they or some close relative had been healed after Pastor Sanjeevi's prayers. The one younger woman among the five had gone for help after her husband was badly burned in attempting suicide. Not only did he recover after the pastor's prayers, but their financial fortunes also improved; they were no longer suffering from the evil eye. Her Hindu father rejoiced particularly at her giving birth to a healthy son, after her first baby, a girl, died soon after birth. While the proud grandfather goes to the pastor for prayers, he continues to worship the goddesses. The other women interviewed say that even the men in their families who have themselves been healed by the pastor's prayers to Christ have not become Christians. It shows an important cultural shift that a decision to become a Christian, made three generations ago by an entire caste community, should now be made, not even by whole families, but by one or two individuals within a family. We examine this change in the following section.

From Group Conversions to Individual Decisions

Since the beginning of western Christian missions in India five hundred years ago, the growth of the Christian church in India has been marked by both individual and group decisions. Individual decisions were more often made by the relatively few high-caste converts, and group decisions often took place among lower-caste converts, beginning with the fisher caste along the coast of South India. Even the group decisions depended on the initiative of certain individuals, but in many cases the outward shift to a new Christian allegiance was made at the same time by the entire caste group in a village.

The same development continued after Protestant missions in India began three hundred years ago, but there was one important difference. The theology of many early Protestant missionaries expected a personally experienced transformation in the lives of individual Christians. As the group decisions to become Christians increased in the latter half of the nineteenth century, it became more difficult for western missionaries to find signs of a genuine individual conversion. In the Hyderabad Methodist Mission, those baptized as adults were listed as being "on trial" until they progressed to the point where they could be confirmed and become full church members.

In many churches, including the Hyderabad Methodist Mission and its successor, the Medak Diocese, the proportion of adult Christians who remain "on trial" for their whole lives has slowly fallen during the past one hundred years, but in these village congregations fifty years ago, it was more than 50 percent. Throughout the Telugu-speaking area, Protestant Christians have very often become Christians in a group decision that involved all (or at least a significant fraction) of their caste group in a particular village. That sense of group identity continued, though sometimes weakened, when Christians moved to the cities, especially if they had been educated in Christian schools.

By the time of the first study, the last group conversion was ten years in the past, and all the conversions to Christianity occurring during the 1959 study were based on individual decisions.[9] Some converts said that they had experienced the healing power of Lord Jesus, while others were convinced by P. Y. Luke's preaching and evangelistic concern. What may be surprising is that in 1959 there were a small number of converts from other castes who were willing to become part of a previously all-Dalit congregation meeting in the Dalit section of the village.

Now, fifty years later, what may have been new trends in 1959 are widespread realities. Healing after prayer is the clearest and most frequent reason for seeking Christian baptism. In many of the newer congregations, the majority of new converts are from non-Dalit castes. Many of these new Christians, therefore, are not joining a previously Dalit congregation, and since they are not Dalits, the issue of forgoing special benefits for Dalits does not arise. They are from many different caste groups, with the largest number from the Mudhiraj, a landowning agricultural caste.

The newer congregations are made up of individuals and families from different castes who affirm their separate caste identities. In their worship and their communal meals, however, they celebrate their unity in the Holy Spirit as new followers of Christ. In some cases their conversion has brought persecution or ostracism from other members of their caste, but the opposition seems less than fifty years ago. Several Hindu spouses have defended the new religious practice of their Christian partners.

---

9. The joint decision of three related families in Mallupally would have been an exception, but that decision was later reversed and the family solidarity broken. See the description of those events later in this chapter.

There is both a modern and a traditional reason for this greater tolerance of diverse religious practices. The modern reason may be more obvious: the influence of modern urban culture, which allows greater deviation from the traditional group norm, although not complete individualism. The traditional reason is Hindu willingness to allow individuals and families to worship their own favorite deity as long as this worship does not prevent observance of obligatory practice for that caste. Sometimes belonging to a different sectarian or devotional community will be tolerated within the same caste, though major devotional communities tend to develop their own subcastes. If a multi-caste Christian church is accepted as a devotional community that does not threaten the caste structure, it may fit into village society. How great a price must be paid for such acceptance deserves further consideration.

Hindu Efforts to "Reconvert" Christians

The nineteenth-century Hindu reformer Dayanand Sarasvati founded the Arya Samaj in 1875. Near the end of his life (1885), he introduced a ritual of reconversion. He adapted the old ceremony of *shuddhi* ("purification") that had been used to remove the defilement of high-caste ("twice-born") Hindus who had committed some serious breach of moral and religious law *(dharma)* so that they could be reintegrated into their caste community. After 1900, however, this ritual was used to reconvert to the Hindu community thousands belonging to Dalit castes in the Punjab who had become Muslims, Sikhs, or Christians.[10] Since part of the ceremony was donning the sacred thread normally worn only by high-caste men, some traditional Brahmin leaders (the Sanatanists) objected, but the more radical Arya Samaj reformers were happy to ignore caste distinctions, which they considered a degeneration after the Hindu "Golden Age." At times, when Hindu leaders saw Hindu membership shrinking in the census, they accepted the reconversion ceremony. At other times, they objected to any suggestion that lower castes could be elevated to higher-caste status by a ritual purification.[11] The growing Hindu nationalist organization tried to counter Christian missions by establishing their own orphanages, schools, student hostels, and dispensaries, especially among tribal peoples. They also tried to have new laws passed placing restrictions on conversions.[12] This did not succeed at the national level, but the states in central India with large tribal minorities

---

10. Jaffrelot, *Religion, Caste, and Politics*, 56-57.
11. Jaffrelot, *Religion, Caste, and Politics*, 150-55.
12. Jaffrelot, *Religion, Caste, and Politics*, 160-61.

Healing and Conversion

(Odisha and Madhya Pradesh)[13] do have such laws. At the same time, Hindu nationalists promoted a significant ritual of reconversion that emphasized the converts rejoining the "Hindu nation."[14]

By 1959 in this area, there had been only a few attempts to convince Christians on ideological grounds to abandon their new religion and to be formally readmitted to the Hindu community by a ceremony of "purification" *(shuddhi)*.[15] There were, however, sporadic acts of violence against Christians, including the burning of Sadhu Joseph's tent near Medak.[16] There were more frequent instances of ostracism ("denying fire and water"), one of which was the threat made to Yohan in Mallupally.[17] A much more effective Hindu strategy was the denial of land and education benefits to Dalit Christians who applied for these benefits (or registered for the census) using their Christian names. Since most of these Christians also had Hindu names by which they were generally known in the village, it was a small step to using those Hindu names to secure benefits to which they felt morally entitled. In 1959 it was surprising how few had taken that step.

In Andhra Pradesh, the number of Christians recorded by the census has decreased, decade by decade. It would therefore appear that many thousands from Christian families have registered with their Hindu names. We do not know how many of them still take part in Christian worship or profess their faith in Christ. In some places, this government policy may have weakened the sense of Christian identity and increased the scorn with which some "higher-caste" Hindus regard Dalit Christians. The improvement in education for all villagers and the increased opportunity for more remunerative and dignified employment, however, have improved the social status of Christians, though more in some villages than in others. It remains a cruel irony that Christians who are still regarded by so many Hindus in the village as "unclean" should have to admit that they still belong to the lowest level of Hindu society in order to secure the benefits that are supposed to improve their economic position. Government rules, moreover, encourage them to give their names in such a way as to deny that they are Christians. The government will help them if they keep their place, but for many government officials and many of their village Hindu neighbors, that place is at the bottom![18]

13. Jaffrelot, *Religion, Caste, and Politics*, 168.
14. Jaffrelot, *Religion, Caste, and Politics*, 163.
15. Luke and Carman, *Village Christians*, 205-7.
16. Luke and Carman, *Village Christians*, 163.
17. Luke and Carman, *Village Christians*, 161.
18. In his collection of articles published in *Heads and Tales*, Vasantha Rao has described one failed effort in 1987 to force Christians to undergo a *shuddhi* ceremony in another pastorate

Greater Hindu Tolerance of a Christian Minority

Since Indian independence in 1947, government policy and the activities of Hindu nationalists have discouraged conversion to Christianity and even sought to reverse the flow. At the same time, however, in the villages studied, there have been some gradual changes in the attitudes of Hindus to Christians. A greater tolerance can be seen both among so-called higher-caste Hindus and among fellow caste members and relatives of those who have become Christians. To some extent, this development is encouraged by such government policies as the constitutional guarantee of religious freedom and the official outlawing of "untouchability." There are also the many factors described in chapter 2 that have increased the influence of a more urban culture.

Among educated Hindus, there is considerable respect for Jesus as a religious teacher and for the moral teachings that many Hindus have learned in Christian schools. Among village Hindus in this region, Jesus is recognized as a deity with great healing powers. While the attitude toward Christians may be less positive, there is some recognition of improvement in the character and lifestyle of Dalits who have become Christians. Even in these villages, moreover, it is widely recognized that Dalits, whether Hindu or Christian, should no longer be treated as serfs of the wealthy landowners or as despised village servants.

Another reason for greater tolerance was noted above. While caste affiliation is considered permanent by traditional Hindus, they have long recognized that individuals or families may become devotees of a different deity than the god or goddess worshiped by the rest of the family or caste group and thereby gain a different sectarian affiliation. While in practice this traditional toleration has been somewhat limited, it now may be strengthened by a modern acceptance of religious freedom.

There is quite a range in the way Hindu relatives relate to Christians. We are unlikely to hear of those cases where an interest in learning more about the Christian faith has been completely thwarted by relatives, in-laws, or caste leaders. Since our information has been gathered within the Christian community, we have learned much more about cases where a Christian connection has been tolerated, supported, or defended by Hindu husbands or in-laws.

In one case, however, a Christian wife was forced by her Hindu mother-in-law to stop her Christian worship and to participate in Hindu rituals, including wearing the auspicious mark on the forehead, drinking toddy, and worshiping Hindu gods and goddesses. We learned this because the wife returned with her

---

of the Medak Diocese (17-19). He has also described some instances of the persecution of Dalit Christians elsewhere in Andhra Pradesh (44-55, 74-79).

Hindu husband to live in her parents' village. When she attended worship in the Christian congregation in which she had grown up, the pastor invited her to pray. She then cried out that she was not worthy to do anything before God because she was contaminated by the mark on her forehead, by drinking toddy, and by other actions that she considered even worse. She had grown up with Christian parents and was then married to a Hindu. In all these interreligious marriages, it is assumed that the wife will adopt her husband's religion and often will live with his family. Her mother-in-law's conduct was therefore according to the village norm. Presumably in most cases, Christian wives in Hindu homes have accepted the situation or swallowed their protests, but we simply do not know how they have felt about this. We would not know in this case either, except that the woman returned to her parents' church. By the same norm, Hindu girls marrying Christians are expected to accept their husbands' religion, but this, too, is not as automatic as the norm would imply.

Most of our accounts are from Christians who are attending Christian worship with the consent, whether grudging or positive, of their Hindu spouses. In six cases it is the wife who is a Christian, which often means that she is living with her Hindu in-laws. Only in one case is the husband unhappy with his wife's Christian activities. Another Hindu husband encourages his Christian wife to dress in her good clothes and go with their daughter to church. Two Hindu husbands give similar reasons for not becoming Christians themselves. They do not want to give up drinking, smoking, and eating meat sacrificed to the village goddesses, and they feel that those habits are incompatible with their being Christians. Another husband stopped beating his wife after her anguished prayers to Christ, but he continues his smoking and drinking. In one case, the in-law family, in whose home the Christian woman lives, no longer forces her to eat sacrificed meat or engage in other Hindu rituals.

Another Hindu husband "likes Jesus Christ," but thinks that his drinking toddy in the evening after a hard day's work is not compatible with following Jesus Christ. His whole family saw how his wife was suffering and witnessed her healing after she went to church and prayed to Jesus. Now he takes her to church (in another village) on his bicycle. There is a similar case with a woman whose husband deserted her. She went back to live with her Hindu parents, who believe that Jesus healed her and who do not object to her new way of life. Another Hindu family had a daughter suffering from polio. She was partially healed after prayer for her in a Christian worship service. The family encourages her to go to church, but it gives similar reasons for not believing in Christ: needing to drink after working in the field all day and not being able to turn down food and drink offered to them by their employers, which they know has been consecrated to Hindu deities. The wife whispered, "Someday we will accept Christ."

In three cases where the husband has become a Christian after healing through the power of Christ, the wife and children have remained Hindus. In one case, the son attends church but is not baptized. The wife does not want to give up wearing the traditional mark on her forehead or carrying the sacred pots in procession during Hindu festivals.

All these religiously divided families indicate a significant change in village attitudes toward religious identity. One hundred years ago, the entire group of families belonging to the same caste group in a particular village would follow the same customs and religious practices. When village caste communities among the Malas and Madigas considered becoming Christians, all the families would convert together, or they would not convert at all. By fifty years ago, it was more common to have a division within the same caste community in a village, but each family would be either Hindu or Christian in its formal identity. Now, especially in the newer congregations, there are many cases where a few families from a particular caste group become Christians, while others do not. Moreover, there are many cases where only one person in a family becomes a Christian.

Within a single family or among larger groups of relatives, religious divisions may cause difficulties on ceremonial occasions, when group solidarity is much prized. If Christians refuse to eat or drink what has been consecrated to Hindu deities, this seems to many village Hindus a shocking breach of etiquette at a time when personal differences are expected to be resolved and the unity of the group affirmed. Many in the older CSI congregations have continued to share in Hindu family feasts, even if that is contrary to their pastor's teaching. More recent members of the newer congregations often take more seriously the biblical and ancient Christian admonitions against sharing in food and drink that has been offered to other gods. They, too, however, have much to gain in maintaining family ties and keeping cordial relations with relatives and neighbors. Every family has to work out some solution. We can report on the few cases about which we have learned.

In Sooraram there are twelve families, all belonging to the Madiga caste, who a few years ago became Christians through the evangelistic efforts of Pastor J. Paul, an independent Baptist. Following his teaching, they celebrate only Christian festivals. Although they do not join in Hindu festivals, they do prepare special treats for their children when those festivals are going on. When they severed their connection with everything related to their former worship of Hindu deities, Hindus complained that the Christians were distancing themselves from village customs and were failing to make their expected contribution. At present, however, Christians in the village say that they are free to express their faith in Jesus Christ.

As related in chapter 7, two women from the fisher caste joined the CSI congregation in Wadiaram twenty years ago after being healed from witchcraft.

One of them now entertains all her Hindu relatives at Christmastime. She and her family attend the celebrations of her Hindu relatives, who are careful to prepare food for their Christian guests that has not been consecrated to Hindu deities. At weddings, the Christians take part in the celebration and share food with all the other guests.

A woman in a Mala family in Wadiaram relates how she and her sister were ostracized by their caste neighbors when they were baptized forty years ago. Their water tap was disconnected, and they were ridiculed when they went to the community well to draw water. The community did not invite them to Mala caste celebrations, but this actually kept them from the awkward position of having to attend ceremonies where Hindu deities were worshiped. The older sister still does not attend any of the Mala community meetings, but when she arranges a prayer meeting at home, she also invites her Hindu neighbors.

A woman from the washerman caste reports that when her husband died twenty years ago, only two years after they had both been healed from the effects of witchcraft and were baptized, none of her Hindu caste relatives came to the funeral. Now, however, all the relatives come to meetings and celebrations at her house and eat the food. These celebrations follow Christian custom. She goes to the celebrations of her Hindu relatives but does not eat the food because it has been sacrificed to gods and goddesses whom she has rejected.

A mainstay of the Ambajipet congregation, Kummari Dass, who is from the potter caste,[19] says that his family has constant interaction with his Hindu relatives. The families visit each other for weddings and all the other lifecycle ceremonies. His family does not eat the meals prepared by Hindu relatives, however, because the cooking pots have been marked with Hindu sacred spots. Some Hindu relatives have gone to the trouble of cooking special dishes for his family, and some have completely discontinued the consecration of their cooking vessels, thereby making all the food they serve religiously "neutral." These relatives do not want to lose the connection with his family, so they have taken the further step of asking him to pray over the cooked dishes, thus blessing them before they are served to guests. The Hindu relatives have in effect replaced a Hindu consecration of the festival meals with a Christian one.

There are undoubtedly many other adjustments and compromises taking place. One custom, now widespread, concerns the wedding feast. When guests are invited from other castes or religious communities, the hosts arrange for the sheep or goats to be slaughtered by a Muslim butcher according to *halal* rules. The meat served is then considered acceptable to all the guests. What is a Muslim practice therefore now enables Hindus and Christians of different

19. See chapter 5.

castes to eat together. In a time of militant Hindu efforts to weaken the Christian presence in India, many families in the vast Hindu majority are showing greater tolerance of the small Christian minority. They are going to some lengths to keep their social connection with Christian relatives or neighbors by accommodating their hospitality to Christian beliefs and practices.

The Legacy of Yohan

In the summer of 1959 a recent convert, Yohan, came to the congregation in Gawallapally for help. He and his wife, Muttavva, were the only Christians in Mallupally, a mile and a half away. A few years before, he had been taught to read, with the Gospels as his textbook, and he became interested in learning more about Jesus. After several years of occasional visits to Christian churches, he and his wife were baptized. Two years after that, he faced a severe test of his new faith when the village officials started collecting funds from each caste community to renovate the shrine of the village goddess Poshamma. Yohan was one of four brothers assigned a share of the assessment on the Madiga community. When Yohan refused to pay his share, his brothers denied his family fire from their hearths and water from the communal well. Later, his brothers gave him an ultimatum: worship our goddess and give up your new god Jesus Christ, or leave the village at once. It was at that point that Yohan sought the help of his fellow Christians. He happened to come during the week that the Lukes were staying in Gawallapally, and Luke was able to arrange a meeting between some Christians, both pastors and local laymen, and Yohan's brothers and caste associates. The delegation from Mallupally felt that they had been patient for two years with Yohan's worship of a foreign god. They were asking him only to fulfill a common village obligation that they knew Christians in many other villages accepted. They were concerned that if he did not contribute, their goddess might vent her anger, not only on them but on the entire village.

Luke then asked whether group solidarity should not work both ways. If Yohan contributed to repairing the shrine, would they help him build a Christian prayer hall? This question threw the delegation from Mallupally into confusion. After withdrawing for some time to discuss the matter among themselves, they returned with a surprising announcement: "Since we cannot persuade Yohan to fulfill his obligation to Poshamma, we will all have to become Christians!"

The first two weeks of the five months before the baptisms were filled with intensive instruction by the presbyter and several evangelists, but after that, they made very few visits. During this time, some Hindu leaders in nearby villages threatened to burn the homes of Yohan and his brothers or to see that they

Healing and Conversion

did not get title to the fields they had been cultivating. Three years later, after these Madiga families finally succeeded in registering their lands, a baptismal service took place, but only one of the other three brothers and his family were baptized. (That brother was given the name Paul.) The other families remained Hindus. This was clearly an unfinished story in *Village Christians*.[20]

In the years since, the little Christian community has not grown. Yohan's adopted son never became a Christian, and most of his brother Paul's family went back to their village religion. Only one son, Manikyam, Yohan's nephew, has continued to think of himself as a Christian for fifty years, without being part of any Christian congregation and without any personal experience of healing or other divine intervention. When we met him, he was delighted to see us and told us that he still has a Christian hymnal and an old Bible. Although unable to bring up his own children as Christians, he said that he himself firmly believes in Jesus Christ. He sings the old hymns by heart and can narrate the family history of growing up as a Christian. Two of his sons married Hindu women and now live in the city of Nizamabad. The third son, though raised as a Hindu, married a Christian girl in Wadiaram who attended Pastor Babu's church. When this son got sick, he went to that church, was healed after prayer by the pastor, and was baptized. He and his family now live with his father. Manikyam also has three daughters, all of whom married Hindu men. One remains a Hindu; the second returned to live with her father and her brother's family after her husband died. The third daughter became an outspoken Christian, despite persecution by her Hindu in-laws, after she was healed in another independent church of a serious illness. She now travels alone to worship in Babu's church.

This complicated family history shows a moving back and forth between primary affiliation to either Hindu or Christian rituals and communities. The main "cause" of Christian conversion of those in the present generation is healing through prayer to Christ, often in an independent church. The official pastors in both CSI and independent churches are men, but women constitute the majority of worshipers, and women who are converted sometimes become bold witnesses for their Christian faith. They are also sometimes agents of healing through their own prayers or by bringing the sick person to someone whose prayers to Christ, they believe, will be more powerful than theirs.

Yohan's story starts with a single Christian couple testing the limits of group solidarity and continues with CSI pastors failing to seize the opportunity to build a new Christian community. The small Christian family remaining reflects a new religious landscape with more individual choice. Traditional loyalties are still strong, but some children reestablish lost Christian ties, while others respect

---

20. Luke and Carman, *Village Christians*, 158-64.

the faith of those made bold by the healing power of Jesus. Three of Manikyam's six children and some of their children are now Christians; it is now easier for them to travel to churches at some distance. They have thus far not found a home in any CSI congregation; some attend an independent church several miles away. Manikyam's family is the legacy of Yohan and his wife, who dared to affirm an exclusive loyalty to Jesus.

Conversion as a Call to Ministry

Healing in response to prayer has been the most evident motivation in the more recent decisions of individuals and families to become Christians. Many who have preached the gospel and prayed for the sick are not themselves converts from Hindu families. They grew up in Christian families and have for various reasons decided to become pastors or lay evangelists. Others who were convinced to become Christians experienced a call to ministry. We first note those who were already Christians and received a dramatic call to a ministry that often included both preaching and prayers for healing.

In the case of Sadhu Joseph, more than fifty years ago, and that of Tharamma of Medak, more than twenty years ago, their calls accompanied their own miraculous healings. For Pastor Babu in Wadiaram, the call came in a voice heard while standing on a rooftop. None of these people describe a deeper sense of sin from which they needed to be redeemed. Nevertheless, they all felt a change in the direction of their lives, leading to a life of full-time ministry. It is this kind of call, often experienced dramatically in a dream or vision, or a personal experience of healing, that might be called "vocational conversion." This is a life-changing experience of a kind with many precedents in both Christian and Hindu traditions. It may come at a pivotal point in a long ascetic journey or in some quite unexpected divine intervention, often but not always during a crisis in a person's life. It is not always a single occurrence: Deevenamma has had many visions, and Tharamma of Medak has had what she considers four miraculous healings.

During the present study, we learned of a few cases in which Hindus were not only converted to Christianity but also called to a gospel ministry. In the case of Satyanandam, now in Achampet, both his own conversion and his call to ministry came after his wife's healing. One man who recovered from a serious illness after three weeks of Mrs. Deevenamma's prayers was baptized and soon thereafter had a vision of Jesus directing him to become a preacher. Another independent pastor, Nathaniel, grew up as a Hindu and, as noted earlier, was converted after visits to the Medak cathedral and to Tharamma's healing services and later felt called to the ministry. Other examples have already been given.

Healing and Conversion

A dramatic case of conversion leading to a call to ministry took place in another part of the diocese at the end of the 1959 study. A young Hindu named Venkateswara belonging to the washerman caste had a dream in which the god Krishna instructed him to accept the next offer of marriage that arrived in the mail. When the letter arrived, he found to his surprise that it was from a farmer belonging to the same caste who had become a Christian after a healing vision of Jesus. The farmer did offer his daughter in marriage, provided that the young man would first become a Christian. Although Venkateswara had had no previous connection with Christians or interest in their religion, he accepted the proposal because he had received a divine command. Later, after instruction by his future father-in-law, baptism, and marriage, he decided that the god who spoke to him in a dream was not Krishna but Christ. He was given the baptismal name of Christopher Dayanand. At the time he was interviewed in 1960, he was starting a ministerial course in Medak in order to become an evangelist. Before that course began, in explaining his decision to his Hindu friends, he had already worked out his own distinctive combination of Hindu and Christian theology.[21]

That was the end of the story in *Village Christians,* but Christopher Dayanand went on to become a respected presbyter in the Medak Diocese. For several years he was the chairperson of the Godavari District Council. He was a good pastor and an inspiring preacher. He was often invited to preach at the revival meetings of independent churches. Throughout his life he maintained a prayer group with two other presbyters who were his classmates as theological students.[22] The trio prayed for revival in the Medak Diocese and appealed for a deeper commitment to Christ. He maintained a good relationship with his Hindu relatives. His mother and sister became Christians, as did his brother at the end of his life. Christopher Dayanand was still serving as a presbyter at the time of his accidental death from electric shock at the age of fifty-five. His son, the Rev. A. C. Solomon Raj, is now the vice chairman of the Medak Diocese, the leading presbyter assisting the bishop.

Although this life story is unique, it reminds us that visions of Christ in Telangana villages occur in a culture in which a few people do have dreams in which they see a divine figure or receive a specific divine command. Both Hindus and Christians now sometimes have dreams in which they see Jesus, feel his healing touch, or hear his instructions for their lives. Not all Hindus who have such experiences are baptized, but they may consider themselves henceforth devotees of Jesus. A few of those who are then baptized are called, like Christopher Dayanand, to a ministry of preaching and prayer.

---

21. Luke and Carman, *Village Christians,* 182-83.
22. The two other presbyters were the late Rev. K. C. Martin and the Rev. C. Robert Nathaniel.

Conclusion

Conversion has become a contested term in modern India because it signifies a transition from traditional Hindu society to a Christian community, a shift promoted by Christian evangelists but opposed by many Hindu leaders as morally deceitful, politically disruptive, or metaphysically impossible. For Christians, conversion has meant a spiritual transformation, but they have differed among themselves as to what changes in behavior should be expected of Christians and to what extent they should still participate in the traditional caste system.

While the term "conversion" may not be part of their vocabulary, village Christians know the importance of their own social location and their own experience of the power of Christ. Some belong to Dalit congregations that have been part of the British Methodist Mission and then the Church of South India for three or four generations. Others grew up as Hindus and were baptized after being convinced of the power of Christ, most often by the answer to a prayer for healing. In a few cases, Jesus has appeared in a dream or vision, bringing instant healing by his word or touch.

It is not surprising that such dramatic conversions are more common among those who are just joining the Christian community. When those who have grown up as Christians have a life-changing experience, it is often understood as Christ's call to a ministry of preaching and healing. In every generation, there is also a large group that joins the older congregations: the Hindu brides of half the young men. Without a personal experience of Christ's power or much instruction before baptism, they are likely to continue much of the traditional practice and belief in which they grew up. The presence of minimally converted wives may not yet be a problem for the independent churches and the new CSI congregations, which have so many first-generation converts and which try to find Christian marriage partners for their children.

The many recent healings after prayer to Christ are reminiscent of the healings of Jesus recounted in the Gospels. They also have many precedents in miracle stories in various Hindu traditions as well as in villagers' belief that divine powers can bestow blessings of health and wealth, sometimes after prayer and sacrifice and sometimes out of apparently arbitrary divine favor. Both the Christian and the Hindu backgrounds of the present confidence in Jesus the healer affect the questions we raise in the two concluding chapters. Some questions are addressed to the older CSI congregations that were the original focus of this study, while other questions face the reality of Christians divided among many denominations. Some of the questions in the final chapters may also be pondered by Christians in other situations, in India and throughout the world.

CHAPTER 11

Challenges Facing the CSI Congregations

Introduction

This study is an attempt to find out what has happened to the CSI village congregations since they were studied fifty years ago. After beginning the new study in 2008, it quickly became apparent that the new churches in the same or nearby villages that had been started in the past twenty-five years could not be ignored. In fact, an attempt to understand the new churches (most of them independent but a few now also part of the Medak Diocese and its Wadiaram pastorate) became necessary.

Summing up this investigation has led, not to several well-documented conclusions, but to a number of questions about challenges inherent in the present situation of the churches. Christians are responding to the challenges in various ways and giving different answers to the questions they face. Challenges addressed in this chapter relate especially to CSI congregations; challenges found in the chapter that follows take up issues that also concern independent churches. The same or similar challenges also confront Christians in many other places, wherever Christians are divided into different denominations, both in India and around the world. These challenges raise questions that are not merely rhetorical, with obvious answers, but questions that have already received and will continue to receive a variety of answers.

How Christians Relate to Their Religious Environment

That every Christian community is affected by its religious and cultural environment has long been understood. The forms of Christian belief and practice introduced into a culture have been shaped by previous cultures into which Christians have injected distinctively new styles of living and thinking. Some forms of Christianity represent a comprehensive synthesis of Christian faith with a local culture. In other situations, Christians have made partitions between what they consider Christian and other parts of their lives. Western Christianity has often recognized the secondary authority of both Greek philosophy and Roman law, as well as of classical Greco-Roman art. It is no accident that the pillars in front of western libraries and law courts often resemble the façade of Greek and Roman temples.

Since relations between the Christian message and the culture in which it is proclaimed are inevitable, this message has to be presented in an understandable language. When the Christian community is a minority in a nation with a dominant religious culture, as in India, its relations with that culture have to be expressed in ways in which Christians think about themselves and in ways that others think about them. In India, where the dominant culture is "Hindu," Christians are divided, along with other Indians, as to whether that Hindu culture, either as a whole or in some of its variations, is a religion competing with their faith or a national culture to which all Indians belong and to which they owe a patriotic allegiance. Many village Christians do not see these different views of Hindu culture as exclusive alternatives but as extremes between which they must negotiate in practical ways. Such negotiation not only occurs in village politics but also in preparing food for every family gathering that includes both Christians and Hindus. In the larger Telangana villages, there is often also a small minority of Muslims, who look back to centuries of Muslim rule and to an urban Islamic culture. Some elements of that culture still remain. As noted in chapter 10, in present compromises for some wedding feasts, both Hindu and Christian guests eat meat prepared according to Islamic *halal* rules.

While some Christian communities have stressed their differences from surrounding religious cultures, leaders of the Methodist Mission, and now of the Medak Diocese, have been quite aware of the need to utilize Indian cultural and religious forms to express Christian life. The need has been all the greater because many village Christians have been living within a hybrid religious environment, observing both Christian and Hindu rituals on separate occasions.

Both the 1959 study and the present research show that there is considerable variety in the type and extent of participation by local Christians in village rituals. Different kinds of ritual and belief are expressed in a variety of Hindu traditions, some of which may be more compatible than others with Christian faith and practice. Many church leaders find animal sacrifices to village goddesses most objectionable. It appears that this kind of ritual is one in which many Christians no longer participate. Yet they still must decide whether, when attending festival meals in homes of relatives, they should eat the meat that has been consecrated by such sacrifices. This issue has arisen for Christians in many cultures, beginning with the earliest Christian church in Corinth, to whose members the apostle Paul offered cautious and nuanced advice.[1] It appears that now both the Christian and non-Christian branches of extended families are trying to find acceptable compromises.[2]

During the past fifty years, there may well have been fewer animal sacrifices to the village goddesses. In part this is because of the opposition of urban Hindu groups to such sacrifices, but it may also be because the goddesses are no longer so much feared. The epidemic diseases that they were believed to have caused have been diminished or even eliminated by public health measures and modern medicine. In some villages, however, the lessening of this fear has been matched by the increasing fear of black magic. There is fear of the jealousy or ill will of the neighbors who might pay a magician to wreak some harm, as well as fear of the black magicians' power to cause illness or even death. Neither more widespread education nor the ending of epidemics has lessened the belief in magical powers that seem to many villagers stronger than traditional remedies or modern medicine, stronger even than the local goddesses. Christ's power to undo the ruinous effects of magical spells is therefore central to the faith of village Christians. This does not mean, however, that they feel it necessary to abandon all their traditional rituals.

Many Christians have continued to observe ceremonies marking special times, both in the yearly calendar and in the course of a human life. The CSI leadership has tried to provide alternative ceremonies, so far, in these village congregations, with limited success. Christian wedding rituals are becoming more popular, and women like to take part in the lighting of a cross, which is central to the Christian alternative to the Hindu festival of lamps *(Dipavali)*. This substitute may turn out to be an addition; villagers like to celebrate festivals of all kinds. As in other parts of the world, Christmas is also celebrated by many outside the Christian community.

Village Christians also share another important dimension of many Hindu traditions: *bhakti,* a devotion that is often expressed as a strong emotional connection with a particular deity. Some past observers have doubted whether such devotion is even present in Telangana villages.[3] Even fifty years ago such an

---

1. 1 Corinthians 8:1-13.
2. See chapter 10.
3. See the discussion of Dube's opinion in the final section of chapter 4.

assessment may have failed to recognize the important expressions of *bhakti* among village Hindus. Certainly in more recent years, with the closer connection of small villages to regional shrines and urban temples, Hindus of all castes have more opportunities to worship in this spirit.

The pan-Indian deities presiding over the major Hindu festivals give villagers access to the more benevolent side of the gods and goddesses. Deities who grant favors to their worshipers may be even more evident at the times when villagers travel to regional pilgrimage sites[4] or to major temples where worshipers can gain a rewarding view *(darshan)* of the great central image of the temple's chief deity. It is often in such settings that members of caste groups who are excluded from such worship in their own villages have the opportunity to worship the benevolent forms of the gods and goddesses. Those who engage in such worship may consider themselves to be maintaining a loving relationship with the deity they have chosen. Unlike persons in an ecstatic state of possession by a goddess, devotees of a particular deity remain fully conscious. They themselves can feel deeply and can share their experiences with others (often in song). They may also describe a blissful moment of union with their deity or bemoan a painful period of separation.

The outward acts in such devotional worship may look like the standard ritual, but rather than fulfilling a vow or requesting a favor, the devotee's outward worship may be the physical sign of a spiritual offering. While some devotional worship may appear to be simply an exchange of gifts and favors, all the worshipers are familiar with the stories of the saints who have passed beyond such exchange to a yearning for the divine presence and a joy in moments of close communion. For some Hindus, *bhakti* can become a continuing sense of divine protection, sometimes with a commitment to stop asking for material blessings, as one relies totally on the merciful care of one's protector and savior.

For many Christians in both cities and villages, the devotional stance associated with *bhakti* is not a part of another religion but the genuine piety of all true worship, combining both deep respect and tender feelings toward their Lord. Thus, this devotional stance is often considered the natural and expected way for Christians to relate to God. The range of attitudes extends from prayers for material blessings to a confident reliance on God's loving care, regardless of material circumstances. The outward expression of *bhakti* is often in song. Both the *Telugu Christian Hymnal* and more recently composed lyrics express the traditions of *bhakti*.[5]

---

4. See chapter 8.
5. See the final section of chapter 4.

Challenges Facing the CSI Congregations

Baptism and Church Membership

For Christians in the Medak Diocese, baptism has been the ceremony marking their entry into the Christian community. When a new congregation was established with an entire caste group in a village, all were baptized in the same service. Later baptisms were of two kinds. All the children born into Christian families were expected to be baptized as infants, while Hindu women marrying men in the congregation were supposed to be baptized only after several months of instruction, normally preceding the wedding.

As in many Protestant mission areas around the world, it was assumed that baptism began the initial or "infant" stage in the Christian life, whether those baptized were infants, small children, or adults. A higher stage of spiritual maturity was required before confirmation and admission to the Lord's Supper. In the statistics of the Medak Diocese, continuing earlier Methodist Mission practice, baptized adults (over age fourteen) who were not yet full communicant members were listed in the church records as being "on trial." Church leaders believed that the proportion of those in this category would diminish as both children and adults in the new congregations learned more about the Christian faith and personally experienced God's grace in Christ. There was indeed much progress from the low point of 16.1 percent of adult communicants in the Hyderabad Methodist Mission in 1930 to 33.8 percent in the Medak Diocese in 1958-59, but this gradual increase did not solve the problems behind the statistics. The average proportion of adult communicants in all nine congregations studied in 1959 was also one-third.

Since only communicant members may take part in the Lord's Supper and conduct the church's governance, two-thirds of the baptized adults were excluded from both. When asked in 1959 what the difference was between the two groups of adult Christians, evangelists explained with a metaphor: "Members on trial are like people sitting on the veranda, but full communicant members are like those who have entered the house."[6] Evangelists said that they would select for confirmation those "who regularly come for prayers and give collections."[7] They might also "look for such signs of progress in Christian living as not drinking toddy, not worshipping idols, not celebrating Hindu festivals, and having marriages solemnized by Christian rites."[8] Then there was the practical qualification: those selected would need to be able to memorize the answers to the questions they would be asked in the confirmation service.

---

6. Luke and Carman, *Village Christians,* 209.
7. Luke and Carman, *Village Christians,* 209.
8. Luke and Carman, *Village Christians,* 209.

The lay members of the congregation generally did not understand why there should be a distinction between two kinds of Christians, and sometimes they did not remember whether or not they themselves were communicants. The evangelist would have to prompt those who were confirmed as full members to go forward to receive the communion elements. With respect to church governance, the evangelist would either himself choose the representatives to the pastorate committee or hold an election in which no distinction was made between communicants and non-communicants.

The original rationale for this distinction was that most of the people coming together as a group for baptism were not making a full personal decision since the decision was effectively made by a few leaders. The same may be true of most of the Hindu women who join the congregation by baptism because they are marrying Christian men. Most members of these congregations were either the children or grandchildren of the first converts, or they were the Hindu brides joining the congregation. Only a few couples had had a Christian wedding, which requires both partners to have been baptized. Thus, the baptism of the non-Christian partner often took place months or years later.

The rules of the Church of South India permit combining baptism and confirmation in a single ritual, in the case of adult converts, but this rarely happens in these CSI congregations. At present, the old distinction persists, with the majority of CSI adults remaining "on trial" for their entire lives. Now another distinction poses what may be a more pressing problem. What happens to these village congregations when the members of Christian families are not even baptized? There was some indication in 1959 that this might become a problem, for many girls in Christian families were not baptized, lest that make it more difficult for them to be married into a non-Christian family. Since then the number of unbaptized children, boys as well as girls, has increased in the older CSI congregations. One reason is that the baptismal record might reveal to government authorities that the parents are Christians. If the parents had registered as "Scheduled Caste" Hindus in order to be eligible for benefits available to Dalits, this could be an awkward disclosure. Since this is such a sensitive subject, we did not even attempt to find out how many children in Christian families had not been baptized. In the pastorate headquarters, the church roll is no longer kept.

Members of the older CSI congregations are almost all Dalits, either Madigas or Malas. They have to decide whether to run the risk of losing benefits for themselves and their children by bringing their children for baptism. Those attending the newer independent churches may attend without joining; many do take the risks of baptism, which are different for Dalits than for others. The Pentecostal and independent Baptist converts who are adults usually become full communicant members when they are baptized. Whether they bring their young children for baptism depends on the polity of their particular church. In any case, they are more inclined than those in the older CSI congregations to seek a marriage alliance with a Christian family in another village, provided that family belongs to the same caste.

There is another category of the unbaptized: Hindu followers of Jesus who testify that they were healed by the power of Jesus, but who hesitate to make an open break with their relatives by being baptized. Those in other castes may not want to join officially what many villagers call "the religion of Malas and Madigas." Since they are not Dalits, losing government benefits for Dalits is not an issue for them.[9]

The Hindus regularly attending Christian worship are often approaching a decision, positive or negative, as to whether they will join the Christian community. If that decision is positive, they understand that the process of becoming Christians involves baptism. The Hindus who take part in Christian *jatharas* or attend special Christmas or Easter services in the Medak cathedral may simply be curious about an unfamiliar religion, but they may be deeply interested in adopting Jesus as one of the objects of their devotion or even as their sole deity. The pilgrimage, however, is for Hindus as well as for Christians a special time and space in which the boundaries between religions become more porous; in most cases, we do not know whether the pilgrim's devotion to Christ continues after returning home, unless there is some subsequent connection to the Christian community. Sometimes this may come in the semiprivate context of family prayers. The pastor may be asked to conduct such prayers in a Hindu home. The question is whether those professing devotion to Jesus without an outward involvement in the Christian community consider this a temporary stage in a transition or a permanent devotional connection.

For the CSI Dalit congregations, the old problems of having a minority of fully communicant members still exist. They may be less urgent, however, than the question of baptism. Can they afford to have their children baptized? What does it mean to the fragile structure of the village Christian community if they do not? The unbaptized children in Christian families are clearly in a different situation than Hindus who want to follow Jesus without being baptized, but both groups pose a challenge for baptized Christians. Is baptism essential to becoming a Christian? Can those who are not baptized maintain their Christian connection for more than one generation? If they consider themselves to be followers of Jesus, what are the consequences for their religious life? Will they

---

9. Hoefer's study, *Churchless Christianity*, suggests that there are a large number of unbaptized followers of Jesus in the city of Chennai and presumably in other urban areas in South India.

also be engaged in various types of village ritual? At issue is what it means to believe in the Christian God and follow Jesus in the midst of village society. What should baptism mean in these circumstances, and how essential is it for Christians to be united in some demonstrable way with other followers of Christ?

Prospects for the Recovery of CSI Village Congregations

The number of active participants in CSI village congregations within this pastorate has gradually decreased during the past fifty years, and this is also true elsewhere in the Medak Diocese. The number of functioning congregations has also decreased. The most dramatic decline was in the Bellampally pastorate, where all but one of twenty-four village congregations have ceased to function. In the Wadiaram pastorate, while the number of village congregations recognized by the diocese has dropped only slightly, several of them, both in 1959-60 and in 2008-10, did not and do not have weekly services. The discontinuing of the church rolls since the 1970s makes it difficult to be precise about the decline in membership. One of the two large congregations, Shankarraj Kondapur, has dropped from fifty-four to thirty-four families, and another older congregation, Ambajipet, from forty-five to ten families.

Now the pastorate is divided into five sections, in each of which there is only one pastor. At the commencement of the new study, only the five congregations with resident pastors and another five or six congregations had weekly services, and many had been long neglected. As a byproduct of our study, pastoral visits have resumed to several other congregations. Even the congregations with resident pastors do not always receive adequate instruction and pastoral care, for some pastors are more energetic and diligent than others.

Dual religious participation, which was the most controversial finding of the first study, has continued. At present, this participation of Christians in Hindu rituals seems to be almost as prevalent in the oldest and largest congregation, Bandaposanipally, which has always had an evangelist or a pastor in residence, as in the congregations with less regular pastoral care. The most significant difference is that most members of this congregation do not eat the meat consecrated to a goddess. While a few of these rituals have been somewhat modified in their use by Christians, as previously discussed, most are part of the total scheme of village seasonal observances and lifecycle ceremonies reviewed in chapter 4. While this dual involvement will not itself dissolve a congregation, Christian worship may become less and less important. Conversely, it may become more important if it is able to adapt village religious practices to a Christian framework.

Several factors have contributed to the decrease in the size of these congregations and to the lack of vitality in their congregational life. The most obvious may not be the most important: the fact that many Christians have used their Hindu names in order to qualify for government benefits for the Scheduled Castes, a legal category that thus far has been defined so as to exclude Christian Dalits. Such registration often does not mean that these individuals and families stop thinking of themselves as Christians. They believe that this is the only way for them to claim what is rightfully theirs as Dalits. In another part of the state, almost an entire Dalit congregation registered as members of the Scheduled Castes, rather than as Christians; they did this at the same time that they built a larger church in which they regularly worship.[10] Other factors include insufficient pastoral care and large numbers of Hindu wives who have been incorporated into CSI congregations because of village custom rather than because of personal conviction. None of these factors automatically weakens the Christian identity of a family, but, taken together, all of them tend to do this. A new factor has been the attraction of independent churches nearby. This has been the case especially when the CSI congregation was without a resident pastor while the independent church possesses both its own resident pastor and an enthusiastic congregation.

It remains to be seen whether the decline in the number of baptized and communicant Christians in the older CSI congregations is an irreversible trend. Some things are out of the hands of the small Christian minority in this region. The strength of the Hindutva nationalist party (the BJP) in India as a whole makes an early end to discrimination against Christian Dalits unlikely. Greater economic opportunities and social freedom in urban areas will continue to attract young people in these congregations. Some of them will leave their villages for advanced schooling and better jobs in the city.

Progress observed in some congregations during the study has called for more than usual zeal on the part of some CSI pastors and for extraordinary lay leadership within some congregations. Such progress is unlikely to continue without greater lay leadership, including that of women, who usually make up more than half of each worshiping congregation.

CSI pastors have been able to learn from the example of independent churches, which have had to secure their financial support from their own members. The inability of some CSI congregations to support themselves financially is partly due to the continuing poverty of many church members and partly due to the lack of emphasis on giving or even of tithing as a Christian duty. This reality is in striking contrast to the great emphasis on

---

10. Sources withheld.

such congregational support of their own pastors in many of the independent churches.

Preaching and teaching that incorporate more of the drama, music, and visual arts, described in chapter 8, constitutes another remedy. This helps to provide a village-level "translation" of Christian doctrine and moral precepts in a village culture in which "service" has meant "serfdom," and in which "sacrifice" has meant making a communal offering to some local divine power. Statements of their beliefs by local Christians (in chapter 9) show that they can think through central Christian doctrines in terms of their own experience. Many testify to how God is answering their prayers.

New evangelism and a strengthening of weak congregational life have already occurred through the evangelistic efforts, financial contributions, and powerful prayers of the retired nurse from Hyderabad, Mrs. Deevenamma. Mr. Vinay Sagar and his siblings have repeatedly gone out from the city to the villages, bringing their personal gifts and financial resources to address the problems of rural congregations.[11] In other pastorates, there are cases of an entire urban church adopting one or more village congregations or helping in the diocesan effort of service and evangelism.

Chapter 5 described the experiences of two laypersons within the small Ambajipet congregation. Dr. Paranjyothi exemplifies how Christians with education or medical training who established their homes and occupations in these villages made their presence felt within their local congregations. Mr. Kummari Dass, a layman who has spent all his life in his village, has continued to provide moral and practical leadership to a diminished congregation without a resident pastor. In the small congregation at the pastorate headquarters of his congregation, Mr. Vijaya Rao and his wife, Yesumani, have each made distinctive contributions.

The future of these CSI congregations lies partly within their own hands and partly within varied political and social developments that are beyond their

---

11. Another layman, Mr. Yasa Vinay Sagar, has also made a distinctive contribution to the CSI congregations in the Wadiaram pastorate. He retired several years ago from the Indian Air Force and now lives with his wife in Hyderabad. With the financial and medical help of three siblings, two of them doctors, he has arranged medical clinics and evangelistic meetings in a number of villages. He has also involved other members of his Ramkote church in Hyderabad in these efforts. He has built new church buildings for two congregations in the pastorate and has repaired the older-style parsonage and worship hall in two other villages. In one village, neighbors were encroaching on the church's small plot of land. He was able to repair the fence around the church property and keep the neighbors from crossing it. Mr. Vinay Sagar does not consider himself an evangelist, but he wants to support the pastoral care and evangelistic outreach of the church as much as he and his extended family possibly can. His type of contribution can greatly help both pastors and congregations.

control. This future may well also be affected by the relations among different Christian denominations. Chapter 12 explores questions related to the divisions among Christians.

CHAPTER 12

Challenges Facing a Divided Church

How Christians Are Counted

The number of Christians in India has long been a political issue. During the last stages of British rule, when minority seats for Muslims were reserved in the state legislatures representing their proportion of that state's population, many Christians felt that they should have the same privilege. From 1871, when the census of India began, local governments counted the people in each religious community. The present census, conducted every ten years, requires one to register as a Hindu or a Christian, not both. According to the 2001 census, there are about twenty-three million Christians in India as a whole.[1] This is less than half of the *World Christian Encyclopedia* estimate, which is more than sixty-two million.[2] This much larger estimate includes many who register for the census as Hindus and counts as Christians fifteen million in India enrolled in Gospel correspondence courses.

---

1. Estimates of the total number of Christians in India vary widely. The 2.3 percent in the 2001 census translates to approximately twenty-three million (Wiebe, *Heirs and Joint Heirs*, 27). The same census indicates that the percentage of Christians in Andhra Pradesh had dropped by more than half from a high of 4.2 percent in 1971 to 1.6 percent in 2001, or about a million and a half. One reason for the sharp drop could be the large number of Dalit Christians who have registered as Scheduled Caste Hindus. Other estimates of the number of Christians are much larger. The World Christian Database estimate in 2005 was sixty-eight million, almost three times the census figure. Frykenberg reports that in the 1992 edition of *People of India*, Kumar Suresh Singh, director general of the Anthropological Survey of India, estimated the Christian percentage of the entire population of India as 7.3, which would mean about seventy million in 1991. Frykenberg therefore concludes that the Christian population in 2010 may have been more than eighty million (Frykenberg, *Christianity in India*, vi-vii, 464).

2. Vol. 1, 371.

Challenges Facing a Divided Church

While the larger number includes many who, by some criterion, are considered Christians, the census uses the same principle as many Christian churches: you are either a Christian or you are not. This is not the way, however, that many people in India look at religious and social identity. You either do or you do not belong to a particular caste *(jati)*, but you may have different degrees of affiliation with a particular faith: initiation, family relationship with an initiate, or limited participation without initiation.[3] Many Indians think of Christians as those affiliated with the sect of Jesus-worshipers, but some consider Christians to form a separate caste or group of castes. Those who profess to be Christians have a variety of views. For our purpose in this study, the crucial question is how those who gather for worship define themselves and other members of their families.

As noted in the preface, *Village Christians* was one of fifteen studies in a project originally entitled "Studies in the Life and Growth of the Younger Churches." After 1960, the project was renamed "Churches in the Missionary Situation — Studies in Growth and Response."[4] Those undertaking the studies were instructed not "to point out what is wrong, but to find out what is there." There was to be, however, an evaluation of the flexibility and creativity with which a church responded to the challenges of its environment.[5] The intended focus of these studies was on the church as a community, not on individual Christians. Yet *Village Christians* and many of the other studies utilized whatever statistics were available about the number of Christians in a church. The Medak Diocese in 1959, like the preceding Methodist Mission, carefully compiled statistics every year for each congregation. Many churches and mission agencies in the world keep close track of how smaller and larger units of the church are growing or shrinking in numbers. Scholars in the history of Christian missions have given much thought to data that can be measured. It is generally assumed that by whatever standard is adopted, one can count the number of Christians. In contrast, it is commonplace in China and Japan for families

---

3. Most of the devotional movements and sects that have developed in various Hindu traditions have one or more initiations, some of which represent the spiritual transformation occurring within the initiate. Some imitate or provide an alternative to ceremonies of renunciation marking the beginning of an ascetic life, but the sectarian lifestyle generally does not require that all the sect's members abandon married life. Sometimes complete asceticism is considered a higher stage. In these Telangana villages, some families or even entire caste groups in a village maintain a hereditary connection with a priest who visits several villages, a priest whose family is or once was connected with a particular sect. Thus, though the inner circle of a particular devotional community is defined by the obligatory initiation, the outer circles are less clearly defined. The initiations of Brahmins and other "twice-born" castes mark their transition from one stage of life to another, beginning with the sacred thread that qualifies them to study the Hindu scriptures.

4. Mackie, ed., *Can Churches Be Compared?* 16.

5. John V. Taylor, quoted in Mackie, ed., *Can Churches Be Compared?* 15-16.

to be connected with two or three different religious traditions. It may be that a more realistic look at the Indian religious situation would reveal something similar, specifically that many people might be considered both Christians and Hindus. In any case, counting Christians has changed from the era of precise statistics to a time when in these CSI congregations, no records are kept, and in the independent churches, record keeping is often informal.

Many CSI village congregations have ceased to gather regularly for worship; and, in some congregations, many families no longer come for worship even on special occasions. Some completely distance themselves from the Christian community. While positive developments in older congregations have been few, most recent beginnings of Christian discipleship have occurred in newer congregations, both CSI and independent. In these, most members are the first to become Christians within their families. This situation is complicated by the fact that some members in the independent churches were formerly members of CSI congregations, and that there may also be many more instances of solitary Christian families, like that of Yohan's nephew Manikyam, who think of themselves as Christians though they do not consider themselves to be a part of any congregation.

In both the CSI and the independent churches, there is often, in many minds, a distinction between "Christian" as a mark of social identification and "good Christian" as an evaluation of those who have lived up to an expected norm. Interestingly, one understanding of such a norm was clearly expressed in the comments of some Hindu spouses of new Christians. They shared their Christian partners' belief in the power of Jesus to heal and to shower material blessings; but they did not want to give up their smoking or drinking, or, for the women, the auspicious mark on the forehead. In their understanding, surrendering these customs was part of what was expected in becoming a Christian. The distinction in the Medak Diocese between adults "on trial" and communicant members might seem to give an administrative and liturgical meaning to this more informal distinction between "Christians" and "good Christians." The confirming of some previously baptized adults, however, is often such a haphazard and perfunctory process that it fails to mark a significant distinction between two levels of Christian identity or practice for two groups of Christians. Independent churches are still at a stage in which many worshipers are regarded as in motion, moving either toward or away from an expected norm. Baptism marks a decisive point in their transition to a new faith and a new lifestyle, without weakening the connection to their own caste community. For those already baptized within a CSI congregation as infants, joining an independent church may lead to a new baptism, or it may be marked by a miraculous healing or some powerful experience of the Holy Spirit.

Challenges Facing a Divided Church

The affirmation of one's Christian identity can be a sign of vitality and spiritual growth, and it may well affect the numerical growth of the Christian community. Along with such affirmation come many decisions, which may have to be frequently repeated: presence at worship, offerings to the church, observance or nonobservance of village rituals, keeping cordial relations with relatives and neighbors, both Christian and Hindu, and, certainly, the decision whether or not to register as a Christian for the census. There are also many aspects of moral behavior that may be connected with a personal understanding of what it means to be a Christian. Many of the repeated decisions may become habitual; all are responses to the multiple challenges of the environment. Those most directly involved may not agree as to which decisions are signs of life and growth. Those who observe from outside can certainly recognize the challenges and sometimes discern the heroic responses.

Strengths of Multi-Caste Congregations

Expansion of the independent churches, in both numbers and influence, has changed the situation of Christians in this area. It is still hard to determine what the changes are and even harder to predict what further changes will occur in the next decade, to say nothing of the next fifty years. Thus far, there has been an emergence and growth among those churches that largely support their own pastor. Although he often has had less formal education and theological training than CSI pastors, he may be more active. Most of the churches emphasize the present power of the Holy Spirit, manifested in healing and in bringing economic well-being, even if the church is not affiliated with a Pentecostal mission or church organization.

These new churches often include members from a range of castes. Among the churches surveyed, the number of families from landholding and occupational castes exceeds the number of Dalit families. Families from the landholding Mudhiraj caste are most strongly represented. In a few new churches that include members of old Christian families who were part of now defunct CSI congregations, Dalits are in a majority. Whatever the caste composition, there is much emphasis on the unity in Christ that surpasses caste differences, and this unity is expressed both in worship and in communal meals, although marriage continues to be arranged with families of the same caste. In most Protestant village congregations in Andhra Pradesh, inter-caste congregations have been largely limited to the two Dalit communities of Malas and Madigas. (In Guntur District in Coastal Andhra, Madigas became Baptists, while Malas became Lutherans.) Beginning at the time of the first study in 1959, a few people from the toddy-tapper and potter castes joined two CSI Dalit congregations, and in one case, Ambajipet, these families have remained in the congregation.

The new multi-caste churches include members from castes in the area that have not previously shown any interest in becoming Christians. Some of these come from landholding castes. The multi-caste congregations have thus far stayed together, except in Achampet. There, some Madiga Christians in a long-neglected CSI congregation first joined a multi-caste Pentecostal church, but recently resumed their old CSI connection. This development, strongly supported by the old Christian families, has weakened the multi-caste Pentecostal church, not only in numbers, but also in its conception as a church that is uniting different castes, including Dalits.

Fifty years ago the vigor of the Achampet congregation owed something to its being the spiritual home and physical center of a single-caste community. The congregation included virtually all Madiga families. That "folk" character of the old CSI church shared something common in spirit, though not in detail, with the strong tribal churches of central and northeast India. Madigas in a multi-caste church could no longer express their caste solidarity through their church membership. They may have also felt uncomfortable as a Dalit minority. The new Pentecostal church must have another basis than caste to express its unity.

Many all-Dalit churches in other parts of Andhra Pradesh have also functioned as a center for a particular caste community. This is particularly the case when the church is all Madiga or all Mala. Without the reinforcement of being part of a particular caste community, these churches might not survive. Where there is more than one Christian community within the same village, however, the separation between them might belie their unity in Christ. Much depends on perspective: whether or not the Medak Diocese of the CSI, consisting almost entirely of Dalit churches, has taken a step backward in reconstituting an all-Madiga congregation that meets for worship only one hundred yards away from a multi-caste independent church. Those concerned with the plight of Dalits might ask whether it is possible for Dalits to be treated as equal members of a multi-caste church, especially when they are in a minority. How much of the discrimination still faced within general Hindu society is replicated within multi-caste congregations remains open to question.

The irony here is that while the Church of South India has from its inception accepted organic union as necessary for Christian witness to Hindu society, many members of village congregations of the Medak Diocese feel most threatened by Dalit Christians' joining a multi-caste Christian community. This is especially true if the Dalits are in a minority. The actual situation differs from village to village, and independent churches are diverse. This fact serves as a

Challenges Facing a Divided Church

reminder that Christians here, as all over the world, are divided by theological beliefs, worship styles, educational attainments, and economic levels, as well as by caste and cultural differences. In any case, independent churches that prize the unity of belonging within a single congregation above wider administrative connections have realized the importance of keeping their churches open and welcoming to the whole range of castes, including Dalits, within the village. This practical necessity persists wherever there are only a few individuals or families from any one caste. Moreover, it serves to demonstrate their witness to unity in Christ with peoples of "all nations and tongues."

Whether, in multi-caste congregations, spiritual unity will prove stronger than the divisive power of caste, in which internal caste loyalty is reinforced by general village support of caste hierarchy and divisions between castes, remains a question. Marriage almost always takes place within one's own caste, and generally so also does eating together or even accepting a drink of water. Each caste has its own forms of governance and, sometimes, a common loyalty to a particular deity.

Since Christians are often regarded as a new sect, it is instructive to note how Hindu sects have balanced caste loyalties of their members with their affirmation of the unity of all within the same devotional community. In South India, only the large Lingayat sect has claimed that belonging to the community of Shiva's devotees dissolved separate caste identities. In practice, however, even Lingayats have become identified with a few specific castes. In North India, a few sects have claimed to transcend caste distinctions. Even Sikhs, who emphasize their higher unity through their sharing of common meals, continue to draw their membership from various castes.

Even when Hindu devotional sects teach that connection with the Supreme Lord transcends social distinctions, they usually maintain that life in society is rightly ordered by the hierarchical framework of castes, ranked according to their degree of ritual purity. Christians, too, often accept the importance of caste rules in ordering their social conduct, and they share the general tendency to rank their own caste higher than others nearby on the social ladder. As noted in chapter 5, the two Dalit castes in the oldest congregation, Malas and Madigas, worship together but generally keep to themselves on social occasions; and they sometimes criticize behavior of persons in the other caste.

Some congregations, especially among the independent churches with members from various castes, have emphasized their spiritual unity by holding common meals after Sunday worship. While this is a break with ordinary caste practice, it may be understood to go no further than the sharing of food that is done by Hindu devotees. It is restricted to a special time and place. It may be too early to tell whether friendlier relations with Christians in other castes extend beyond the church premises during all days of the week. Certainly there are instances where this has occurred. A more general expansion of inter-caste relations not only requires overcoming inherited prejudices but also threats of disciplinary action by caste leadership. Some churches may hold together their multi-caste constituencies by limiting social interaction and continuing to accept the principle of caste hierarchy on the basis of ritual purity. This attitude is very different from that of the Dalit Christian theology discussed in chapter 3. At this point, clarifying conflicts between different Christian attitudes or views of caste is useful.

Dalit Theology and Village Churches

The oldest Christian community in India is that of the Syrian or Thomas Christians of Kerala, who look back to their founding by the apostle Thomas. For centuries, this community has functioned in the context of the larger Hindu society as a caste or a series of subcastes, which are not only defined by their liturgy and leadership, but also by their custom of confining marriages within the community. In the past, they have refused to admit into their church membership people of "lower" castes. Roman Catholic missions, beginning on the west coast of India, chose not to challenge caste divisions; they frequently established separate congregations for those belonging to different castes. The first Protestant missions, led by German Lutheran Pietists, established a single congregation in the Danish port of Tranquebar for all Christians, but they accepted caste differences within the church. The first European missionaries, both Roman Catholic and Lutheran, argued that the caste hierarchy was equivalent to the European system of social classes. In that system, a prince would never dine with a peasant, serf, or slave.

Only in the nineteenth century did British and American missions begin to change such attitudes. They insisted that Indian Christians should recognize one another as social equals and should sit and eat together at church gatherings. Ironically, such attitudes developed at a time when western racial prejudices were increasing, so that many western missionaries would not accept Indian Christians as their equals, still less join them in a common fellowship. The new Protestant mission policy continued, however, and was strengthened by the fact that most new Christians came from those groups whom Hindus considered to be the lowest castes. On one key point, however, western missionaries accepted the view of all Indian Christians: that marriage should always be within one's own caste. In South India, the choice of a marriage partner was often restricted to a maternal relative. While the official position of many churches was that

Challenges Facing a Divided Church

Christians should marry only other Christians, caste solidarity and family connections were often considered more important. Certainly this is seen as true within the congregations being studied here: caste solidarity is as important for Malas and Madigas as for any other caste. The one instance of a "love marriage" that was uncovered — between members of the two castes — was dissolved by their parents.[6]

The message of Dalit theology is not against "caste" understood as an endogamous community, but against the system of caste ranking based on degrees of purity or pollution, with Brahmins at the top and "untouchable" castes so far down that they must live at the edge of the main village, even though they are required to perform the most menial services for higher-caste people in the village. Dalit Christian theology seeks to imbue all Dalits with a strong sense of human dignity, of which they have been systematically deprived. There is also a message for non-Dalits: give up your system of caste ranking, for only then will you cease to look down on us! While the Indian Constitution formally abolished caste and "untouchability," such abolition has by no means become a social reality, especially in villages. As long as the leaders of Hindu society, and all who follow them, continue to assume a high-to-low ranking, Dalits will continue to be "crushed" at the bottom of a fixed social hierarchy.

The message of Dalit theology is frequently heard in Protestant seminaries. It is unclear to what extent it has been incorporated into the thinking of lay members of the CSI village congregations, most of whom are Dalits. Malas and Madigas certainly know firsthand the denigration by people in other castes. Yet, it is not clear whether this leads them to affirm greater solidarity with non-Christian Dalits. A brief sample of lay Christian beliefs does not reveal the characteristic themes of liberation theology. This may change, of course, after a new generation of pastors has been preaching for several years.

Within all-Dalit CSI churches, there are no Christians of other castes who can even hear this message from Dalits to the rest of village society. In many independent churches, on the other hand, there are many non-Dalit caste members, but sermons do not indicate that any notice is being taken of the Dalit critique of hierarchical Hindu society. It is possible, of course, that this critique is expressed in more informal or less direct ways, but the evident overcoming of caste barriers seems to go no further than it has gone among communities of Hindu devotees — for example, sharing meals while within the sacred precincts. To include Dalit members of an independent church in common meals is itself a notable achievement; but it is not a critique of the hierarchical system that, in theory, not only validates the superior purity of Brahmins, but also provides

---

6. See chapter 5.

religious and social support for the claim of landholders and wealthy merchants to be, in worldly matters, the lords of the village. The claim of superior purity reinforces the self-understanding of every caste to be superior to its closest neighbors and rivals in village caste ranking.

Multi-caste independent churches do not yet challenge the hierarchical principle of greater or lesser caste purity. More widespread education, democratic political institutions, and new urban influences are improving the lot of Dalits and softening caste prejudice. They are unlikely, however, to bring CSI Dalit congregations and multi-caste independent churches closer together. Whether or not a shared sense of Christian unity or limited cooperation is even possible — that is a matter for further consideration.

Prospects for Village Christians in Telangana

Looking back fifty years, some developments that were anticipated have in fact occurred: the decline of some congregations; the greater urban influences on all villagers; and the continuation, often by remarkable lay leaders, of a ministry of healing through prayers to Jesus. One major development was not anticipated: new independent churches with members from different castes. New predictions of the future are unlikely to be more than half right! Nevertheless, trying to look ahead may be a way to reflect on what we have seen, what we have heard, and what we have learned.

The government of India's exclusion from benefits for Dalits who register as Christians has probably contributed heavily to the sharp decline in the number of Christians in the census enumeration for the state of Andhra Pradesh. It is unclear, however, whether, or to what extent, this development has weakened the functioning of the Dalit Christian congregations. The state legislature has requested a change in the central government policy. For political reasons, there is at least a chance of this happening within the next decade. In any case, the increasing numbers of Christians from non-Dalit castes make the denial of benefits to Dalit Christians a less effective strategy for their suppression by Hindu nationalists.

Christians in independent churches in the area studied may soon outnumber those in CSI congregations, if they do not already do so. This development may or may not lead to greater cooperation between these growing independent churches and the Church of South India. Throughout their history and around the world, Christians have repeatedly doubted, if not denied, that Christians outside their own denomination really belong to the one church of Christ. They have also, however, repeatedly found ways of working together on matters of

Challenges Facing a Divided Church

common concern. So far, there has been little inclination by different denominations to work together. Occasional cooperation between CSI and independent pastors is a noteworthy exception, and laypeople often have a more inclusive view. This is sometimes indicated by their attendance at festivals in the Medak cathedral, considered by many as a favorable location for healing prayers.

The development of the Horeb Prayer Church in Chinna Shankarampet, first as an independent congregation and then as part of the CSI, is too distinctive to be easily repeated. In any case, it represents a merger of traditions that is still the exception.

A few instances of brief cooperation between CSI and independent Christians were discovered. In one village, a clever response by a CSI Christian allowed the independent pastor's wife to raise the Indian flag on Independence Day.[7] For the independent pastor Mr. Sanjeevi, the opportunity arose to turn over pastoral care in some more distant villages to the CSI pastor living nearer by. Again, the willingness of independent pastors to allow CSI seminary students, who were research assistants, to observe their worship services and to interview them greatly contributed to this study.

The CSI congregations and the independent churches in this area draw on many of the same Christian traditions, as well as on many Indian religious traditions. That can be seen from an academic vantage point, whether or not the participants themselves are aware of the traditions that they have inherited. The CSI members whose responses were summarized in chapter 9 believe that Jesus is God, and that the power of Jesus ought to be manifest in the lives of his followers. As one said, "If you believe in him, you can be successful in anything." Among responses received, such success included finding lost earrings, getting good water from a new well, the gift of children, good harvests, successful operations, avoiding a fatal electric shock, restoration of sight, and help in passing school examinations. Restoration of harmony in the family, healing after severe

---

7. Lalitha is the wife of Pastor Shivnur Hanoch, who started the independent Baptist church in Jangarai. She came with her husband to Jangarai in 1990 when she was appointed by the government to run the local nursery school. On Indian Independence Day (August 15) in 2008, she was responsible for raising the flag in the middle of the village. The night before, however, some village leaders met and decided that she should not be allowed this honor unless she put on her forehead the vermilion mark that Hindu women wear. When Hanoch heard about this, he went to see Mr. Prakash, who was the CSI congregation's representative on the Wadiaram pastorate committee and also the leader in in Jangarai village of the Telugu Desham Party. Prakash told Hanoch not to worry. The next morning, when the village leaders told Prakash of their decision, he told them that the Indian flag had already been raised in the nation's capital. "Do you know who raised it?" he asked. "Of course," they replied, "our nation's president, Abdul Kalam." "Well now," said Prakash, "if the Muslim Abdul Kalam did not have to put a mark on his forehead, why should the Christian Lalitha?" The village leaders went away and made no more objection. Lalitha raised the Indian flag.

road accidents, and, most frequently, healing from the various effects of witchcraft were among other benefits. Jesus (God) was seen as bringing many blessings. In villages formerly under Islamic rule, Hindus and Christians as well as Muslims continue to use the Islamic term for "blessing," *barakat* (from *barakha*), and such divine blessing is usually seen as taking some specific material form.

Michael Bergunder argues that, behind the Indian Pentecostal emphasis on healing and exorcism, there is a common religious attitude within the older Protestant churches. Viewing Jesus as the source of material blessings, he maintains, is the Christian equivalent of the popular Hindu belief that the goddesses bring both material blessings and calamities. According to Bergunder, Indian Christians believe that even after Jesus has defeated evil spirits, they continue to exist.[8] Evidence of this belief is manifest, perhaps most vividly in the life story of Tharamma of Medak: even after she had become a healer in Christ's name, she felt she was repeatedly being attacked by evil spirits.[9]

Fifty years ago, Christians in these villages certainly believed in the power of village goddesses and of evil spirits. In principle, they also believed in the superior power of Christ. The crucial question was how they could avail themselves of Christ's power, both to ward off misfortune and to bring good fortune. Along with Hindus and Muslims, many Christians attended the healing services of Sadhu Joseph. In a few cases, Hindus reported that Lord Jesus had appeared in their dreams and healed them.

At the time, there were no Pentecostal or other independent churches in these villages. Yet, the general attitude of Christians corresponded to what Bergunder considers the Indian background to Indian Pentecostalism. As noted in chapters 4 and 11, however, the Indian background also includes *bhakti*, which in its Christian form assumes that devotees may request healing and other material blessings for one's own family and may intercede for others, not as part of a bargain, but as an expression of faith in Jesus. While some prayers are believed to be more powerful than others, the response always depends on the loving care of the Lord. In their prayers for healing, Christians speak of experience, both in their connection with God and in their difference from God, who is the giver of the blessings they seek and the source of their empowerment.

While Brahmins and other Hindus often accept, in theory, that even those in what they consider the lowest castes can practice *bhakti*, many Hindu sectarian communities worshiping a particular god or goddess assume that only higher-caste persons practicing rituals to ward off impurities and keeping to a strictly vegetarian diet can qualify to become true devotees of the Lord. One

8. Bergunder, *The South Indian Pentecostal Movement*, 125-26.
9. See chapter 6.

of the attractions of the Christian message among those whom Hindu society has considered most "impure" is the belief that Jesus welcomes them, too, as his disciples and devotees. Christian teaching has its own standards of purity and devotion, but it does not forbid personal requests. Indeed, it encourages them, and they may include prayers for good health and material blessings, not only for one's own family, but also for others in need.

Prayer for Christians, as well as for other villagers, can become an attempt to strike a bargain with God: for such and such a blessing, we promise to give so much in return. Such prayers have been frequent throughout Christian history, yet petitions are not banned because of their misuse. Jesus taught his disciples to pray for "bread for today." They were also enjoined to pray for forgiveness from God, which they might confidently expect, provided that they forgive others who wronged them. The responses from Christians included in chapter 9 show how seriously they take the Lord's Prayer.

Many other strands of Christian piety and village Hindu practice are joined in a broad tradition undergirding present Christian life among these village Christians. One is a sacramental practice in which God's saving grace in Christ, especially mediated through his sacrificial death, sustains the ongoing Christian community. Christ's sacrifice is believed to make possible the forgiveness of the Christian's sin, as well as victory over sin in all human life.

A second strand is a requirement of good works. This is often understood as God's commandments, found in both the Old Testament and the New Testament. If God is obeyed, he showers abundant material blessings. If he is not obeyed and his commands are flouted, it is believed that his punishment is sure to follow in this life or in the life to come. The commandment most frequently mentioned by independent preachers is a requirement to tithe, returning one-tenth of one's earnings to God. The positive response to this emphasis has made it possible for many independent churches to support their pastors without outside financial support. Even more important, in the eyes of independent church members, God has blessed their obedience with good health and increasing wealth.

A third strand of piety brings together the Wesleyan call for a transformation of society with the later "social gospel" of more liberal Protestant missions, in which efforts in education, medicine, and social uplift were seen as indispensable to spreading the gospel. Contemporary Dalit theology, developed in protest against the injustice of Hindu society, also owes much to the recent liberation theologies of other countries. In these village congregations, this seems to be represented more in the preaching of CSI pastors than in the expressions of lay Christians; but certainly many lay Christians want to end the evident discrimination against them and to be treated with dignity and respect, not only as individuals, but also as members of a distinct caste community.

These and other strands of Christian piety sometimes merge with the village mindset. In Sadhu Joseph's healing services, features of village religion came together with healings of Jesus in the Gospels. Sadhu Joseph's rescue from death and from leprosy, and Christ's appearance in the dreams of some Hindus who later became Christians both suggest how indigenous is this stream of Christian piety. This phenomenon predates any Pentecostal presence in these villages, but resonates with more recent experiences of healing, especially of those joining independent churches. Sadhu Joseph's preaching stressed the healing miracles of Jesus, which include his victory over the demons.

What may be even more emphasized now than fifty years ago is the power of Christ in overcoming the effects of witchcraft, which seems to have reached epidemic proportions in some villages. Certainly, fear of magicians and of jealous neighbors who pay the magicians to cast a spell is so widespread as to affect the quality of normal village life. Neither counter-magic nor modern medicine seems to be effective against this black magic; only Jesus can break the magician's spell. If that power is to be effective, ardent prayers are needed. Both individual persons and whole congregations have needed to pray, and the prayers of saintly souls have been considered to be most effective, especially the intercession of those who have experienced the gift of healing.

Repeated waves of healing have been manifest many times in Christian history. Yet, there have also been many periods when it was assumed that healing miracles were confined to New Testament times. Catholic piety has linked miraculous healing to the power of the saints, sometimes related to a specific relic or to a place where the Virgin Mary has appeared. In much recent western Protestant piety, however, healing is interpreted in spiritual rather than in physical terms, except for those groups for whom healing through prayer is a sharp alternative to seeking medical assistance. Such contrasts are hardly present in these villages. In one woman's dream fifty years ago, Jesus not only laid his hand on her stomach, but also gave her some pills.[10]

The prominence of the healing from disease in the ministry of Jesus and the early church has fed later Christian traditions, such as the prayers and exorcisms contained in the liturgy of more Catholic and Orthodox traditions. Medical work in modern Protestant missions often developed as a response to evident physical need. This has been presented as a distinctive expression of the gospel and a tangible demonstration of Christ's love, especially in situations where verbal witness was or is not possible. This emphasis has to some extent corrected a lack of attention to healing in some churches, which was sometimes accompanied by a suspicion of unorthodox beliefs among lay healers. In the

---

10. Luke and Carman, *Village Christians*, 154.

recent past, healing has often been the province of professionals trained in modern science — or of practitioners of various forms of alternative medicine. In India, both medical care in hospitals and prayers for healing are avenues of Christian witness.

In these villages, faith in Jesus as the preeminent healer is central for Christians of all kinds as well as for some of their Hindu and Muslim neighbors. Such faith does not keep Christians from seeking medical treatment. If, however, healing is understood only as a reward for obeying God's commands, ill health or an accident can be taken as a sign that one has displeased God, as evident in one sermon, by failing to tithe. It has not been easy for village Christians to believe in Christ's present healing powers and yet remain faithful when no healing comes.[11]

For Christians engaged in the ecumenical movement, the rejoining of separate Christian traditions might, like the Seven Streams pilgrimage at the Hindu site described in chapter 8, be understood as a sign of divine presence. For many Christians in these villages, that presence is welcomed with each new appearance of the healing Christ, understood as God's present victory and a great divine blessing.

---

11. An emphasis on material blessings occurs in the lives of many Christians in all parts of the world. A recent report on "Ghana's New Christianity" emphasizes that "their Christianity is about success," which is primarily related to financial and material matters, with the remarkable success of Old Testament heroes as the biblical model. What is different from our study, however, according to Gifford, is that their emphasis "has displaced their earlier focus on healing." When the expected blessings do not come, this is attributed by many Christians in Ghana to demonic influences. (Gifford, "A View of Ghana's New Christianity," especially 85-88.)

With respect to our study, it should be noted that both health and wealth are precious blessings that village Christians do not always experience. A few of the testimonies cited earlier include patience in waiting for blessings that have not yet been granted. Though all too familiar with poverty and physical suffering, they find it difficult to think of such distress as divine discipline or to link their misfortune positively to the suffering of Christ.

Appendix

Sermons Preached in CSI Congregations

Sermon at Church in Toopran, October 17, 2010, "Youth Sunday"

Guest Preacher: Mrs. Sumalatha (wife of Mr. Ravinder),
Teacher at Engineering College at Haveli Ghanpur, near Medak

I start with a sentence by Martin Luther: "Darkness will not be removed by darkness." Parents are afraid when their daughters leave home to study in school or college, afraid that they might fall in love or even commit suicide. Let me give you an example from my college, something that happened in 2004. A Dalit girl fell in love with a Reddy boy, but she would not agree to marry him. Since she was a Dalit, she thought that after their marriage he would continually criticize her. He was so disappointed at her refusal that he tried to commit suicide. Fortunately, some friends came to his room in time to save him.

We Christians ought not to behave like that [engaging in love affairs]. We must obey rules. How can we overcome the temptations and meet the challenges of modern life? First, we must seek God's way and turn toward God. Second, we have to choose the best way. Third, we need to be partners with God, accepting God's promises. Young people are like a blank sheet of paper. If you write well on it, the paper will be good, but if you write badly, the paper will be bad. Young people should not live according to their own will, but they should depend on God's will. If they live by their own will, they will go into darkness, but if they live by God's will, they will go into the light.

Paul gave a teaching to Timothy [in the Epistle 1 Tim. 4:6-16] that a young

Appendix

person should live in the *bhakti* of God [be in a loving relationship with God]. If we are strengthened in the Spirit, we go to the feet of the Lord. Jesus said, "And everyone who has left houses or brothers or sisters or father or mother or children or fields, for my name's sake, will receive a hundredfold, and will inherit eternal life" [Matt. 19:29, NRSV]. If you leave everything, you will receive abundant blessings in your future ministry. If you give importance to God, you will be blessed.

Young people should be informed about AIDS. You should warn other people about AIDS.

We have to live spiritually, and we also have to live with a knowledge of conditions in contemporary society. If we do both, we will gain light in our life.

May God bless you!

Sermon in CSI Pastorate Headquarters Church,
Wadiaram, October 24, 2010

Theme: Christian Character

Guest Preacher: The Rev. M. Vijay Kumar from Ramayampet Pastorate

"Trial sermon" evaluated by three CSI presbyters and a few lay leaders

My text is from 1 Peter 2:12: "Maintain good conduct among the Gentiles, so that in case they may speak against you as wrongdoers, they may see your good deeds and glorify God on the day of visitation."

I want to share with you a saying in English: "When wealth is lost, nothing is lost. When health is lost, something is lost, but when character is lost, everything is lost." [He then translated this into Telugu.] Character includes all five of the following: gracious disposition *(saushilyamu)*, good conduct *(nadatha)*, good behavior *(pravarthana)*, good qualities *(gunamu)*, and good nature *(svabhavamu)*.

For students, a good conduct certificate is important for later in their lives. These certificates are given in the schools, and what they state depends on the student's behavior. This certificate should be a sign of your good life. When someone is looking for a wife, he will not accept a woman if her character is not good, even if he is offered money.

Paul teaches that you should equip yourself with truth, righteousness, and a pure mind to preach the gospel of peace (Eph. 6:14-15). A Christian should have a gracious disposition toward God and human beings. In 1 Samuel 24:1-

15, we read that King Saul and his army were searching for David to kill him. David hid in a cave and later, while Saul was asleep, cut a piece of cloth from Saul's robe, but did not kill him. This was because of David's character. He knew that he should not kill Saul because God had appointed Saul to be king. David loved his enemy.

We human beings usually don't forgive our enemies. We tend to curse them. We don't love them. A Christian should have a loving heart, a heart of forgiveness. Christian character does not tolerate injustice. Psalm 15 says that a Christian should not put the blame on his friend. He should speak the truth, and he should not say bad things about people behind their backs. Christian character prohibits hurting others or stealing from them. A Christian should not lend money at interest. Think of the money lender and how the debtor commits suicide when he cannot repay the loan.

Jesus is the example of good Christian character, as we see in the Gospel lesson (Matt. 5:13-16). A Christian's life should be light and salt, Christ said. A pinch of salt is tiny, but everyone can taste it. Light cuts down the darkness. We ought to have at least a little faith in God. If our lives are not tasty, God throws us out. Jesus Christ is a role model for living a good life. Because we Christians are worshiping Jesus Christ, who is our role model, we also are good, and we have to follow where Jesus Christ has led. When people are living as true Christians, they have to change their lives.

Once when an artist was carving a statue, he unwittingly put a scar on one cheek. For that reason he started to carve a new statue. Some bystanders told him that he didn't need to because the statue would be placed so high up that the blemish could not be seen. He replied, "People might not see the scar, but I would know that it is there." Then the others said, "You won't gain anything; it will be a waste of your time and energy." To that the sculptor replied, "Even if my time and energy is wasted, I must start again, for I would not want to present an imperfect figure as my work."

We Christians, likewise, should not have a spot on our lives. People might not recognize our flaw, but God would recognize it. Others might not know what wrong we have in our lives, but we know, and we have to correct ourselves. Jesus Christ showed his character by shedding his blood and dying on the cross of Calvary. Living as Jesus lives will bring us blessing.

Appendix

Sermon in CSI Church in Bandaposanipally, October 24, 2010

Theme: Christian Character

Preacher: The Rev. Benny Paul, the Resident Deacon

I thank God and this congregation for the opportunity to preach God's word. Christian character includes both disposition and behavior. If we do not possess it, we are a disgrace to God.

If we believe in Christ, we should continue to worship him. While Hindus worship as individuals, Christian worship is more collective.

If one's behavior is pleasing to God, he can turn his enemies into friends (Prov. 16:7). [The preacher expounded 1 Samuel 24:1-5, where David restrained himself from killing King Saul.] King Saul was ordained by God. The people with David wanted him to kill Saul, but David contented himself with cutting out a small piece of Saul's robe. This incident should be an example for us.

Our thoughts, words, and deeds should be acceptable to God. As it says in Psalm 119:105, "Your word is a light to my feet and a lamp to my path." We should correct ourselves with God's word and continue on our journey. Otherwise we are of no use to our family, church, or society. With this word we have to revive our life. Since we follow Christ, we should have love, peace, and happiness. We should share our experience of salvation with others and move further with our lives.

As we read in Matthew 5:13-16, we should be like salt and light in the world. Since Jesus is a light to the world, our words and deeds should be like a light to the world. Just as a lamp should not be kept under a bushel, so our deeds should lead society like the light on a lamp stand. Our life should be filled with the Spirit. We should concentrate on spiritual things. If Jesus comes, we should all be justified as righteous people. We should have a transformed life.

Sermons Preached in Independent Churches

Sermon by Pastor Anandam, Bethesda Prayer Temple, Ambajipet

(Preaching began at 1.00 p.m., two hours after the worship service began.)

Greetings to all of you in the name of our Lord and Savior Jesus Christ. Are you all doing well? I know that the days are hot, and because of the heat wave, many have died. We cannot be safe in this world without the grace of God, so praise be to God! Hallelujah! That's why we must be thankful to God. I will tell you a certain word from God. Psalm 9:10 reads: "Those who know your name put their trust in you, for you, O Lord, have not forsaken those who seek you" [NRSV]. *Stotram* [Praise]!

When we were in the world, we consulted shamans and doctors, but when we seek refuge in God, God is with us and he will not leave us. Many people make wealth and money their refuge, but if you believe in God, he will be your refuge and will not leave you. We catch hold of God in our need but leave him at other times. That is not the right way.

If we continue to follow the word, God will remember us and guide us so that we will not walk on the path of death. If parents advise their children, the children sometimes respond as if the parents' advice were not worthwhile, but whatever situations we are in, God will not forget us.

When Jonah went to Nineveh, everyone there, from the king to a beggar, prayed to God. Then Jonah was angry, realizing that God would save any wretched sinner. There are such people in this world, so be careful. We must love our enemies. We must wish that they should get ahead in their lives. They are the children of God. Jonah ran away angrily and put up a shed outside the village. God made a vine sprout and grow, but the next day he made it dry up.

The shed stands for our world; the shadow of the vine indicates a temporary joy and temporary shelter. God is eternal. If God makes us dry up, then we will be truly dried up. Dear children, in which shadow are you living? Are you in the shadow of money? In what shadow do you stand? Our own shadow that accompanies us only remains while the sun shines. After that, it is not to be seen. Therefore, you must not live in the shadow of this world, but you must live in God's shadow. Then he will save you from death, and he will lead you into the safe shadow. In the book of Ruth, we see that Boaz tells Ruth: "You have come into the safety of God's shadow." Hallelujah!

This afternoon, since you are listening to God's word, God will not leave you. God will be your shelter. May God grant such grace to us and to our families. Amen. Hallelujah![1]

---

1. The message ended at 2:16 p.m.; it lasted for one hour and sixteen minutes.

Appendix

Sermon by the late Pastor Burgupalli Sanjeevaiah,
The King's Prayer House, Chegunta, affiliated with
International Outreach Church (IOC)

Text: Psalm 65:4. "Happy are those whom you choose and
bring near to live in your courts. We shall be satisfied with the
goodness of your house, your holy temple." [NRSV]

St. Paul wrote, "I regard everything as loss because of the surpassing value of knowing Christ Jesus my Lord" [Phil. 3:8, NRSV]. We must not love anything more or anyone more than Christ, lest we make a fault of friendship. If we love money, it will take wings and fly away. The wife we love may go far away, and so, too, may our husbands or our children. But if you love God, God's blessings will come to you according to your works. Hallelujah! [The congregation responded, "Hallelujah!"] Many persons on a Sunday remain at home instead of coming to the church. In the book of Genesis we see that Sunday was a blessed day; it is a holiday and a day for worshiping God. Hallelujah! [The congregation responded, "Hallelujah!"] Sunday is a blessed day; all must be in the house of God. Hallelujah! [The congregation responded, "Hallelujah!"]

Psalm 65:4 says, "We shall be satisfied by being in the precincts of your temple." If we are not satisfied, then our lives are wasted. Hallelujah! [The congregation responded, "Hallelujah!"] If we are not satisfied, we are not human beings. We need to have the same desire that David had for God. Hebrews 13:5 says, "You must not have a desire for money, but you must be satisfied with what you have." Proverbs 30:15-16 says that life which does not say "Enough!" is a life that is not satisfied: "Three things are never satisfied; four never say, 'Enough': Sheol, the barren womb, the earth ever thirsty for water, and the fire that never says, 'Enough.'" We must be satisfied with what we have. Hallelujah! [The congregation responded, "Hallelujah!"] To stay in the house of the Lord for one day is better than spending time with the Godless. Many people give excuses for not coming to church. We must not give such lame excuses as saying, "Our cousin's marriage is taking place," for then we would glorify the marriage more than Sunday worship, and we would honor the human persons more than God.

Bad company spoils the good life. Hallelujah! [The congregation responded, "Hallelujah!"] Whatever you might possess, it is all a zero. Your conscience must tell you that you are a good person Hallelujah! Hallelujah! [The congregation responded, "Hallelujah! Hallelujah!"]

APPENDIX

Sermon by Pastor M. C. Babu, Hermon Church, Wadiaram

(Sermon began at 11.15 a.m. and lasted until 1.00 p.m.)

Let me start with two illustrations from Hindu practice. First, we see the icon of Ganesh [the elephant-headed god] during his festival. People make him sit down so that they can worship him. They also dance to cinema tunes, they play cards, and they drink and make merry.

My next illustration is the story of a lazy person who thought of a way to get rich without doing any work. He carved a *lingam* [the icon of Shiva] and then one night dug a deep pit, which he filled with feed grain, placed the *lingam* on top, and then covered it with mud. After he poured a lot of water on the mud, the feed grain started to swell, pushing the *lingam* up through the mud. Then he told people to come and see the miracle: out of its own volition, an icon of Shiva was rising up out of the earth. He then put vermilion on the image, broke a coconut in front of it, and began to worship it. People joined him in worship and left offerings of money, which provided him with a substantial income.

We read in Psalm 123:2: "As the eyes of servants look to the hand of their master, as the eyes of a maid to the hand of her mistress, so our eyes look to the Lord our God, until he has mercy upon us" [NRSV]. Our eyes should look toward the true God, not toward the image of Ganesh carried around during his festival. We certainly should not be fooled by a *lingam* appearing to rise up out of the ground. That man duped the people with his *shivalingam*. We should not cheat like that. Rather, we must lift up our eyes and look toward God.

Next are two illustrations to show what it means for a servant to look toward his master, expecting something from him.

When we go a restaurant, a server asks us what we would like to eat, and when we order something, the server will shout to the kitchen — one plate *idly* — one *dosa* — one *upma*, etc. In the same way, you come to the church (which is like the restaurant) and tell us your troubles, and I, like the server, will shout to God that this church member needs this while another member needs something else, etc. [The pastor dramatized every word with lots of actions, speaking in very colloquial language, although his accent was not local but that of Coastal Andhra.]

My last illustration is this: even a dog looks to its master; even my dog looks to me, wanting to have whatever I might have brought for it. Since the dog looks so hopefully to its master, the master gives it something. So also we look to God with hope and God gives us something that is good for us. We must not be like the person who tricked people with the Shiva *lingam*.

In Genesis 16:8-9, the angel asks Hagar, "From where did you come, and

Appendix

where are you going?" After he had asked this question, he talked about pride. Hagar became proud after she had become pregnant. She left after Sarah scolded her. Here we see the servant going away from her mistress. Hagar should have looked to her mistress with humility, but she looked down on her with pride. The angel told Hagar to go to her mistress and live with her in humility. If a poor man eats meat just once, he will boast of his higher status and feel proud. We should not become proud because we have received something from God. If we behave like Hagar, we should remember that God made Hagar confess her fault. Hagar considered Sarah to be cursed because of her barrenness. Hagar treated Sarah with contempt, considering her to be a useless woman (Gen. 16:3-4).

You see, we pastors eat chicken and mutton all the time, but if a poor person is fed with all varieties of meat at the same meal, he will start boasting; he will feel proud about it. Adam was blessed by God, God gave him everything, and Adam became proud and ate the fruit. Then God made him confess his fault. It is the same with our people also. We become proud very soon.

Look at Satyanarayana, for whose healing we are praying. He never gives a tithe to God; he only gives fifty rupees per month. When I ask him to give a tithe, he says that he is not in the habit of tithing. He sometimes misses giving even that fifty rupees, but then the next month he finds a crisp one hundred rupee note and gives that as his offering. He never gives a tenth of his income. Will God leave him unpunished? No, God makes the proud confess their sins. You see that he is now in the hospital. I went to see him in the hospital. I did not fail to visit him in the hospital, for he is my child, but God takes what belongs to God. When he did not give a tithe, God took what was owed in a different form. You must give a tithe, you must not think that it is just this pastor who asks for that. If you don't give what God requires, he will extract it in his own way.

Hagar's experience testifies that God is the God who sees. Hagar duped Sarah and ran away, but God caught her. We must give our tithe; otherwise God will it take it from us. You see, Satyanarayana, he used to ride a bicycle and sell clothes. Later God blessed him, for now he has a shop and is selling just by sitting in the shop. God gave him profits, but Satyanarayana did not give a tithe; he became proud, but God is now extracting from him through his accident.

We read in Matthew 12:36 that "on the judgment day men will render account for every careless word they utter." We must not utter proud words, for we will have to account for every word we speak.

God is a God who heals; we should testify to this from our own experience. Our God is a God who hears prayers. God healed me when I met with an accident. I have experienced his healing. One can describe the taste of a chicken curry only after eating it. So also we must experience God.

You see, if Satyanarayana wants to, he can pray to God for healing. We must have humility, as God demanded from Hagar, and we must have a generous heart of giving to God. You see what happened to Satyanarayana. I told him to give a tithe, but he did not listen. He did not give a tithe even once in a while. You see that God is now taking his due in the way he chooses.

Our eyes must look to God.[2]

Sermon by Pastor Hanoch, Independent Baptist Church, Jangarai

(Based on Ps. 111:1-10)

Children who have come together for worship, I greet you all in the name of Jesus Christ. Hallelujah! [The congregation responded, "Hallelujah!"] In Psalm 111:1 the Bible tells us that we need to worship God. Why should we praise God? Because, in those days, the people worshiped God for the good deeds that he did in the lives of the people, and for the healing he brought. Not just for that, but because God delivered them from Egyptian slavery, they worshiped and praised God. God called the Israelites by name. He gave them the promised land. For the great deeds that God wrought in their lives they praised God with such instruments as the *tambura* and the *sitar*. They worshiped God after crossing the Red Sea.

God has wrought many miracles and good deeds. The Israelites worshiped God, but we forget to worship him. David tells us in Psalm 103:1-2, "Bless the Lord, O my soul; forget not all his benefits." That is why you children of God know that he is giving us all that we need and is helping us whenever we need help. Crops are good; we praise God for giving us such a happy life. We all must praise God for all the benefits we have received from God.

In the same way in verse 7, God's deeds are righteous and just, says the psalmist. Beloved, every deed of God is just; that is why we are worshiping him today. God has wrought many good deeds in everyone's life. In former times you expressed ignorance about the person of Christ, but today you are able to believe that Jesus-God died for your sins. Because of his life sacrifice you are able to believe in Jesus Christ. Hallelujah! Jesus did many miracles; with five loaves and two fish he fed more than five thousand people. He healed the blind, lame, and paralytic. We can say that this is God's plan.

In Luke 4:18-19, God's will was revealed. Beloved, God has done and is still doing many great things in the lives of our families. When we are sick and pray

---

2. The congregation was alert all the time, though he preached for an hour and forty-five minutes.

to God, God gives us healing. Our troubles roll away because God's deeds are just and can be trusted.

We see in verse 10 that God's name is holy. It is not only God's name that is holy, but the Bible says that God is holy, too. It is God's wish that we who are his children also should be holy. God says, "Be ye holy, for I am holy." What God wishes is that we, our lives, and our families be holy. But are we being that way? No, some are drinking toddy, some are taking drugs, some smoke country cigars, and some smoke cigarettes. Some women chew betel leaves. All these things are contaminating us. Will Jesus come into your unholy heart? No, he will not come. On the day you become holy, he will be in you. You need God. If he is to live in your heart, you must leave all those habits. Leave those habits and come to God's presence, confess your sins. He will forgive you; he will save everyone. He will be with you in sufferings and sadness, and when you are in trouble, he will be with you.

Dearly beloved, I will give you an illustration. A small boy always used to go to school from in front of the church. He used to stand at the gate of the church and say, "Jesus, I am James." He used to say this every morning and evening. One day as he was walking on after saying this, a motor scooter knocked him down. Bleeding and badly hurt, he was taken to the hospital. There he was treated and sent to school. In the evening while being taken back home from school, he again stopped at the church gate. He was hurting too much to say his usual, "Jesus, I am James," but Jesus came to him and said, "James, I am Jesus." [The pastor used English to express the words of James and Jesus and later translated these words into Telugu.] When James heard Jesus speaking, he recovered from his accident and was completely healed. He left happily to go home.

When we go into God's presence, all our sickness and all the effects of black magic will disappear. God will come to us, and he will redeem us from all these troubles. May God help us all!

Sermon Preached in the CSI Church in Chinna Shankarampet

Sermon Preached in the CSI Church of Chinna Shankarampet (Horeb Prayer Church), October 17, 2010, "Youth Sunday"

Preacher: Pastor Prabhaker, Presbyter of the Congregation

"The son instructed by the father will become wise." [The pastor sang a hymn beginning with, "You are my refuge, Jesus Christ."] Paul instructs young Timothy in the Epistle lesson. [The pastor expounded 1 Timothy 4:6-16.]

For whose sake did you come to church today? [The congregation replied, "We came for our own sake."] That is right. No one can be forced to become spiritual. There is a Telangana proverb, "Even if you attach a *lingam* (icon of Shiva) to a man, that will not make him a devotee of Shiva." Likewise, if parents force the children whom they have spoiled to come to church, that will not make the children spiritual.

We should follow the example of King David. [The pastor sang, "I dance like David and praise God."] Our youngsters are dancing during wedding processions and festivals rather in the church. If young men dance in a funeral procession, their parents are happy that their sons are dancing. Yet if they are invited to dance in the church, they don't come. David, however, danced in the presence of God, and when Saul was troubled by an evil spirit, David played the harp.

Numbers [8:24-25] says that young people should perform service to God between ages twenty-five and fifty, but our children are not doing God's work according to the word of God. [An interruption followed for a response by the congregation.] According to the Indian Constitution, you young people have the right to vote when you turn eighteen. When you are not allowed to exercise that privilege, you shout your complaints, but you are not coming forward to serve God. Do you find your name in the Book of the Lamb? [The pastor sang another hymn, "When we change toward God, our life changes."]

All roads have speed bumps. When crossing, you need to drive slowly. Young people should be careful when driving. Paul says, "Timothy, be careful!" Samuel as a child served the Lord and was blessed abundantly when he grew up. [Here the pastor read verses from Ecclesiastes and Proverbs and sang another song.] When you are a young person, your blood is hot. Don't start running, and don't shout at others. [The pastor recited some village proverbs, ending with, "Don't walk with a person carrying an umbrella. If it starts to rain, he will just keep it for himself." The pastor sang, "You have to change your life."]

Today is the festival of *Dasara*. Hindus will tie mango leaves to their house posts. Christian young people are like leaves tied to the door. Nowadays they are attached to cell phones.

John writes [1 John 2:14-17]: "I have written to you, young men, because you are strong: you have defeated the Evil One." The Gospel lesson [Matt. 19:16-30] is about Jesus and the rich young man. Jesus told him to sell all his property and give the money to the poor. It says in Ecclesiastes, "Remember the Creator in the days of your youth" [11:9-10; 12:1]. [Then the pastor recited, "God is my refuge and my fortress" (Psalm 91:1). The congregation answered with a unison response.]

When young people celebrate their birthdays, they want cell phones as presents, but it says in Lamentations [3:27], "It is best to learn this patience in our

Appendix

youth." Don't tell others to change. When someone forces you, you won't learn. You have to change by yourself.

We read in Genesis 26 that Joseph's brothers seized him and sold him to the Ishmaelites, who sold him to Potiphar. Joseph was a young man when he was tempted by Potiphar's wife, but he overcame that temptation. You young people will definitely be tempted. You, too, should overcome temptation. How can a young man keep his life pure? By obeying God's commandments. [The pastor sang another song.] You need to be conscious that God is observing you. [The congregation responded.]

We read in Ephesians [6:1-2], "Children, obey your parents . . . This is the first commandment with a promise . . . Bring up your children in the fear of the Lord." Deuteronomy 6:9 says, "You shall write the commandments on the portals of your house." Parents should teach children, and "when they grow up, they will not depart from it." Timothy's mother and grandmother brought him up. [There was a response by the congregation and another song by the pastor.]

Nowadays young people watch TV. The parents watch God's channel and the news, but the children take the remote and shift to the movie channel. Jesus said that he came to preach to the poor [Luke 4:18]. I always pray for the youth. In Hyderabad, they are spending their time in the park and spending five or six hundred rupees every day. Some parents feed their children even when they are old enough to provide for themselves. That food could become poison for children who do not respect their parents.

"Your youth is renewed like the eagle's" [Psalm 103:5]. In his youth, Jesus respected his parents and was on good terms with the leaders of the church. He led an exemplary life.

Let us pray for the young people — for their health, that they may have good jobs and lead a good life, that their spiritual life may grow, and that they may become pillars of the church. Amen.

Glossary

Andhra Pradesh   the Indian state established in 1956 by merging the Telugu-speaking part of the former Madras Presidency (Andhra) with the Telugu-speaking part of the former Hyderabad State (Telangana). The capital has been the largest city in the state, Hyderabad. After repeated agitation to dissolve the merger, the Indian Parliament voted in February 2014 to separate Andhra Pradesh into two states, Andhra and Telangana, with Hyderabad City, which is within Telangana, serving for ten years as the capital of both states.

Arya Samaj   a Hindu nationalist organization founded in the nineteenth century by the Hindu reformer, Swami Dayananda Saraswati. It has undertaken the "reconversion" of a number of Christians to their former Hindu status, adapting a ceremony of purification. (See **Shuddhi**.)

Balamma   a village goddess worshiped especially by Dalits.

Banjara   the name used by some Gypsy (Roma) communities in Telangana.

banumathi   witchcraft/black magic, discussed in chapter 4.

barakat   a Muslim term for Divine blessings, understood by all villagers as the equivalent of *shubham*, "good fortune."

batkamma   a traditional dance form described in chapter 8.

Bestha   the name of the fisher caste.

bhakti   devotion to God, discussed in chapter 4.

bonalu   decorated pots with cooked rice that women carry on their heads during Hindu festivals.

bottu (Sanskrit *tilaka*)   the auspicious dot, made of red-orange paste, on the forehead of married women.

burrakatha   a traditional form of dance, storytelling, and social comment by three musicians, described in chapter 8.

Glossary

caste the English word, derived from Portuguese *casta*, "color," that is used as the equivalent of two Indian words with overlapping but distinct meanings. (See **jati** and **varna**.)

Circuit the name used by the Methodist Mission for a group of village congregations supervised by a British missionary or an Indian pastor. The equivalent term in the Church of South India is "Pastorate."

Dalit a Marathi word meaning "crushed" or "oppressed," popularized by Ambedkar as a collective term for those often called "outcastes" or "untouchables." The government term for those belonging to castes at the bottom of the village ranking is "Scheduled Castes." Gandhi tried to dignify them by calling them Harijans, "children of God."

darshan seeing or beholding a divine image, which for many Hindus implies both seeing and being seen by the deity.

devatalu a general term for goddesses.

Devudu (Sanskrit *deva*) for many Hindus, a general term for any masculine deity; for Telugu Protestants, the proper name of God.

dharma this ancient term has many meanings; in the context of this book, it is the most general term for the moral, religious, and social order of traditional Hindu society, in which fulfilling one's dharma is considered the first goal of human life.

dhoti a man's lower garment, a length of cloth wrapped around his waist and thighs, and sometimes also the lower legs.

Dipavali (Diwali) the Hindu festival of lights in late October or early November, celebrated with different stories and different forms of worship, depending on region and sect.

Durga a militant form of the great goddess, sometimes considered independent and sometimes the consort of Shiva. She is the presiding goddess at the shrine of the "Seven Streams" pilgrimage.

Ellamma a village goddess much worshiped by Dalits. Her name suggests that she protects the boundaries of the village.

Godavari River a major river that flows from the highlands of Maharashtra through northern Telangana before entering the Bay of Bengal in coastal Andhra.

halal rules the proper way for Muslims to prepare meat, sometimes followed as a way to cook festive meals that will be acceptable to both Hindu and Christian relatives. The Arabic term *halal* has a broad range of meanings for Indian Muslims and others using the Urdu language, signifying some object or practice that is pure, genuine, good, lawful, or permissible. For example, *halal-sicca* is a genuine coin, not a counterfeit. With respect to food, the meaning and the specific rules are similar to Jewish *kosher*. The

GLOSSARY

opposite term is *haram*, which can refer to anything impure, harmful, false, or forbidden.

Harikatha "Vishnu's story," a traditional form of song and dance that includes stories about Vishnu's incarnations Rama and Krishna.

Hindu originally a Persian term designating anyone living in the Indian subcontinent (living beyond the Indus river), it became a Muslim term for non-Muslim Indians. By the nineteenth century the word also designated the religion of all Indians who did not declare themselves something other than "Hindu," thus leaving out not only Muslims and Christians, but also Buddhists, Jains, and Sikhs. For many at present, Hindus are those who accept the ranked social system and the beliefs expounded by Brahmins. Modern Hindu nationalists identify "Hindu" with both the religion and the nationality of those living in the sacred land of India *(Bharat)*. Those who do not call themselves Hindus are therefore sometimes considered "traitors" to the Hindu nation. *Hindutva* ("Hindu-ness") is a term expressing this unity of nationality, religion, culture, and social system.

Holi the early spring festival in which the god of romantic love, Kamudu (Kama) is worshiped and conventional social norms are broken, most noticeably by splashing other people on the street with colored water.

illutam the practice of adopting a son-in-law when a family has no sons. The new "son" then comes to live with his new "parents," reversing the usual practice of the wife leaving her parents and moving to the husband's family, usually in another village.

jagirdar under the Nizam's rule in the former Hyderabad State, the holder of a feudal estate often including several villages, whose residents could be taxed for his benefit, but who received almost no social services.

jangama a non-Brahmin village priest of a temple to Shiva.

jathara (Sanskrit *tirtha-yatra*) a pilgrimage to and/or circumambulation of a sacred site *(tirtha)*, which is often at a river or stream in which the pilgrims may take a sacred bath. See chapter 8.

jati one of the many endogamous groups in Indian society, into which one is born and within which one must marry. This is the most common equivalent of the English term "caste," but the principle of caste-ranking depends on the Brahmanical theory of four *varnas*. Each *jati* is convinced of its superiority to lower-ranked castes, from whom its members will not accept food or drink. (In practice there are compromises and exceptions.) Many castes have the name of their members' traditional occupation.

Kamudu (Kama) the god of romantic love.

Katta-Maisamma the village goddess believed to be responsible for illnesses to cattle and to human beings (cholera, upset stomach, and diarrhea)

Glossary

during the rainy season. Animal sacrifices are offered to appease her. See *paska*.

Krishna   the incarnation of Vishnu who receives much devotion, both for the romantic and heroic exploits in his youth and for his role as Arjuna's counselor in the great war that ended the previous age.

Krishna River   the great river whose various branches start in the highlands of Karnataka and flow eastward. After they have joined, the river divides Telangana from Andhra before entering a delta and flowing into the Bay of Bengal.

kolattam   a traditional dance form described in chapter 8.

kulam   in these villages, the term means both the extended family and the larger caste group *(jati)* within which intermarriage should take place.

Kummari   name of the potter caste.

kummi (dance)   a traditional dance form described in chapter 8.

Lambada   the caste name of many Gypsies (Roma) in Telangana, who live outside the villages, sometimes migrate from village to village for seasonal work, and worship their own distinctive deities.

lyric   the English word used by Telugu Protestants for their more informal hymns and choruses.

Madiga   one of the two major Dalit castes (the other is Mala) in the Telugu-speaking area (Telangana and Andhra). Its traditional occupation is disposing of dead cattle and leather-working. Madigas also perform various menial services, including cleaning houses in which a death has occurred.

Mahar   a Dalit caste in Maharashtra, many of whose members followed their leader, B. R. Ambedkar, in becoming Buddhists.

Mala   one of two major Dalit castes in Telangana and Andhra (along with Madiga). Its traditional occupation was fieldwork and other services for the Malas' landholding masters. Malas consider themselves superior to Madigas, who reject such inferior ranking.

mandal   the term comes from *mandala* ("circle"); it is used here for an administrative circle of villages that comprises one part of a sub-district *(taluk)*.

Mankali   a village goddess whose name is a shortening of Sanskrit *maha-kali*, the great goddess Kali, worshiped with animal sacrifices. She is sometimes regarded as an independent goddess with the power to kill or keep alive, sometimes as a consort with power surpassing that of her husband Shiva, and sometimes as the supreme divine power.

mantrikam   magic, the word derived from *mantra*, which means a secret and powerful word. While such sacred words are important in much Hindu ritual, in magic their power is utilized by the magician who knows and controls them. Through these words and the accompanying rituals the magician

GLOSSARY

is able to harm people by casting a spell, or to provide a remedy against another magician's spell. See chapter 4.

monsoon the rainy season. The first monsoon follows the shift of the wind in June, when it starts to blow in from the southwest, off the Indian Ocean. The second monsoon starts in October, when the wind returns to the northeast, off the Bay of Bengal.

Mudhiraj a lower-level landowning caste in Telangana, some of whose members in the villages studied have become Christians, joining Pentecostal and other independent churches.

Muharram the first month of the year in the Islamic calendar and the name of the Muslim festival most commonly celebrated by almost all villagers; it occurs during the first ten days of the New Year. Especially for Shia Muslims it commemorates the martyrdom of the Prophet Muhammad's grandsons, Hassan and Hussain.

Nadar Once known as Shanar, this is the modern name, meaning "lords of the land," for the caste originally concentrated in the southern part of the Tamil country. Their traditional occupation was that of "toddy-tappers," extracting the sap of palm trees to make an alcoholic drink (toddy) and palm-sugar (jaggery). After escaping that occupation, they objected to the demeaning term *Shanar*. Many Nadars became Protestant Christians in the nineteenth century. Both Christian and non-Christian Nadars have improved their social and economic status, and educated Christian Nadars provided much of the leadership for Protestant churches, including the first Indian bishop in the Anglican Church, Samuel Azariah, whose Dornakal Diocese adjoined the Hyderabad Methodist Mission (later the CSI Medak Diocese).

Nizam abbreviation of *Nizam-ul-mulk,* the title of the hereditary ruler of Hyderabad State from 1724 until 1948.

Panchama another term for Dalits. The word means "fifth" and here signifies a fifth category of castes below the four categories recognized by Brahmins to be part of the Hindu social system *(varna-dharma)*.

panchayat governing "council of five" *(panch)* of a caste in a village or region, of the whole village, or of an administrative "circle" *(mandal)* of villages.

paska the name is the village version of *pachika* ("fresh green grass"), a festival for the protection of villagers and their cattle from the illnesses of the rainy season, with animal sacrifices offered to a village goddess. (See **Katta-Maisamma**.) In their adaptation of the festival for Christians, some pastors have related *paska* to the Jewish *Pascha* (Passover) because the words are pronounced the same way, but Christians keep their celebration in July or August during the rainy season. See chapter 8.

Peddala Amavasya the Hindu festival at the Dark of the Moon close to the end of September, which commemorates the ancestors. All Saints' Day and All Souls' Day sometimes provide a Christian equivalent. See chapters 4 and 8.

Poshamma the village goddess responsible for bringing and for warding off smallpox.

prasadam the word, which also means "divine grace," refers in ritual to the consecrated food or other offerings that after being given to a deity are returned to the giver or to other worshipers to share with their families as a tangible symbol of divine grace.

puja Hindu worship of sacred images believed to contain, or to represent, the presence of a particular deity. Reverent gestures and prayers are accompanied by an offering of flowers, fruits and other food, and sometimes money.

ragi one of two kinds of millet (gray-colored grain) that are major dry crops in Telangana. The other kind of millet is called *jonna* or *zonna*. Both can be grown without the irrigation that rice requires; the monsoon rains provide enough water. In semi-arid regions of Telangana, both kinds of millet may be planted alternately in the two seasons of the agricultural year. *Ragi* and *jonna* are therefore both major staples for poorer villagers.

rakshana divine protection or salvation, both during this earthly life and in heaven, a term in Hindu devotion *(bhakti)* that has been adopted and much used by Christians.

Rama the most human incarnation of Vishnu, worshiped in some temples in the region and widely known and honored throughout the Indian subcontinent as well as Southeast Asia as the ideal king, whose life story is recounted in the many versions of the *Ramayana*.

Reddy the highest-ranked and most powerful landowning caste in this part of the Telugu-speaking area.

rupee the standard unit of Indian currency, trading in December 2013 at about 51 rupees to the U.S. dollar.

Sadhu an honorific title for a Hindu ascetic, especially a wandering ascetic. The title has been adopted by a few Christian ascetics.

Sakali the title of the washerman caste, many of whose members are now engaged in farming and other occupations.

sarpanch the chairperson of the council governing a caste, a village, or a *mandal*.

Scheduled Castes the government term, beginning under British rule but continuing after Indian independence, for those castes at the bottom of the Hindu social hierarchy, now often called Dalits. The government holds that only those who are registered as Hindus or as members of some other religion of Indian origin (thus not Muslims or Christians) are to be considered as members of the Scheduled Castes and eligible for benefits reserved for them.

seven steps a Brahmanical wedding ritual adapted for use in a few Christian weddings.

Seven Streams the name of the pilgrimage site, described in chapter 8, where a stream in Telangana divides into seven streamlets before reuniting and then flowing into the Godavari River.

Shiva/Siva one of the two major Hindu gods (along with Vishnu), Shiva is sometimes considered to be the destructive aspect of divine reality but is usually worshiped as the supreme deity, either alone or in conjunction with his consort or consorts (the goddesses), or as represented by his two divine sons, Ganesh and Skanda (Murugan in South India).

Shivalingam the "mark of Shiva," the cylindrical stone that is the image at the center of the worship of Shiva in his temples and shrines. Some of his worshipers understand the lingam to represent the union of the male and female organs (*lingam* and *yoni*), which symbolize Shiva's transcendent power in his union with the Goddess.

Shivaratri "Shiva's night" is a festival celebrated at the dark of the moon, especially on the "great night of Shiva" occurring in late February or early March. For some, this festival includes an all-night vigil and/or a pilgrimage to a temple of Shiva or a goddess-shrine.

shubham "good fortune," considered the equivalent of the Muslim term *barakat*, "blessings."

Shuddhi "purification," a Brahmanical Hindu ceremony to regain caste status lost by a serious infraction of social rules that was adapted by the Arya Samaj for a ceremony readmitting repentant Christian converts to their previous Hindu status. Some Brahmins have objected to using this ceremony for Dalits, considering them too polluted to have even inferior ranking in the Hindu caste system.

Shudra the fourth and lowest division in the Brahmanical system of castes, in which Shudras are ranked as servants. In much of South India, the many castes in this category make up three-quarters of the population and include landowners and the many occupational castes, some of whom object to a name that suggests that they are the Brahmins' servants.

tali the necklace placed around a bride's neck at her wedding and worn throughout her marriage, equivalent to the Western wedding ring.

Telangana the Telugu-speaking and largest part of the former Hyderabad State. Since 1956, it has been part of Andhra Pradesh, but now it is scheduled to become a separate state, sharing its capital of Hyderabad for ten years with the adjacent state of Andhra.

Glossary

Telugu a Dravidian language in a different linguistic branch than the other major Dravidian languages (Tamil, Kannada, and Malayalam). It is spoken by more than sixty million people in the northeastern part of South India.

tirtham originally denoting a ford or shallow river crossing where people could bathe, the term now refers to the sacred places where such ritual bathing occurs, both on river banks and in temple pools, and to the destination and center of any pilgrimage.

toddy the Indian English term equivalent to Telugu *kalu* for the alcoholic beverage made from fermented palm tree sap.

Ugadi the Telugu New Year's Day in mid-April.

Vaikunta Vishnu's abode. In village usage this becomes one of the terms for heaven, along with *moksha,* permanent release from the cycle of lives, and *svarga,* a temporary heavenly abode until one's merit from previous good deeds is exhausted.

Varna The Sanskrit word, originally meaning "color," used to designate each of the four major groups distinguished in the Brahmanical theory of social ranking: Brahmins (priests and scholars), Kshatriyas (rulers and warriors), Vaishyas (originally farmers, later largely merchants), and Shudras (originally designating servants, who were much lower in the social hierarchy, but now comprising the majority of Hindus, both landholders and those belonging to the occupational castes). The social order, called *varnadharma,* is often called in English the "caste system," but "caste" usually refers to a particular *jati* (endogamous group). [See *jati* in the Glossary and the section in chapter 2 entitled "Village Social Structure and the Position of Dalits," pages 18-22.]

Veda the inclusive term for the four collections of sacred verses and chants in the most ancient Sanskrit. Together with their extensions and commentaries they constitute the most revered "scriptures" (not strictly speaking "writings," since they were memorized and passed on orally) of Brahmins and many other Hindus. The sacred words of the Vedas are considered in some traditions to be the source of the world's creation and the authority behind the social and moral order.

Vedanta the "end of the Vedas," the final extension of the Vedas in the Upanishads, leading to mystical and philosophical reflection. The commentaries on the Upanishads elaborate theologies and methods to attain salvation. The word is used by Christians as a general term for theology, whether Hindu or Christian.

Vishnu one of the two major Hindu gods (along with Shiva), he has many names and forms. He is the maintainer of the universe, the ultimate source of the created world through a series of emanations, and in his descents *(avatara)* or incarnations is the rescuer and protector of the social order and particularly of his devotees. Each of the sects of Vishnu-devotees has its favorite divine names and favorite avatars. In much of South India, the Srivaishnava community worships Vishnu as Narayana together with his consort Sri (Lakshmi), along with two subordinate divine wives.

Wadla   name of the carpenter caste.

Bibliography

Alter, James P., and Herbert Jai Singh. *The Church in Delhi*. In *The Church as Christian Community: Three Studies of North Indian Churches*, edited by Victor E. W. Hayward, 1-136. London: Lutterworth Press, 1966.

Appadurai, Arjun. "Gratitude as a Social Mode in South India." In *Spoken and Unspoken Thanks: Some Comparative Soundings*, edited by John B. Carman and Frederick J. Streng, 13-22. Cambridge, MA: The Center for Study of World Religions, Harvard University, and Dallas, TX: Center for World Thanksgiving, 1989.

Ayrookuzhiel, A. M. Abraham. *The Sacred in Popular Hinduism: An Empirical Study in Chirakkal, North Malabar*. Madras: The Christian Literature Society, 1983.

Babb, Lawrence A. *The Divine Hierarchy: Popular Hinduism in Central India*. New York: Columbia University Press, 1975.

Barrett, David B., George T. Kurian, and Todd M. Johnson, eds. *World Christian Encyclopedia: A Comparative Survey of Churches and Religions in the Modern World*. 2nd ed., vol. 1. Oxford and New York: Oxford University Press, 2001.

Bauman, Chad M. *Christian Identity and Dalit Religion in Hindu India, 1868-1947*. Grand Rapids, MI, and Cambridge, UK: William B. Eerdmans, 2008.

Bawa, V. K. *The Last Nizam: The Life and Times of Mir Osman Ali Khan*. New Delhi: Penguin Books, 1991.

Beals, Alan R. *Gopalpur: A South Indian Village*. New York: Holt, Rinehart and Winston, 1964.

Bergunder, Michael. *The South Indian Pentecostal Movement in the Twentieth Century*. Grand Rapids, MI, and Cambridge, UK: William B. Eerdmans, 2008.

Boal, Barbara M. *The Church in the Kond Hills: An Encounter with Animism*. In *The Church as Christian Community: Three Studies of North Indian Churches*, edited by Victor E. W. Hayward, 221-343. London: Lutterworth Press, 1966.

Campbell, Ernest Y. *The Church in the Punjab: Some Aspects of its Life and Growth*. In *The Church as Christian Community: Three Studies of North Indian Churches*, edited by Victor E. W. Hayward, 137-220. London: Lutterworth Press, 1966.

BIBLIOGRAPHY

Carman, John B. "Bhakti." In *Encyclopedia of Religion*, edited by Mircea Eliade, 2:130-34. New York: Macmillan, 1987.

Carman, John B. "The Dignity and Indignity of Service: The Role of the Self in Hindu Bhakti." In *Selves, People and Persons: What Does it Mean to Be a Self?* edited by Leroy S. Rouner, 107-22. Notre Dame, IN: University of Notre Dame Press, 1992.

Carman, John B. "Hindu Bhakti as a Middle Way." In *The Other Side of God: A Polarity in World Religions*, edited by Peter L. Berger, 182-207. Garden City, NY: Anchor Books, 1981.

Carman, John B. "When Hindus Become Christian: Religious Conversion and Spiritual Ambiguity." In *The Stranger's Religion: Fascination and Fear*, edited by Anna Lannstrom, 133-53. Notre Dame, IN: University of Notre Dame Press, 2004.

Carman, John B., and Frederique Apffel-Marglin, eds. *Purity and Auspiciousness in Indian Society*. Leiden: E. J. Brill, 1985.

Carman, John B., and Frederick J. Streng, eds. *Spoken and Unspoken Thanks: Some Comparative Soundings*. Cambridge, MA: The Center for Study of World Religions, Harvard University, and Dallas, TX: Center for World Thanksgiving, 1989.

Chatterji, Saral K., Richard W. Taylor, M. M. Thomas, and J. Paranjoti-Augustine, eds. "Christians, Society, and Bhakti in Andhra Pradesh." *Religion and Society* 29, no. 1 (March 1982).

Clarke, Sathianathan. *Dalits and Christianity: Subaltern Religion and Liberation Theology in India*. Delhi: Oxford University Press, 1998.

Clough, John E. *Social Christianity in the Orient: The Story of a Man, a Mission and a Movement*. Written with the assistance of his wife Emma Rauschenbusch Clough. New York: Macmillan, 1914.

Dempsey, Corinne G. *Kerala Christian Sainthood: Collisions of Culture and Worldview in South India*. New York: Oxford University Press, 2001.

Devasahayam, V., ed. *Frontiers of Dalit Theology*. Delhi: Gurukul Lutheran Theological College and Research Institute and Indian Society for Promoting Christian Knowledge, 1997.

Downie, David. *The Lone Star: The History of the Telugu Mission of the American Baptist Missionary Union*. Philadelphia: American Baptist Publication Society, 1893.

Dube, S. C. *Indian Village*. New York and Evanston: Harper and Row, 1967. Originally published by Humanities Press, n.d.

Estborn, Sigfrid. *The Church among Tamils and Telugus: Reports of Some Aspect Studies*. Nagpur: The National Christian Council of India, 1961.

"The First Letter of Paul to the Corinthians." In *The Holy Bible, Containing the New and Old Testaments*. New Revised Standard Version. Nashville: Thomas Nelson Publishers, 1989.

Fishman, Alvin Texas. *For This Purpose: A Case Study of the Telugu Baptist Church in its Relation with the South India Mission of the American Baptist Foreign Mission Societies in India*. Guntur, S. India: Self-published by the Rev. A. T. Fishman, Andhra Christian College, 1958.

Francis, T. Dayanandan. *The Relevance of Hindu Ethos for Christian Presence: A Tamil Perspective*. Madras: Christian Literature Society, 1989.

Frykenberg, Robert Eric. *Christianity in India: From Beginnings to the Present*. New York: Oxford University Press, 2010.

Frykenberg, Robert Eric, ed. *Christians and Missionaries in India: Cross-Cultural Com-

munication since 1500. Grand Rapids, MI, and Cambridge, UK: William B. Eerdmans, and London: RoutledgeCurzon, 2003.

Frykenberg, Robert Eric, ed. *Land Control and Social Structure in Indian History*. Madison: University of Wisconsin Press, 1969; New Delhi: Manohar, 1978.

Frykenberg, Robert Eric, ed. *Land Tenure and Peasant in South Asia: An Anthology of Recent Research*. Delhi and Hyderabad: Orient Longmans, 1977.

Frykenberg, Robert Eric, ed. "The Genesis of the Andhra Movement and the Formation of Andhra: A Case Study of the South." *Calcutta Historical Review* 18, no. 1 (June 1996): 36-63.

George, P. S., Maria Alacoque, and Cletus Colaco. *Medak District: A Socio-Religious Study*. Pune: Ishvani Kendra, 1978.

Gifford, Paul. "A View of Ghana's New Christianity." In *The Changing Face of Christianity: Africa, the West and the World*, edited by Lamin Sanneh and Joel A. Carpenter, 81-96. Oxford: Oxford University Press, 2005.

Harper, Susan Billington. "The Dornakal Church on the Cultural Frontier." In *Christians, Cultural Interactions, and India's Religious Traditions*, edited by Judith M. Brown and Robert Eric Frykenberg, 183-211. Grand Rapids, MI, and Cambridge, UK: William B. Eerdmans, and London: RoutledgeCurzon, 2002.

Harper, Susan Billington. *In the Shadow of the Mahatma: Bishop V. S. Azariah and the Travails of Christianity in British India*. Grand Rapids, MI, and Cambridge, UK: William B. Eerdmans, and Richmond, Surrey, UK: Curzon, 2000.

Hawley, John Stratton, and Vasudha Narayanan, eds. *The Life of Hinduism*. Berkeley, Los Angeles, and London: University of California Press, 2006.

Hedlund, Roger E., Sebastian Kim, and Rajkumar Boaz Johnson, eds. *Indian & Christian: The Life and Legacy of Pandita Ramabai*. Chennai: MIIS/CMS/ISPCK, 2011.

Hoefer, Herbert E. *Churchless Christianity*. Pasadena, CA: William Carey Library, 2001. First published in 1991.

Hudson, D. Dennis. *Protestant Origins in India: Tamil Evangelical Christians, 1706-1835*. Grand Rapids, MI, and Cambridge, UK: William B. Eerdmans, and Richmond, Surrey, UK: Curzon, 2000.

Jaffrelot, Christophe. *Religion, Caste, and Politics in India*. New York: Columbia University Press, 2011.

Jenkins, Philip. *The Next Christendom: The Coming of Global Christianity*. Oxford: Oxford University Press, 2002.

Jeyaraj, Daniel. *A German Exploration of Indian Society: Ziegenbalg's "Malabarian Heathenism."* Chennai: Mylapore Institute for Indigenous Studies, 2006.

Joseph, Ravela. *Bhakti Theology of Purushottam Chowdhari*. Chennai: Christian Literature Society, 2004.

Kent, Eliza F. *Converting Women: Gender and Protestant Christianity in Colonial South India*. New York: Oxford University Press, 2004.

Kuruvilla, K. P. "Dalit Theology: An Indian Christian Attempt to Give Voice to the Voiceless." Unpublished paper.

Luke, P. Y. and John B. Carman. *Village Christians and Hindu Culture: Study of a Rural Church in Andhra Pradesh, South India*. Delhi: Indian Society for Promoting Christian Knowledge, 2009. First published in 1968 by Lutterworth Press.

BIBLIOGRAPHY

Mackie, Steven G., ed. *Can Churches Be Compared? Reflections on Fifteen Study Projects*. Geneva: World Council of Churches, and New York: Friendship Press, 1970.
Massey, James. *Down Trodden: The Struggle of India's Dalits for Identity, Solidarity and Liberation*. Geneva: World Council of Churches, 1997.
Massey, James. "Movements of Liberation: Theological Roots and Vision of Dalit Theology," Internet accessed on July 20, 2009, http://www.cca.org.hk/resources/ctc/ctc01-04/ctc0104j.htm.
Massey, James, ed. "Dalit Ideology." *Religion and Society* 37, no. 3 (September 1990).
McCormack, William. "On Lingayat Culture." In *Speaking of Siva*, poems translated and introduced by A. K. Ramanujan, 175-87. Harmondsworth, UK, and New York: Penguin Books, 1987. First published in 1973.
Mosse, David. *The Saint in the Banyon Tree: Christianity and Caste Society in India*. Berkeley and London: University of California Press, 2012.
Oddie, Geoffrey. "Christian Conversion in Telugu Country, 1860-1900: A Case Study of One Protestant Movement in the Godavery-Krishna Delta." *Indian Economic and Social History Review* 12 (January–March 1975): 61-79.
Oommen, George. "The Emerging Dalit Theology: A Historical Appraisal." *Indian Church History Review* 34, no. 1 (June 2000).
Prabhakar, M. E., ed. "Andhra Christians." *Religion and Society* 37, no. 1 (March 1990).
Raj, Selva J., and Corinne G. Dempsey, eds. *Popular Christianity in India: Riting Between the Lines*. Albany: State University of New York Press, 2002.
Ramanujan, A. K. *Hymns for the Drowning: Poems for Visnu by Nammalvar*. Princeton, NJ: Princeton University Press, 1981.
Rauschenbusch-Clough, Emma. *While Sewing Sandals: Tales of a Telugu Pariah Tribe*. New Delhi: Asian Educational Services, 2000. First published in 1899.
Robinson, Rowena, and Sathianathan Clarke, eds. *Religious Conversion in India: Modes, Motivations, and Meanings*. New Delhi: Oxford University Press, 2003.
Sackett, F. Colyer. *Posnett of Medak*. London: Cargate Press, 1951.
Sanneh, Lamin. *Disciples of All Nations: Pillars of World Christianity*. New York: Oxford University Press, 2008.
Sanneh, Lamin. *Translating the Message: The Missionary Impact on Culture*. Maryknoll, NY: Orbis Books, 1992.
Schmitthenner, Peter L. *Telugu Resurgence: C. P. Brown and Cultural Consolidation in Nineteenth-Century South India*. Delhi: Manohar, 2001.
Shiri, Godwin. *The Plight of Christian Dalits: A South Indian Case Study*. Bangalore: Asian Trading Corporation for the Christian Institute for the Study of Religion and Society, 1997.
Solomon, Etala David. *Change and Continuity: Influences on Self-Identity of Christian Dalits of Madiri Puram Village in South India (1915-2005)*. Delhi: ISPCK, 2012.
Sontheimer, Gunther-Dietz, and Herrmann Kulke, eds. *Hinduism Reconsidered*. 2nd ed. New Delhi: Manohar, 1997. First published in 1989.
Srinivas, M. N. *Religion and Society among the Coorgs of South India*. Bombay: Asia Publishing House, 1965. First published in 1952.
Sugandhar, B. P. *Presidential Address Presented to the 30th Ordinary Session of Medak Diocesan Council by The Most Reverend Dr. B. P. Sugandhar, Bishop in Medak*. November 2005.

Bibliography

Sugandhar, B. P. *Presidential Address Presented to the 31st Ordinary Session of Medak Diocesan Council by The Most Reverend Dr. B. P. Sugandhar, Bishop in Medak.* November 2007.

Sundara Rao, R. R. *Bhakti in the Telugu Hymnal.* Bangalore: The Christian Literature Society for the Christian Institute for the Study of Religion and Society, 1983.

Thomas, M. M., Saral K. Chatterji, G. R. Karat, R. W. Taylor, and T. K. Thomas, eds. "Conversion and Baptism in the Cultural Context of India." *Religion and Society* 19, no. 1 (March 1972).

Tiliander, Bror. *Christian and Hindu Terminology: A Study of their Mutual Relations with Special Reference to the Tamil Area.* Uppsala: Almqvist & Wiksell, 1974.

Vasantha Rao, Chilkuri. *Heads and Tales.* Secunderabad: Liturgy and Literature Committee, Medak Diocese, Church of South India, 2008.

Vasantha Rao, Chilkuri. *Jathara: A Festival of Christian Witness.* New Delhi: Indian Society for Promoting Christian Knowledge, 2008. First published in 1997.

Verma, Acharya R. S. "Christ Bhakti: A Biblical Perspective." Lecture presented at the Centennial of the Parliament of World Religions. Chicago, IL, September 2, 1993.

Victor, K. James Cecil. "Meaning and Significance of Rural Dalit Christian Marriage Symbols." In *The Yobel Spring: Festschrift to Rev. Dr. Chilkuri Vasantha Rao on His 50th Birthday,* vol. 2, edited by Praveen PS. Perumalla, Royce M. Victor, and Naveen Rao, 699-704. New Delhi: ISPCK, 2014.

Visvanathan, Susan. *The Christians of Kerala: History, Belief and Ritual among the Yakoba.* New Delhi: Oxford University Press, 2007. First published in 1993.

Viswanathan, Gauri. *Outside the Fold: Conversion, Modernity, and Belief.* Princeton, NJ: Princeton University Press, 1998.

Walls, Andrew F. *The Cross-Cultural Process in Christian History.* Maryknoll, NY: Orbis Books, 2002.

Walls, Andrew F. *The Missionary Movement in Christian History: Studies in the Transmission of Faith.* Maryknoll, NY: Orbis Books, 1996.

Webster, John C. B. *The Dalit Christians: A History.* Delhi: Indian Society for Promoting Christian Knowledge, 2007. First published in 1992.

Wiebe, Paul D. *Christians in Andhra Pradesh: The Mennonites of Mahbubnagar.* Madras: Christian Literature Society, 1988.

Wiebe, Paul D. *Heirs and Joint Heirs: Mission to Church Among the Mennonite Brethren of Andhra Pradesh.* Winnepeg: Kindred Productions, 2010.

Wiebe, Paul D. "Religious Change in South India: Perspective from a Small Town." *Religion and Society* 22, no. 4 (December 1975): 27-46.

Ziegenbalg, Bartholomaeus. *Alte Briefe aus Indien. Unveroeffentliche Briefe von Bartholomaeus Ziegenbalg 1706-1719.* Edited by Arno Lehmann. Berlin: Evangelische Verlagsanstalt, 1957.

Index

Achampet: CSI congregation in, 3-5, 53, 85, 90-91, 97, 141, 174; independent church in, 4-5, 30, 107, 124, 204
Ambajipet: CSI congregation in, 10, 92-97, 98, 146, 173, 196, 198, 204; independent church in, 100, 134, 148-49
Ambedkar, Bhimrao Ramji, 21, 171-72
Anandam, Pastor, 80, 93, 134, 136, 138, 148-49
Arya Samaj, 8, 103, 158, 172, 178-79

Babu, M. C., 107-8, 185, 186
Badia, Banoth, 128, 129-30
Bhakti, 68-71, 143, 191-92, 210-11
Bharatiya Janata Party (BJP), 25, 29, 134, 197
Black magic, 10, 63-68, 93-95, 106, 120, 121, 126-27, 128, 132, 138, 175, 191, 212. *See also* Witchcraft
Burrakatha, 145-47

Caste: and Christianity, 13, 31-37, 51, 104, 149, 184-85, 188, 197, 205, 206-7; and congregational life, 5, 50, 93, 100, 112, 116, 123-26, 135, 136, 177-78, 203-5, 207-8; definition/description of, 18-21, 25-26, 87; and group conversion, 37, 39, 173-74, 176-77, 182; and Hindu society, 46, 51-54, 77, 87, 143-44, 146, 172, 178, 180, 205-6; and politics, 23-25, 29-30, 171-72, 208;

and religious identity, 4, 8, 40, 85, 86, 149, 182-84, 201, 204
Christianity: and adaptation of Hindu ritual, 11, 32-33, 56, 139-53; and Christian participation in Hindu ritual, 52-62, 75, 78, 86-88, 133, 140, 141, 182, 196; and Hindu culture, 171-72, 180-84; history of in India, 31-50, 200; and religious environment, 86-87, 177-78, 189-92
Clough, John Everett, 36, 37-38
Conversion: group, 37, 39-40, 85, 129, 131, 173-74; individual vs. group, 176-78; meanings of, 171-73; testimonies of, 110, 186-88

Dalit(s): and Christianity, 5, 8, 25-26, 36-38, 40, 43-44, 149-50, 173-74; government policy toward, 9, 13, 22-25, 73-74, 79, 179, 194, 197, 208; and Hindu society, 18-22, 51-52, 143-44, 171-72; and multi-caste congregations, 93, 100, 113, 123-24, 177, 203-5; and politics, 28-30; theology, 13, 45-48, 206-8, 211
Dass, Kumari, 94-97, 98, 183, 198
Dayanand, Christopher, 187
Deevenamma, Mrs. (Mrs. Raduva Deevenamma Mithra, 7, 11, 86, 94, 95, 98, 135, 186; lay ministry of, 96, 124, 127-28, 131-34, 136, 198

Index

Gowd, Narayana, 101

Healing and conversion, 12, 138, 174-76, 177, 185-86, 212-13; examples of, 93-97, 101-4, 109-12, 115, 132-33; from witchcraft/black magic, 10, 62, 65-66, 67, 105, 119-20, 126-27, 129-30, 137
Hindu nationalists, 171-73, 178-80, 208
Horeb Prayer Church, 95, 101, 133-37, 138, 209
Hyderabad: closer connections with villages, 26-28; history of, 14, 15-18, 23, 73; Wesleyan Methodist Mission in, 38-44, 139-40, 176-77

Independent churches: and Church of South India, 86, 93, 96, 101, 208-9; growth of, 7, 9, 10-11, 48-50, 99-101, 123-24, 203; and multi-caste congregations, 100, 107, 112, 116, 203-5, 207-8; pastoral ministry in, 104-8; preaching and worship style in, 113-19; women in, 109-12, 122
Intermarriage, 7, 86-88, 181

Jati, 19-21, 52, 201. *See also* Caste
Jesus as healer, 3, 6, 7, 12, 13, 122, 180, 191, 202, 208, 212-13; testimonies about, 93, 95-97, 101-4, 105, 112, 124, 132-34, 175, 181, 187, 195; visions of, 187, 188, 210; from witchcraft, 63-68, 106, 137
Joseph, Botumanchi (Sadhu), 3, 6, 101-4, 124, 186, 210, 212

Kumar, Nithin, 90-91
Kumar, Prasanna, 136-37

Luke, Mrs. Devapala, xiii
Luke, P. Y., 1-3, 12, 42-43, 89-90, 92, 102, 103, 121, 155-56, 169, 174, 177, 184

Madiga(s). *See* Dalit(s)
Mala(s). *See* Dalit(s)
Manikyam, 185-86, 202
Medak Diocese (CSI), 1, 3, 10, 12, 88-91, 142, 153, 190, 196, 204; baptism and church membership in, 193-96, 202; history of, 41-42, 44-45; and independent churches in, 11, 12-13, 104, 123, 134, 136, 137; Jangarai section of, 72-74. *See also* Wesleyan Methodist Mission
Mithra, Mr. Raduva, 127

Nirmal, Arvind P., 47

Outcaste(s), 8, 19-21, 51, 171, 172

Paranjyothi, Mahima, 94, 95, 96, 98, 131, 198
Periah, Yerragantla, 36-38
Poolsingh, Daravath, 128, 129-30, 131
Posnett, Charles Walker, 41-44, 92, 142, 174

Ramabai, Pandita, 48-49
Rao, Malaga Sanjeeva, 94
Rao, Vijaya, 126, 127, 198
Religious identity/group solidarity, 7, 9, 54, 89, 177, 179, 182-83, 197, 201-3; example of Yohan, 184-86

Sanjeev Kumar, Burgupalli (Pastor Sanjeevi), 11, 95, 105-6, 109, 110, 111, 176, 209
Sarasvati, Dayanand, 178
Satyanandam, Pastor, 5, 106-7, 186

Telangana region: Christianity in, 31-45, 48-50, 187, 191-92, 208-13; politico-social history of, 6, 10, 14-30, 73-74, 77
Tharamma, Kurma, 93-94
Tharamma, of Medac, 11, 67, 105, 119-23, 124, 126, 186, 210

Village congregations of the Church of South India (CSI), 9, 10, 11-12, 50, 85-86, 97-98, 194-96, 204-5; in Bandaposanipally, 60-61, 62, 67-68, 76-78, 196; beliefs of Christians in, 154-70; and independent churches, 11, 13, 101, 208-9; Jangarai section of, 72-76; new congregations of, 125-38; pastoral care of, 88-91; in Shankarraj Kondapur, 78-80; worship and preaching in, 80-85, 198
Village religion: *bhakti* in, 68-71; and Christianity, 8-9, 86-91, 141, 212-13;

241

INDEX

Hindu cultural environment of, 10, 51-62; and spirit possession, 62-63; and witchcraft, 64-68

Wadiaram pastorate (CSI): beliefs of Christians in, 161-70; current state of congregations in, 6-7, 72-76, 97-98, 196; festivals in, 142, 150-51; independent churches in, 99-100; new congregations in, 11, 125-38, 189; socio-political change in, 22-30

Wesleyan Methodist Mission, 6, 12, 88-89; and Christian adaptation of Hindu culture, 11, 139-40, 142, 190; in Hyderabad, 10, 11, 38-44, 177, 193. *See also* Medak Diocese (CSI)

Witchcraft, 10, 63-68, 121; healing from, 7, 42, 122, 128, 129-30, 137, 162, 175, 183, 210, 212. *See also* Black magic

Yesumani, B., 126-27, 198
Yohan, 184-86

Ziegenbalg, Bartholomaeus, 34-35

www.ingramcontent.com/pod-product-compliance
Lightning Source LLC
Chambersburg PA
CBHW020645300426
44112CB00007B/246